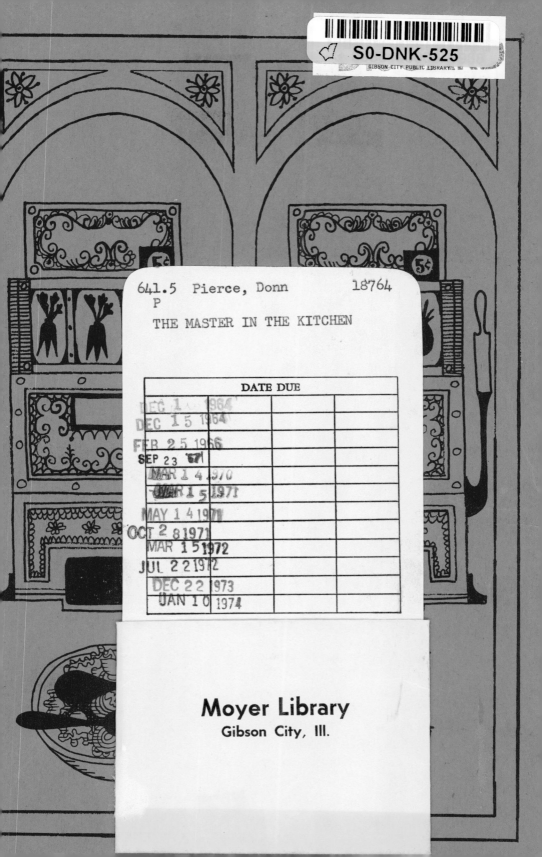

Outstanding Borzoi Books on FOOD

MASTERING THE ART OF FRENCH COOKING
    by Simone Beck, Louisette Bertholle and Julia Child
COOK, MY DARLING DAUGHTER *by Mildred O. Knopf*
THE PERFECT HOSTESS COOK BOOK *by Mildred O. Knopf*
THE OMELETTE BOOK *by Narcissa Chamberlain*
ITALIAN FOOD *by Elizabeth David*
SEASON TO TASTE *by Peggy Harvey*
THE JUNE PLATT COOK BOOK *by June Platt*
THE HONEY COOKBOOK *by Juliette Elkon*
PARIS BISTRO COOKERY *by Alexander Watt*
THE CLASSIC FRENCH CUISINE *by Joseph Donon*
THE FOOD OF FRANCE *by Waverly Root*
TABLE TOPICS *by Julian Street*
    Edited and with Additions by *A.I.M.S. Street*.

THE MASTER
IN THE KITCHEN

THE MASTER IN THE KITCHEN

BY

DONN PIERCE

&

CHARLOTTE TURGEON

DRAWINGS BY DENNIS REDMOND

New York: Alfred · A · Knopf

1964

L. C. catalog card number: 64–12299

THIS IS A BORZOI BOOK,
PUBLISHED BY ALFRED A. KNOPF, INC.

Copyright © 1964 by Donn Pierce and Charlotte Turgeon. All rights reserved. No part of this book may be reproduced in any form without permission in writing from the publisher, except by a reviewer, who may quote brief passages and reproduce not more than three illustrations in a review to be printed in a magazine or newspaper. Manufactured in the United States of America, and distributed by Random House, Inc. Published simultaneously in Toronto, Canada, by Random House of Canada, Limited.

FIRST EDITION

INTRODUCTION
BY DONN PIERCE

MY KITCHEN *début* occurred when I was eight. I baked —a rock-like cake, which the family somehow managed to eat. There were no disparaging remarks; in fact, shortly thereafter, during The Depression, I became chief cook-and-bottle-washer while everyone else worked—in part to support my more or less edible efforts. Since then I have been a recipe-robber, under-cover-sniffer, and pot-snooper in many, many kitchens and in many countries.

Some of them were outstanding. One of the first was Aunt Bessie's Iowa farm kitchen. In exchange for chopping cookstove wood or wrestling with the churn, I was permitted to pester— and to copy her "receipts" for all-American food. "Sister" Lily's college fraternity was another. I observed and admired her

INTRODUCTION

cooking for four years, in between dishwashing and table-waiting. She blessed me with extra-large helpings and a more than workable knowledge of marvelous Southern cooking.

Then I fled the Midwest to Hawaii with a one-way ticket, and landed in Mama Skronczyki's Boarding House for Men. At her overladen table I gained too much weight too soon. In her kitchen I gained a healthy respect for Russian and Polish cooking. Mama, in turn, came to respect my ability at the stove—especially on days when her feet hurt. I was often permitted to cook for the other men—carefully following her commands from a strategic rocking chair. Also, during ten wonderful years in The Islands, I had close friends from Hawaii, Samoa, China, Korea, Japan, India, Indonesia, Portugal, Puerto Rico, Germany, Scandinavia, and the Philippines, with whom I cooked and learned about their native food.

Some kitchens are best forgotten—especially those of the wartime navy. After existing on their products for several years, it was a real pleasure to meet Mme Coussinet in New Caledonia. The Madame had two thriving establishments. Most profitable was the highly popular (and only authorized) *palais de joie* in the South Pacific. The food at her second, a mountain dinner house, was sheer joy. She became my close friend and let me into my first of many French kitchens for watching and learning. Years later, in a similar establishment in Mexico City, I became equally friendly with Señora Morales while I was her "house" guest—paying, but not for the prime services rendered; the Señora, her "nieces," and I spent many charming hours cooking together.

Henri Simon led me to the best kind of French home cooking when, on the train from Zurich, he invited me to the Paris home of his *petite amie*. Mlle Marie not only furthered my French cooking experiences but also opened the way into other kitchens in France, both private and commercial. In New York, M. Girard, *maître d'hôtel* at one of the best French

Introduction

restaurants, introduced me to *haute cuisine*. It became especially *haute* when he instructed me in his own kitchen.

As the only off-season guest in a Sorrento hotel, I remained for days on end, peeking and poking in the kitchen with the chef. He finally sent me along to relatives in Venice, to friends in Florence, and to Tia Maria in Rome, whose Italian cooking was unequalled.

In Spain, Caterina was the treasure. Laundress, cleaning woman, language instructor, and cook, she took complete care of me for pennies per day. It was months before she admitted me—a mere man—into her kitchen. In the months that followed, neither of us became proficient in our respective languages, but we did cook up storms of delicious Spanish food.

It is obvious, then, that in almost forty years I have done a lot of cooking—very often beyond the limits of culinary law. I have made every possible mistake. I have also formed not a few rather positive ideas about food, which are scattered throughout this collection, and about its preparation. Cooking, to me, is a creative way of life. The real joy is cooking for others. It then becomes a labor of love. As such, it requires common sense, imagination—and courage. The real gratification comes when the food looks beautiful and tastes absolutely great.

We men who cook seriously and not just when the spirit moves us are, in my opinion (and that of many women), better cooks. Maybe this is because few of us are married to the kitchen through sheer necessity. None of us is hampered by past cooking conventions. When we cook we are seldom out to save time but to spend it, if not recklessly, at least proudly. When more effort is involved than that spent in just whipping up a meal, there is one great difference in the results: a far better meal. We have learned to be at ease in the kitchen—one of the real secrets of good living.

A cookbook is nothing more than a handbook for action.

INTRODUCTION

No recipe is static. It is merely a jumping-off point toward the discovery of new and elusive tastes. (Who needs or wants the same monotonous results guaranteed by following a recipe every time?) This is such a handbook. It is not a collection of short-cuts but neither does it operate on the premise that the cook has absolutely nothing else to do but cook. It is a book for everyone who shares my curiosity about food and for anyone who can recognize the potentials of a recipe and then take over—with one eye on the kettle and the other on friends or family who will be sampling its contents. According to Charlotte Turgeon, who helped in the final preparation of this book, the book will be as useful to women as to men. But it is primarily a cookbook for those men who take the art of cooking seriously—with no apologies. It is, in short, a handbook for men who are (or wish to be) masters not only of the household but of the kitchen.

P.S. *Charlotte Turgeon has also added helpful comments and suggestions, indicated by the P.S. at the end of many of the recipes.*

Contents

THE SPECIES OF SAUCES	3
SOUP SORCERY	27
TREATS AND TREATMENTS WITH EGGS	55
UNDERWATER EXPOSÉ: FISH, MOLLUSKS, AND CRUSTACEANS	71
HOW TO EAT MEAT LIKE A MILLION (INSTEAD OF MILLIONS OF OTHERS)	103
THE PROMISE OF A GOOD MEAT LOAF	159
CAPITAL GAINS WITH LEFTOVERS	173
THE STATUS OF STEWS AND RAGOUTS	189
CHICKENS AND THEIR BARNYARD BRETHREN	199
CASING THE CASSEROLE CIRCUIT	231
MEAT CASSEROLES	232
CHICKEN CASSEROLES	251
FISH AND SHELLFISH	258
CHEESE AND EGG	270
VEGETABLE CASSEROLES	274
A MEAL-IN-ITSELF	287

CONTENTS

VARIOUS VEGETABLE VIGNETTES	315
TOSS AND SERVE	399
MORE THAN BREAD	423
GOURMET GOLD: CHEESE	453
DESSERTS THAT DESERVE ATTENTION	469
FRUITS, THE ESSENCE OF ELEGANCE	471
CAKE COMMENTS	495
CROWNS FOR CAKES (TOPPINGS AND FROSTINGS)	508
INIMITABLE ICE CREAM	512
TARTS AND PIES	516
SWEET ENDINGS	531
MASTER MENU-MAKER	*follows page* 274
INDEX	*follows page* 540

THE SPECIES OF SAUCES

SAUCES

ENOUGH, if not too much, has been written about the sanctity of good sauces and the importance of making them carefully. It's all true. A sauce must be a superior creation, or why bother? Its purpose is to enhance the food. But if the basic food is not good, no sauce will ever conceal the fact.

Sauce-making is demanding, but not difficult. A determination, a respect for the food as well as the sauce, exactness and attention to detail are important prerequisites. But a sensitive nose and palate are the best critical guide, for constant smelling and tasting are required.

One word of caution: don't overdo. Never serve food swimming in a sea of sauce, and be careful not to let the sauce dominate. Maintain a good relationship between the sauce and the food it serves.

Brown Stock

TIME: Between 14-16 hours   YIELD: 2 quarts

Brown stock is no sauce, but it's a basic element in some important sauces. Making it instead of buying it brings extra dividends to the sauces in flavor and applause. You also get a free meal while making it.

COMPOSITION

4-pound shinbone of beef
4 pounds veal shank or shin-bones
¾ cup fat or oil
1 pound carrots
1 pound onions
2 pounds lean beef (1 chunk)
1 pound lean veal
salt
pepper
½ cup parsley, minced
1 bay leaf, crushed
1 teaspoon thyme

PREPARATION

Paint the bones with ½ cup of the fat. Brown them in a very hot oven.

Meanwhile, chop the vegetables very fine. Brown them lightly in the rest of the fat.

Combine bones and vegetables and cover with 4 quarts of water. Simmer for 12 hours, adding hot water when necessary to maintain water level, skimming occasionally to remove the scum. Remove the bones and add the lean beef and coarsely chopped veal. Season.

Simmer until the beef is tender and the liquid reduced to ½ gallon. Two hours will do it, perhaps.

Remove the meat, which is called *bouilli* and can now be eaten hot, or later, cold. This is the free meal.

Strain the stock. Press and squeeze the final pulp to extract all

Glace de Viande

the good juices. Cool. Remove the fat. It is now ready for use.

Glace de Viande
(Meat Sauce)

TIME: 1½ hours minimum   YIELD: 1 cup

If you are intent on buying *Glace de Viande,* insist on the very best. Otherwise, try this for perfection.

COMPOSITION

4 cups brown stock (see preceding recipe).

PREPARATION

Simmer and skim the brown stock until reduced to a thick jelly. Stir occasionally to prevent sticking.

Cool. Skim off any residue of fat. Let it thicken.

Keep it for weeks in the refrigerator and use as needed.

P.S. *This recipe is a real bonus since meat glaze is hard to come by in most of the United States. To make this easily, let the cooled brown stock stand in the refrigerator until all the fat has come to the top. Skim off all the fat before starting the reduction process.*

Quick Meat Glaze

TIME: ½-¾ hours   YIELD: About 1 cup

COMPOSITION

1 can bouillon
½ can water
1 parsley sprig
1 bay leaf, crushed

5

THE SPECIES OF SAUCES

PREPARATION
Bring the ingredients to a boil. Let them simmer until thickened.
Strain. Cool. Use.

Sauce Espagnole
(Brown Sauce)

TIME: Less than 4 hours   YIELD: About 5-6 cups

COMPOSITION

3 medium onions   *1 parsley sprig*
1 carrot   *thyme*
½ cup beef fat   *1 bay leaf*
¾ tablespoons flour   *3 tablespoons tomato paste*
2 quarts rich brown stock

PREPARATION
Chop the onions and the carrot.
Melt the fat. Brown the vegetables. Sprinkle them with flour.
Continue cooking until they are dark brown. Stir steadily.
Add the stock slowly. Toss in the herbs. Add the tomato paste.
Cook very slowly for 2-3 hours.
Adjust the seasonings, strain, cool. Remove fat before using.

Brown Sauce on the Double

TIME: Less than an hour   YIELD: 1½ cups

For the benefit of those who refuse to part with the time required to make a brown stock, here is a substitute using canned bouillon. It is a quick but not at all bad imitation.

COMPOSITION

3–4 *green onions (scallions)*
2 *tablespoons butter*
1 *tablespoon flour*
2 *cups beef bouillon*
2 *teaspoons tomato paste*

1 *bay leaf*
pepper
salt (possibly)
thyme

PREPARATION

Mince the onions. Brown them in butter.
Add the flour. Stir and cook until the flour is well browned.
Add the bouillon slowly.
Season to taste, adding more salt if necessary.
Simmer for about 25 minutes.
Strain before using.

Demi-Glace

TIME: 1 hour   YIELD: 2 cups

COMPOSITION

1 *cup chopped mushrooms*
2 *tablespoons butter*
2 *cups brown sauce*

2 *cups brown stock*
¼ *cup dry sherry*

PREPARATION

Chop the mushrooms. Sauté them in the butter for a couple of minutes.
Add the brown sauce and the brown stock.
Simmer. Skim at intervals. Reduce the quantity by half. Cool. Remove the fat.
Stir in the sherry.
Refrigerate for future use.

THE SPECIES OF SAUCES

~~~~~~

Béchamel Sauce

TIME: 20-25 minutes   YIELD: 1 cup (approximately)

COMPOSITION

1 tablespoon grated onion *2 tablespoons flour*
1 very small bay leaf   *salt*
1½ cups milk   *white pepper*
2 tablespoons butter

PREPARATION

Grate the onion and crush the bay leaf. Toss them into the milk.

Bring the milk to a boil. After a few minutes, strain it.

Melt the butter. Stir in the flour. Add the milk slowly. Stir constantly. Season.

Cook and stir over low heat for 15-20 minutes.

Mornay Sauce

TIME: About 30 minutes   YIELD: 2 cups

COMPOSITION

½ cup grated Parmesan cheese   *pepper*
½ cup grated Swiss cheese   *3 egg yolks*
1 pint heavy cream   *cayenne*
salt   *paprika*

PREPARATION

Grate the cheeses. Cook them in a double boiler with the cream. Add salt and pepper to taste.

Beat the egg yolks slightly. Stir a little of the hot cheese mixture into the eggs. Pour the combination into the pot slowly, stirring constantly. Never let the sauce boil. Season with cayenne and paprika to taste.

Hot Meat Sauce

TIME: 10 minutes   SERVES: 4-6

COMPOSITION

½ pint sour cream   4 tablespoons horse-radish
¾ cup applesauce   ½ teaspoon salt

PREPARATION

Combine all ingredients.
Warm well without boiling.

PRESENTATION

Serve with hot or cold meats, especially pork.

Mustard Sauce for Meat

TIME: 5 minutes   YIELD: About 1½ cups

This keeps well and even improves with age.

COMPOSITION

1 cup chili sauce   1 tablespoon horse-radish
½ cup A-1 sauce   1 tablespoon dry mustard
¼ cup prepared mustard   1 tablespoon lemon juice

PREPARATION

Mix well.

THE SPECIES OF SAUCES

Cold Meat Sauce

TIME: 5 minutes   YIELD: 1½ cups

COMPOSITION

½ pint heavy cream
½ cup good mayonnaise
about 4 tablespoons hot Dijon mustard
soupçon of dry mustard

PREPARATION

Whip the cream. Fold the other ingredients into it.

Almond Sauce for Meat

TIME: 45 minutes   YIELD: 1 cup

COMPOSITION

½ cup almonds
2 tablespoons butter
1 cup beef stock
salt
pepper
1 egg yolk

PREPARATION

Blanch the almonds in boiling water. Peel, toast and chop them.

Mix them to a smooth paste with the butter, by hand or in a blender.

Add the stock and season with salt and pepper.

Cook over low heat for ½ hour.

To bind, stir in the egg yolk at the last minute before serving.

PRESENTATION

For use with Pork Chops with Almonds (p. 143), with hot or cold meats or meat loaf.

Almond Sauce for Fish

TIME: 20-25 minutes   SERVES: 2-4

COMPOSITION

½ cup almonds
2 tablespoons butter
⅔ cup heavy cream

¼ teaspoon salt, cayenne
1 teaspoon onion juice

PREPARATION

Blanch, skin, and chop or shred the nuts. Brown them in butter.

Add the rest of the ingredients, scraping a cut onion with a knife to get onion juice.

Mix well. Heat. Serve.

PRESENTATION

Use with Salmon Soufflé, Fish Pudding, or any shrimp casserole.

A Good Barbecue Sauce

TIME: 10 minutes   YIELD: About 2½ cups

COMPOSITION

½ cup honey
⅔ cup soy sauce
⅔ cup catsup
1 teaspoon dry mustard
1 teaspoon paprika

½ teaspoon Tabasco
2 garlic cloves, pressed
1 teaspoon salt
1 cup red wine
1 cup wine vinegar

PREPARATION

Mix well.
Heat well.

THE SPECIES OF SAUCES

Use as a marinade for charcoal broiling or for Marinated Pork Chops (p. 144), Marinated Short Ribs (p. 119) or Pot Roast in Beer (p. 116).

Mushroom Sauce for Ham

TIME: 10-12 minutes   SERVES: 4-6

COMPOSITION

½ pound mushrooms
1-2 parsley sprigs
2 tablespoons flour
⅛ pound butter

1 jigger sherry
½ cup water
1 garlic clove
Worcestershire sauce

PREPARATION

Clean and slice the mushrooms.

Chop the parsley.

Brown the flour in half of the butter. Add the sherry and the water. Cook and stir until mixture becomes a fairly thick sauce.

Heat the remaining butter and press the garlic into it. Add the mushrooms, the parsley, and a dash of Worcestershire sauce.

Combine the two mixtures. Cook them together for about 5 minutes.

Pine Nut Sauce

TIME: 10-12 minutes   YIELD: 1½ cups

COMPOSITION

½ cup grated onion
¼ cup pine nuts
2 tablespoons butter

1 tablespoon tomato paste
1¼ cups water

A Witch's Brew for Marinating Meat

PREPARATION

Brown the onion and pine nuts in the butter.
Add the tomato paste and the water. Simmer for 5 minutes.

PRESENTATION

This is especially good with Fondue Bourguignonne (p. 295).

A Witch's Brew for Marinating Meat

TIME: 20 minutes (plus 24 hours)

COMPOSITION

¼ teaspoon pepper
1 teaspoon salt
3 tablespoons sugar
12 whole cloves
cayenne

grated rind of 1 lemon
grated rind of 1 orange
1 large onion, grated
½ cup olive oil
1 12-ounce can beer

PREPARATION

Combine all the ingredients.
Let the brew mellow for a day before using. It improves with age and keeps well in the refrigerator.

Sweet-Sour Sauce for Fish or Meat

TIME: 10 minutes YIELD: About 1 cup

COMPOSITION

1 teaspoon fresh minced ginger
1 cup cider vinegar

1 cup brown sugar
¼ cup cornstarch

THE SPECIES OF SAUCES

PREPARATION

Mince the ginger.
Mix everything into a paste. Add a little water if necessary. Bring to a boil. Stir constantly.

PRESENTATION

Pour over cold meat or baked fish. Cook in a hot oven briefly.

Shrimp Sauce for Meat and Fish

TIME: 10-12 minutes   SERVES: 4-6

COMPOSITION

1 can frozen cream of shrimp soup
¼ cup milk
¼ cup sherry or white wine
1 garlic clove
nutmeg

PREPARATION

Combine the ingredients in a saucepan. (For a strong garlic flavor use a fat clove, squeezed; for a mere hint, drop in the peeled bud and remove it before serving.)
Bring to a boil and simmer until the shrimp is heated.

PRESENTATION

Use with hot or cold meat or fish.

Lemon-Herb Butter

TIME: 10-15 minutes   YIELD: ½ cup

COMPOSITION

¼ pound butter
1 tablespoon grated lemon peel
2 tablespoons minced parsley
1 tablespoon minced chives
¼ teaspoon basil
½ teaspoon chervil

Anchovy Sauce

PREPARATION

Let the butter soften.
Grate the lemon peel.
Mince parsley and chives.
Cream together the butter and lemon peel. Mix well.
Add the herbs.

Anchovy Sauce

TIME: About 20 minutes   YIELD: About ¾ cup

COMPOSITION

4-5 anchovy fillets   1½ tablespoons capers
¼ pound butter   1-2 parsley sprigs
¼ cup dry sherry   lemon juice

PREPARATION

Pound the anchovies. Combine them with the butter and the sherry in a saucepan.
Cook over low heat for 10-12 minutes.
Chop the capers and mince the parsley. Stir them into the sauce.
Add lemon juice to taste.

A Sauce for Fish

TIME: About 25 minutes   SERVES: 4

COMPOSITION

4 egg yolks   1¾ cups white wine vinegar
½ cup chopped sweet pickles   ¼ teaspoon salt
2 tablespoons butter   3 tablespoons cornstarch
1 cup sugar   ¼ cup capers
1 cup water

THE SPECIES OF SAUCES

PREPARATION

Beat the egg yolks thoroughly.

Chop the pickles very small.

Melt the butter in a double boiler. Add everything except the cornstarch, pickles and capers. Cook and stir for a few minutes.

Remove a small portion of the sauce. Stir in the cornstarch and return mixture to the pot. Continue to cook and stir until the sauce is fairly thick.

Add the pickles and the capers. Heat briefly.

PRESENTATION

Serve immediately over hot or cold fish. The sauce is also good cold.

Hot Sour Cream Sauce

TIME: 7 minutes   YIELD: 1 cup

COMPOSITION

2 green onions (scallions)	½ teaspoon sugar
2 tablespoons butter	salt
1 tablespoon flour	pepper
2 teaspoons vinegar	½ pint sour cream

PREPARATION

Mince the onions. Sauté them in the butter.

Stir in the flour. Add the vinegar and seasonings. Cook and stir until the sauce is tan colored.

Stir in the sour cream. Warm, but do not let it boil.

PRESENTATION

Serve with or over any green vegetable.

Sauce for Baked Potatoes

TIME: 10 minutes   YIELD: 2 cups

COMPOSITION

1 tablespoon (or more) grated onion
1 tablespoon chopped parsley
1 tablespoon chopped chives
¼ pound butter
1 pint sour cream
salt
pepper

PREPARATION

Grate the onion and chop the herbs.
Melt the butter. Add onion, parsley, and chives.
Stir in the sour cream. Heat well without boiling.
Season to taste with salt and pepper.

Sauce Mon Dieu
(good for plain rice)

TIME: About 15 minutes   YIELD: 1 cup

COMPOSITION

½ cup cream
½ cup dry vermouth
¾ teaspoon flour
2 teaspoons brown sugar
2 teaspoons Worcestershire sauce
½ teaspoon salt

PREPARATION

Mix the cream with half of the vermouth. Heat the mixture.
Add the flour. Simmer and stir until smooth.
Remove the pan from the fire. Blend in the rest of the ingredients.

THE SPECIES OF SAUCES

Nut-Butter for Vegetables

TIME: 5 minutes   YIELD:

COMPOSITION

2 to 4 tablespoons butter per serving

¼ cup chopped nuts (except peanuts) per serving

lemon juice

PREPARATION

Melt the butter. Add the nuts. Stir until they are golden brown. Keep the fire low and don't be distracted. Stir. Burned nuts are a bore.

Add a dash of lemon juice at the last minute.

Béarnaise Sauce

TIME: 15-20 minutes   YIELD: Approximately 1½ cups

COMPOSITION

1 *shallot* or *green onion*
1 *parsley sprig*
½ *cup white wine vinegar*
1 *teaspoon tarragon*
salt

pepper
thyme
1 *bay leaf*
3 *egg yolks*
½ *pound butter*

PREPARATION

Mince the shallot and the parsley and crush the bay leaf. Simmer in vinegar together with the other herbs and seasonings. Reduce the quantity by half.

Beat the egg yolks together with a teaspoon of water. Add to the sauce.

Toss in the butter. Cook and stir until it is melted.

Hollandaise Sauce

TIME: 15-20 minutes   YIELD: 1 cup

COMPOSITION

¼ *pound soft butter*
1 *tablespoon flour*
3 *egg yolks*
3 *tablespoons lemon juice*
or *herb vinegar*
cayenne
salt
¾ *cup boiling water*

PREPARATION

Put everything into the blender.
Blend. (If you don't have a blender, beat everything by hand.)
Pour the sauce into a double boiler. Cook and stir for 8-10 minutes over hot (but never boiling) water.
Add salt to taste before serving.
Keep the sauce warm until ready to serve. Refrigerate any leftovers. Warm again before using.

Simplified Hollandaise

TIME: 15 minutes   YIELD: 1 cup

COMPOSITION

2 *3-ounce packages cream cheese*
2 *egg yolks*
2 *tablespoons lemon juice*
salt

PREPARATION

Soften the cheese in top part of double boiler.
Add the egg yolks, one at a time. Mix well.
Season with lemon juice and salt.
Heat in a double boiler, stirring occasionally.

THE SPECIES OF SAUCES

Aïoli

TIME: 10-12 minutes   YIELD: 1 cup

Aïoli is basically nothing more than garlic-flavored mayonnaise. It is good: good with fish, with cold meat, with eggs, with hot or cold vegetables. It is so good that it should be on hand at all times. None will ever be wasted.

COMPOSITION

4 garlic cloves   *pepper*
1 egg yolk   *1 cup olive oil*
salt   *½ tablespoon lemon juice*

PREPARATION

Squash and mash the garlic, preferably with a mortar and pestle. Add the egg yolk and a pinch each of salt and pepper.

Beat—with the pestle, a fork, or a whisk.

Add the oil slowly, beating constantly, until a beautiful emulsion is obtained.

Stir in the lemon juice, taste, and reseason if necessary.

Pseudo-Aïoli

TIME: 3 minutes, if you have the mayonnaise   YIELD: 1 cup

COMPOSITION

½ cup mayonnaise (preferably home-made)   *½ cup sour cream*
    2 garlic cloves

PREPARATION

Mix together equal quantities of mayonnaise and sour cream. Stir in the minced or crushed garlic.

Real Mayonnaise

TIME: 10-15 minutes   YIELD: 1 cup

True mayonnaise is a makeshift hollandaise, dreamed up by a chef who could find no butter. It has become a classic sauce. Nothing like it has ever appeared in a bottle, even under the same name.

The only knack required is good judgment. The only effort required is a steady stir with a sturdy arm. Arm yourself with the few ingredients (2 mixing bowls which nest, a wet towel, and 2 mixing spoons) and the courage. It takes no time at all.

Let the ingredients come to room temperature. Place the smaller bowl inside the larger, separating them with the wet towel. (This is a neat trick for any beating process. It helps steady the bowls and frees a hand.)

COMPOSITION

2 egg yolks from fresh eggs (plus a spare for emergencies)
1 teaspoon dry mustard
1 teaspoon salt
2 tablespoons vinegar or *lemon juice*
16 tablespoons (1 cup) olive oil

PREPARATION

Drop two egg yolks into the inner bowl. Add the mustard, the salt, and the vinegar. Stir briefly.

THE SPECIES OF SAUCES

Grab the spoons, one in each hand. Fill the lefthand spoon with oil. Let it drip, drop by drop, into the bowl.

With the other spoon, stir. Stir constantly and vigorously. (For operational ease, all southpaws should reverse the hand directions.)

Never add oil until the previous drop has been thoroughly beaten in. As the sauce thickens, step up the rate of oil-addition. Once started, don't stop until you have mayonnaise. You'll have better mayonnaise if the oil goes in very slowly.

SALVATION

If you now have an oily, curdled mess, don't swear. Prepare as you think best for another round.

Get out a fresh egg yolk and a fresh bowl.

Start with the egg yolk. Beat it slightly. Add the mess, drop by drop as you stir—with more care than before. You *can* end up with mayonnaise.

Vinaigrette Sauce

TIME: 5-6 minutes   YIELD: 1 cup plus

Make this a little in advance in order to let it mellow.

COMPOSITION

2 tablespoons chopped green onions (scallions)
2 tablespoons chopped capers
2 tablespoons chopped green olives
½ teaspoon chopped tarragon

3-4 parsley sprigs, chopped
salt
pepper
⅓ cup red wine vinegar
1 cup olive oil

Hard Sauce

PREPARATION

Chop all that needs to be chopped. Combine with remaining ingredients. Mix well.

Hard Sauce

TIME: 10 minutes   SERVES: 4-6

COMPOSITION

¼ pound butter   ¼ teaspoon vanilla
1 egg   1 jigger rum
1½ cups powdered sugar   1 tablespoon bourbon
salt

PREPARATION

Blend together the butter, the egg, and the sugar. Add a pinch of salt, the vanilla, and the liquors.
Beat like hell until it becomes light and frothy. Chill.

PRESENTATION

Serve with Date Delight (p. 482), gingerbread, or any hot cake.

Donn's Dessert Sauce

TIME: 15 minutes   SERVES: 6-8

COMPOSITION

2 egg yolks   ½ pint heavy cream
1 cup powdered sugar   1 teaspoon vanilla

PREPARATION

Beat the egg yolks with the powdered sugar.

THE SPECIES OF SAUCES

Whip the cream with a teaspoon of vanilla.
Combine the two mixtures, working without violence.

PRESENTATION

Serve with Fig Pudding (p. 483) or almost any rich fruit pudding.

SOUP SORCERY

ⓘⓘⓘⓘⓘⓘⓘⓘⓘⓘⓘⓘⓘⓘⓘⓘⓘⓘⓘⓘⓘⓘⓘⓘⓘ

THE MAN who in ancient times accidentally let part of his kill and some greenery fall into a cauldron of boiling water made a discovery that was lucky for the whole human race— SOUP. For centuries his happy accident has remained an integral part of every cuisine.

Soup has two main purposes. In one form it serves to whet the appetite; in another it provides hearty nourishment. One test of a good cook is his selection of the soup. As an appetizer, a light soup must be carefully chosen to stir the taste buds and to complement the foods that follow. Hearty soups can, and often do, constitute an entire meal.

For many of us who work a full day and then go home to cook, soup dinners are an excellent way to obtain more-than-just-edible nourishment. One morning, afternoon, or evening given to the preparation of a good soup will provide several work-free dinners. Soup dinners are also an easy way to entertain. Prepared beforehand, a huge pot (better still, two pots—one for thick soup and one for thin) leaves the host free to enjoy his own party, no matter how long it lasts. Those who would or should stop imbibing can help themselves at will. Huge slabs of sour-dough bread, a tossed salad, possibly a dessert, and certainly coffee will complete a meal that needs no overseeing.

The making of soup has become almost a forgotten art. It is not to be entrusted to just anyone who owns a can opener. Yet, if you know how, exotic soups can be served from cans with the addition of a pinch of this and a dash of that. Second best are soups made with a combination of fresh and canned ingredients. Not to be overlooked are some of the dried soups, imported and domestic. The very best are still made from scratch in the manner of a *pot-au-feu*.

Soup preferences vary. Some people want it thin and meager. Some want it thick and hearty. Others want it rich and wholesome. Some people like it cold; others hot. Many people just want it straight out of a can. We like to be all things to all people when it comes to soup, so you'll find some of each category in the following pages. Take your pick!

Pot au Feu

TIME: 4-5 hours   SERVES: 6-8

The delicious brew resulting from this is the foundation for hundreds of soups. In the cooking field, *pot au feu* is basic training. Master it, and you join the long procession of famous French chefs, all of whom have struggled with this not-so-plain boiled beef.

Since the making of this soup brings dividends in the form of a meat-and-vegetable course, provide yourself with hot mustard, sour pickles, coarse salt, and plenty of French bread.

COMPOSITION

1½ pounds chuck or bottom round of beef	1 garlic clove
1½ pound shin or rib of beef	4-5 peppercorns
½ pound cracked (or broken) beef or veal bones	2 teaspoons salt
	4 medium carrots
2-3 parsley sprigs	2 turnips
1-2 chervil sprigs	1 parsnip
1 bay leaf	2-3 leeks or green onions
	6-8 medium potatoes

PRELIMINARY PREPARATION

Pile the meat and bones in your largest soup kettle. Add the herbs and spices, cover with 2 quarts of cold water, and bring quickly to a boil.

Skim off the matter that will come to the surface, lower the heat, raise it again and skim once more.

Cover the pot loosely and let it simmer for 1 hour.

PREPARATION

Wash, pare, and chop all vegetables except the potatoes. Add them to the pot and simmer for 3 more hours, skimming

SOUP SORCERY

the surface occasionally. Add more hot water as necessary to maintain the original 2-quart level. Correct the seasonings from time to time.

Add the pared potatoes about 20-25 minutes before the deadline.

PRESENTATION

Traditionally the soup is served first. The meat and vegetables are removed to a hot platter and kept warm while the soup is strained, skimmed of excess fat, and served with grated cheese.

The meat and vegetables are served with coarse salt, sour pickles, and hot mustard.

If you have future soups in mind, serve the hot platter of meat and vegetables, but guard the broth.

Onion Soup

TIME: 30-40 minutes   SERVES: 4-6

COMPOSITION

1 pound onions
¼ pound butter
1 tablespoon flour

1½-2 cups rich stock (beef or chicken)
grated cheese
French bread

PREPARATION

You may skip the peeling process on the onions and shed fewer tears by slicing them and removing the slivers of skin as they fall away. Then chop the slices very fine.

Melt the butter. Add the chopped onions. Cook and stir over high heat until they are lightly browned.

A Quick Onion Soup for Two

Blend in the flour and continue stirring until everything is a rich dark brown.

Add the stock, then let the soup simmer for about 25 minutes.

PRESENTATION

Place a generous slab of good French bread in each bowl. Add the soup and sprinkle generously with grated cheese.

P.S. *The tip on peeling onions is a culinary headline and will eliminate weeping sessions from coast to coast.*

A Quick Onion Soup for Two

TIME: 15 minutes   SERVES: 2

COMPOSITION

2 large onions
½ cup grated Parmesan cheese
1 egg yolk
2 thick slices sour-dough bread
⅛ pound butter
1 bay leaf

2 cans beef bouillon or consommé
½ can hot water
¼ teaspoon nutmeg
1 tablespoon olive oil
1 jigger brandy

PREPARATION

Peel, then slice or chop the onions. Grate the cheese. Separate an egg and beat the yolk thoroughly. Toast the bread on both sides; cover one side with cheese and let it melt under the broiler. Keep the toast hot.

Sauté the onions in the butter until they are light brown. Toss in a well-crushed bay leaf. Add the bouillon and the water. Simmer for 5 minutes or longer.

Blend together the oil and nutmeg. Stir it into the soup. Add the beaten egg yolk, stirring slowly. Add the brandy and serve quickly.

PRESENTATION

Pour into individual bowls, add the toast, and sprinkle with additional grated cheese.

P.S. *This is so good, you may never want to try the more conventional again.*

Garlic Soup

TIME: 25 minutes   SERVES: 6

This soup is for people you really know well. I suggest that you serve it to them only occasionally, but when you do, provide quantities of thickly sliced Russian rye bread.

COMPOSITION

6 cups beef stock
6 tablespoons butter
8 fat garlic cloves
6 tablespoons flour
¼ teaspoon basil
salt
pepper
1 pint sour cream

PREPARATION

Heat the beef stock, which can come from a Pot-au-feu (p. 29) or, less good but possible, a cube or a can.

Melt the butter in a large saucepan. Press the garlic into it and sauté until golden. Do not let it burn.

Stir in the flour gradually, then add the hot stock, also gradually. Season with the basil and salt and pepper to taste.

Chicken Soup

PRESENTATION

Serve in individual bowls with dollops of sour cream in each.

Chicken Soup

TIME: 2¼ hours (plus 25 minutes to complete) SERVES: About 6

COMPOSITION

1 fat stewing hen
2 quarts water
1 teaspoon salt
4 peppercorns
1 lemon
⅛ teaspoon thyme
⅛ teaspoon basil
1 garlic clove

2 small onions
1 celery stalk
2 small carrots
1 teaspoon sugar
4 tablespoons raw rice
cayenne
2 egg yolks
sour cream

PRELIMINARY PREPARATION

Cut up the chicken, cover with salted water, and bring to a boil slowly.

Squeeze the lemon and reserve the juice. Toss one-half of the rind into the pot. Add all other ingredients except rice, cayenne, egg yolks, and sour cream.

Cover the pot and let it simmer for about 2 hours or until the meat falls from the bones.

PREPARATION

Strain the stock, let it cool and skim the fat from the surface.*

* If you stop at this point, you'll have perfect chicken stock with which to make other soups such as those that follow immediately. If you can't resist going on and making this soup, you'll have to start all over again or resort to canned chicken broth for stock.

SOUP SORCERY

For 6 people, reheat 6 cups of stock, adding the rice and lemon juice. Let the soup simmer for 20 minutes. Re-season to taste with salt and cayenne.

Just before serving, stir in the beaten egg yolks.

PRESENTATION

Float sour cream on the top of each bowl.

Borscht

TIME: About 2 hours   SERVES: 8 people

COMPOSITION

2 pounds short ribs
3 medium onions
2 sprigs fresh dill
3 medium potatoes
1 small cabbage

3 medium beets
1 lemon
½ pint sour cream
red wine

PREPARATION

Drown the short ribs, the peeled onions and the dill in a kettle containing 3 quarts of water.

Boil for 1 hour or until the meat falls from the bones and the liquid is reduced about one third.

Strain the broth into another pot, discarding the bones, onion, and dill. Save the meat.

While the ribs are cooking, peel and cube the potatoes. Chop cabbage. Peel and quarter beets.

Poke the lemon with a sharp fork in several places. Add it along with the meat and vegetables to the broth.

Simmer until the vegetables are tender.

Remove the lemon and let the soup cool slightly.

Stir in the sour cream, which should be warmed to room temperature.

PRESENTATION

Serve from a large tureen into heated soup plates.
[When you make this, provide plenty of dark bread (pumpernickel or black rye) and red wine.]

Minestrone

TIME: 1½ hours (plus overnight)   SERVES: 6-8

Minestrone means a thick—not a thickened—soup, and may be as varied as the cooks who prepare it. All minestrones contain dried legumes, vegetables, pastas, oil, herbs, and cheese. There are no fixed recipes, but here is one that serves me well. Try it and make your own variations.

COMPOSITION

½ pound dried navy beans
2 medium onions
2 celery stalks
1 small cabbage
2 small zucchini
2-3 parsley sprigs
2 tablespoons olive oil
2 garlic cloves
½ can tomato paste
1 teaspoon rosemary
1 teaspoon salt
½ teaspoon pepper
2 whole cloves
12 thick slices French bread
1½ cups grated Romano or Parmesan cheese

PRELIMINARY PREPARATION

Soak the navy beans overnight.

PREPARATION

Drain the beans, then boil them in 3 quarts of water for about 1 hour or until tender.
Meanwhile chop the onions, celery, and parsley, shred the cabbage, and dice the zucchini.

SOUP SORCERY

Heat the oil in a large pot. Press the garlic into it and brown briefly. Add the onions and celery. Brown them lightly. Stir in the tomato paste which has been diluted with an equal amount of water. Cook for 5 minutes.

Add the remaining vegetables, the herbs, and the seasonings. Stir in the beans and their juice. Cook slowly for about 25 minutes.

Toast the bread.

PRESENTATION

Pour the soup over the toast. Sprinkle heavily with grated cheese.

Lentil Soup

TIME: About 3 hours (plus time to soak lentils)   SERVES: 6

COMPOSITION

- 1 cup dried lentils
- 1 teaspoon salt
- 1 medium onion
- 1 bay leaf
- 2 parsley sprigs
- 1 carrot
- 2 thick slices bacon
- 1/8 pound butter
- thyme
- 2 egg yolks
- 1 lemon

PRELIMINARY PREPARATION

Soak the lentils in cold water overnight. Consult directions on packaged variety. Some require less soaking than others.

PREPARATION

Drain the lentils and put them to cook in 1½ quarts of salted water.

Dice the vegetables and chop the parsley. Crush the bay leaf.

Sauté the bacon in butter until it is crisp. Add the onion, the carrot, and a pinch of thyme. Simmer for 8-10 minutes. Add the bay leaf and the parsley.

Combine the vegetables with the lentils, cover the kettle, and simmer the soup for about 2½ hours or until the lentils are well cooked.

Put it through a blender or food mill and return to the fire for a few minutes. Beat the egg yolks slightly and stir some of the hot soup into them to keep them from curdling. Then add them to the soup, stir, and serve.

PRESENTATION

Serve from a large tureen, with thin lemon slices floating on top.

Pumpkin Soup

TIME: 25 minutes   SERVES: 4-5

COMPOSITION

1½ cups pumpkin pulp (fresh or canned)
3½ cups beef broth
salt
pepper

Worcestershire sauce
3 tablespoons butter
2 garlic cloves
nutmeg

PREPARATION

In a large bowl, combine the pumpkin and the broth. Season to taste with salt, pepper, and Worcestershire sauce.

Melt the butter, add the pressed garlic cloves, and sauté quickly.

SOUP SORCERY

∼∼

Pour the pumpkin broth into the pot and simmer until it is very hot.

Adjust the seasonings just before serving.

PRESENTATION

Sprinkle nutmeg over each brimming bowl.

Cheddar Soup

TIME: 25-30 minutes   SERVES: 4 men or 6 women

This is a hearty soup enjoyed by all men and an occasional woman.

COMPOSITION

1¼ *cups grated Cheddar cheese*	2 *tablespoons flour*
	1 *clove garlic*
2 *egg yolks*	1 *cup dry white wine*
2 *tablespoons cream*	*salt*
3 *cups milk*	*pepper*
2 *tablespoons butter*	*nutmeg*

PREPARATION

Grate the cheese.

With a fork, blend together the egg yolks and the cream.

Scald the milk.

Melt the butter in the top part of a double boiler over simmering water. Stir in the flour. Press the garlic into the mixture, then add the hot milk, stirring constantly until the mixture is smooth. Simmer for 20 minutes, stirring constantly.

Add the wine, salt, pepper, and a pinch of nutmeg.

Add one-half of the grated cheese and stir the soup until it is completely melted. Slowly blend in the egg mixture. Cook for 2-3 minutes only.

PRESENTATION

Serve with a topping of the remaining grated cheese.

P.S. *If you ask me, every woman would like it. It's the "occasional woman" who can never resist anything.*

Exotic Tomato Soup

TIME: 30 minutes   SERVES: 8

COMPOSITION

1 medium onion	½ teaspoon soda
1 quart milk	1 teaspoon sugar
4-5 whole cloves	salt
4 cans tomato soup	½ pint whipping cream

PREPARATION

Peel and chop the onion. Scald the milk with the onion and cloves.

Empty the tomato soup into the top of a double-boiler. Blend in the soda and the sugar. Heat over simmering water.

Combine the strained hot milk with the soup, stirring constantly. Season to taste with salt.

PRESENTATION

Pour the soup into individual oven-proof soup bowls and cover the entire surface of each with whipped cream.

Brown—but do not burn—the cream under the broiler.

SOUP SORCERY

Black Bean Soup

TIME: 15 minutes SERVES: 4

COMPOSITION

2 eggs
1 teaspoon grated lemon rind
1 10½ ounce can black bean soup
1 10½ ounce can Madrilene consommé

PREPARATION

Hard-cook, shell, and slice the eggs.
Grate the lemon rind.
Blend together the soups, add the lemon, and heat well.

PRESENTATION

Serve in a tureen or individual soup plates.
Garnish with slices of egg.

Lobster Pea Bisque

TIME: 12-15 minutes SERVES: 6

COMPOSITION

1 6-ounce can lobster meat
sherry
2 cans green pea soup
1 can tomato soup
3 soup-cans milk
1 pint sour cream

PREPARATION

Flake the lobster meat, cover with sherry, and let stand.
Mix the soups and the milk together. Heat them without boiling.

Add the sherried lobster and continue cooking without boiling until the lobster is warmed.

PRESENTATION

Serve in individual bowls, each topped with sour cream.

Crab Soup with Beer

TIME: 10 minutes   SERVES: 4

COMPOSITION

1 can tomato soup
1 can pea soup
1 12-ounce can beer
1 cup milk
1 6-ounce can crab meat

PREPARATION

Combine all ingredients. Heat thoroughly without boiling.

PRESENTATION

Serve immediately.

Oysters Abstruse

TIME: 30 minutes (or 1½ hours if you can spare the time)   SERVES: 2-4

COMPOSITION

1 parsley sprig
12 chives
3 tablespoons butter
1 pint fresh oysters (including juice)
Worcestershire sauce
¼ teaspoon salt
pepper
⅛ teaspoon oregano
1 can cream of chicken soup
1 cup heavy cream
1 pint sour cream
paprika

SOUP SORCERY

PREPARATION

Mince the parsley and chives.

Melt the butter. Pour in the oysters and their liquid. Simmer them gently until the juice just begins to boil.

Add a dash or two of Worcestershire, the salt, pepper to taste, the chives, the parsley, and the oregano.

Carefully stir in the soup and the sweet cream. Watch the pot and let it simmer for 10 minutes. Don't let it boil or you've had it.

At the last minute blend in ½ cup of the sour cream.

PRESENTATION

If you are starving, eat the soup immediately.

Otherwise, cool it and let the flavors meld together for at least an hour. Reheat before serving.

In either case, serve the soup in individual soup plates with a dollop of sour cream and a dash of paprika in each.

Cream of Corn Soup

TIME: 30-40 minutes   SERVES: 6

COMPOSITION

2½ cups cooked corn (preferably fresh)
1 small onion
⅛ pound butter
4 tablespoons flour
2½ cups milk

½ pint cream
curry powder
pepper
1½ teaspoons salt
chives

PREPARATION

Cook fresh corn quickly, then scrape the kernels from the cob. Mince the onion. Sauté it in butter until golden.

Stir in the flour, then cook and stir for 5 minutes.

Add the corn, the milk, and the cream. Season with a dash each of curry and pepper. Add the salt, heat to boiling, and serve immediately.

PRESENTATION

Sprinkle liberally with fresh chopped chives.

Canned Corn Chowder

TIME: 20 minutes   SERVES: 4

COMPOSITION

4 slices of bacon
2 medium onions
1 sprig parsley
2 tablespoons butter
1 quart milk

1 can (1 pound 1 ounce) cream-style corn
salt
pepper
nutmeg

PREPARATION

Sauté the bacon until it is very crisp, then crumble it.

Sauté the finely chopped onions and parsley in butter until they are limp.

Combine all ingredients and heat them well without boiling. Season to taste with salt, pepper, and a dash of nutmeg.

PRESENTATION

Serve from a small tureen or in individual soup plates.

Cream of Olive Soup

TIME: 25 minutes   SERVES: 4

COMPOSITION

1 cup chopped ripe olives
3 cups chicken stock
1 garlic clove
½ pint heavy cream
2 egg yolks
⅛ cup sherry
salt
pepper

PREPARATION

Chop the olives or drain 2 cans of the minced variety.
Simmer the stock, olives, and pressed garlic for 15 minutes.
Blend together the cream and the egg yolks. Add them to the soup.
Flavor with a dash of sherry.
Season to taste with salt and pepper.
Cook for 4-5 minutes before serving.

PRESENTATION

Serve in small individual bowls.

Simple Singhalese Soup

TIME: 20 minutes—hot   SERVES: 4
(plus 1 hour—cold)

COMPOSITION

1 small onion
1 clove garlic
2 tablespoons butter
1 can cream of pea soup
1 can chicken consommé
1 can beef bouillon
1 teaspoon sugar
3 teaspoons curry powder
cayenne
1 pint heavy cream
1 tart apple

Almond Chicken Soup

PREPARATION

Grate the onion and combine it with the pressed garlic. Sauté them in butter very briefly.

Combine the soups and add them to the pan. Heat well without boiling. Season with sugar, curry, and cayenne. Stir in the cream and heat again.

PRESENTATION

Serve very hot or very cold. In either case, garnish with apple. Cut the apple in julienne strips at the last minute or they will turn dark.

Almond Chicken Soup

TIME: 45 minutes   SERVES: 4

COMPOSITION

2 cups blanched almonds
1 ice cube
4 cups chicken stock
¼ cup finely chopped cooked ham
¼ teaspoon ground cloves
¼ teaspoon mace
¼ teaspoon nutmeg
salt
cayenne
1 bay leaf
¼ teaspoon thyme
¼ teaspoon basil
⅛ teaspoon celery salt
1 tablespoon sherry

PREPARATION

Chop ½ cup of the almonds coarsely. Spin the remainder in a blender together with an ice cube. This will keep oil from forming.

Combine all ingredients except almonds and sherry. Simmer for 15 minutes, then strain the soup through a fine sieve.

Add the almond paste and sherry. Simmer for another 20-25 minutes. Stir in the chopped almonds and serve.

SOUP SORCERY

PRESENTATION

Serve this in your finest soup dishes.

Coconut Soup

TIME: 10-12 minutes   SERVES: 4

COMPOSITION

- 1 tablespoon butter
- 1 cup canned shredded coconut
- 2 cups chicken broth
- 1/8 teaspoon curry powder
- 1/2 teaspoon salt
- 1 tablespoon cornstarch
- 1/2 cup light cream

PREPARATION

Melt the butter, add the coconut and the broth, and heat well.

Mix the dry ingredients with a bit of the hot broth and stir into the pot.

Simmer the soup over low heat for about 5 minutes. Add the cream and simmer until hot.

PRESENTATION

Serve hot or chilled.

Watercress Soup

TIME: 45 minutes (plus 2 hours to chill)   SERVES: 6

COMPOSITION

- 3-4 potatoes
- 2 medium onions
- 2 tablespoons butter
- 3 cups chicken stock
- 1 teaspoon salt
- 1 cup milk
- 1/2 pint heavy cream
- 2 bunches watercress

Iced Curry Soup

PREPARATION

Peel and slice the potatoes and the onions.

Sauté the onions in the butter until golden. Add the potatoes, the chicken stock, and the salt. Simmer the vegetables for 30-35 minutes or until they are tender. Purée the soup in a blender, add the milk, and bring it to a boil. Stir in the cream.

Meanwhile, cook one bunch of the watercress in boiling salted water to cover for about 4 minutes. Drain. Toss the cress into the blender briefly. Add the purée to the soup.

Chill the soup thoroughly before serving.

PRESENTATION

Garnish with well-washed, chopped watercress.

Iced Curry Soup

TIME: 25 minutes (plus 25 minutes to chill)   SERVES: 4

COMPOSITION

4 cups chicken stock   *½ cup heavy cream*
2 teaspoons curry powder   *1 avocado or 1 apple*
2 egg yolks

PREPARATION

Heat the stock over a low flame.

Make a paste of curry with a little of the stock. Add the paste to the soup, blending well.

Beat the egg yolks, then blend them into the cream. Add this mixture to the soup, let it cool, then chill well.

SOUP SORCERY

PRESENTATION

Serve in individual bowls over chunks of avocado or peeled tart apple.

Cucumber Soup

TIME: 30 minutes (plus 1 hour to chill) SERVES: 6

COMPOSITION

3 *large cucumbers*	*salt*
2 *medium onions*	*pepper*
1 *cup milk*	½ *cup cream*
3 *tablespoons butter*	½ *cup sour cream*
3 *tablespoons flour*	*chives*
3 *cups chicken broth*	

PREPARATION

Peel and slice the cucumbers. Peel and chop the onions.
Scald the milk with the onions.
Cook the cucumbers in butter for about 10 minutes, using a covered pan.
Add the flour and stir until the mixture is thick and smooth, then add the broth, stirring constantly.
Stir in the onion-milk mixture.
Season to taste with salt and pepper and continue cooking for another 10 minutes.
Purée the soup in a blender, then add the sweet cream.
Chill for at least 1 hour.

PRESENTATION

Just before serving add the sour cream.
Garnish with chopped chives.

Vichyssoise

TIME: 1 hour (plus 2 hours to chill)   SERVES: 8-10

COMPOSITION

4 *leeks or 4-6 green onions*
1 *medium Bermuda onion*
5 *medium potatoes*
2 *tablespoons butter*
2 *tablespoons flour*
1½ *quarts chicken broth*

2 *cups milk*
1 *pint light cream*
½ *pint heavy cream*
1 *tablespoon salt*
sherry
chives

PREPARATION

Peel and slice the leeks; retain the white part only.
Slice the Bermuda onion very thin, discarding the skin.
Pare and thinly slice the potatoes.
Sauté the leeks and onion in butter until golden. Stir in the flour. Do not let it brown.
Add the potatoes and the chicken broth. Cook for about 40 minutes, or until the potatoes are soft but not mushy.
Force everything through a sieve, or better still, use the blender. Return the purée to the fire and add the milk and light cream.
Bring the soup almost to a boil, season it with salt, then let it cool.
Add the heavy cream and a dash of sherry, stir well, and chill very well.

PRESENTATION

Before serving, scatter finely chopped chives over the surface.

SOUP SORCERY

Gazpacho

If you are looking for this in the soup section, you're in the wrong pew. Look under salads (p. 413), where it rightfully belongs.

Cold Tomato Soup

TIME: 15 minutes (plus 45-60 minutes to chill)
SERVES: 6

COMPOSITION

1 medium onion	6 teaspoons olive oil
1 garlic clove	juice of 2 lemons
1 can Italian style tomatoes	salt
1 quart size can tomato juice	celery salt

PREPARATION

Grate the onion, press the garlic, and squash the tomatoes. Spin them to a liquid state in a blender.

Combine all ingredients, season, mix thoroughly, and chill well.

18764

Cold Buttermilk Soup

TIME: 30 minutes (plus 1 hour to chill)   SERVES: 6

COMPOSITION

1¾ pounds shrimps
½ medium cucumber
1 tablespoon finely minced fresh dill
1 tablespoon mustard
1 teaspoon salt
1 teaspoon sugar
⅛ teaspoon curry powder
1 quart buttermilk
2 tablespoons chopped herbs (chives, parsley, and summer savory)

PREPARATION

Clean, cook, and chop the shrimps. Mince the cucumber and the dill.

Mix together the shrimps, cucumber, and seasonings. Stir in the buttermilk.

Chill thoroughly.

PRESENTATION

Drop a couple of ice cubes into each soup plate. Pour in the soup. Sprinkle with the combined fresh herbs.

TREATS AND TREATMENTS WITH EGGS

BASIC FACTS concerning eggs are available from hens, from other cook books, and from the encyclopedia. Outward appearance, color, size (except in baking), or grade are not terribly important. It's the interior quality of the egg that matters.

If you question the age of an egg, carry out your own research. Shake it. If it rattles, shun it. A bad egg will always rattle. Or drop it gently into cold water. It should sink, not swim.

An egg should be kept cool. This is not to retard hatching; it is to preserve the taste and flavor. Before use, it should be allowed to come to room temperature. If you have forgotten to take it out of the refrigerator beforehand, let it stand in tepid water for a few minutes.

TREATS AND TREATMENTS WITH EGGS

There are dozens and dozens of ways to cook eggs. Look in your cooking primer for the elementary procedures, but for uninhibited adventures, consider the following recipes. Most are written for a single serving, designed for a man feeding himself. Most people, having discovered these recipes, will want to show them off. Nothing could be simpler than doubling or quadrupling the egg and its attendant ingredients.

The treats are good for all occasions. The treatments are more specialized. If they sound unlikely, don't stop to wonder. Egg yourself on. You won't be sorry.

THE TREATS

Eggs Diable

TIME: 30 minutes   SERVES: 1

COMPOSITION

1 small onion
1 teaspoon chopped parsley
1 large pinch of mixed herbs, including basil
2 tablespoons olive oil
1 garlic clove

1 cup tomato sauce
salt
pepper
3 eggs
4 slices French bread
grated Parmesan cheese

PREPARATION

Chop the onion and mince the parsley.

Mix the herbs.

Using a shallow pan, sauté the pressed garlic and the onion in the heated oil. Cook until both are golden.

Add the tomato sauce, the salt, the pepper, and the herbs. Cook for about 15 minutes.

Break the eggs into the sauce, trying hard to keep the yolks intact. Spoon hot sauce over them.

Cover the pan tightly and let it simmer for about 12 minutes.

Toast the French bread.

PRESENTATION

Place the eggs carefully on hot toast. Cover them with sauce. Sprinkle generously with grated cheese.

P.S. *There are men who eat three eggs, but if you slipped in an extra egg, you could certainly feed two people with this recipe.*

TREATS AND TREATMENTS WITH EGGS

Eggs in Ale

TIME: 25-30 minutes   SERVES: 1-2

COMPOSITION

1 medium onion
1 medium green pepper
¼ cup dry bread crumbs
¼ cup grated sharp cheese
⅛ pound butter

salt
pepper
2-4 eggs
1 cup ale or beer

PREPARATION

Chop the vegetables.
Crumb the bread.
Grate the cheese.
Sauté the onion and green pepper in butter until they are limp. Put them into a small buttered casserole. Break the eggs into the casserole, spacing them evenly. Season with salt and pepper.
Mix together the cheese and the bread crumbs. Throw the mixture on top of the eggs.
Add the beer.
Bake at 350° for 10-12 minutes.

Eggs Funghi

TIME: 10-12 minutes   SERVES: 1

COMPOSITION

1 can cream of mushroom soup
1 6-ounce can button mushrooms
Worcestershire sauce

salt
pepper
2 eggs
toast

Eggs in Cream

PREPARATION

Dilute the soup with the canned mushroom juice. Add the mushrooms. Season with Worcestershire, salt, and pepper. Heat thoroughly without boiling.

Poach the eggs in salted water.

Toast bread.

PRESENTATION

Cover toast with eggs.

Cover eggs with sauce.

Eggs in Cream

TIME: 15 minutes   SERVES: 1

This might be considered as a treatment on a jaundiced morning, but it's too good to limit to those rare occasions.

COMPOSITION

2 *bacon slices*	*pepper*
½ *cup sour cream*	*Tabasco*
1 *jigger sherry*	2 *eggs*
salt	

PREPARATION

Chop the bacon. Throw it into a casserole. Add the sour cream and the seasonings to taste.

Place the casserole in a 450° oven for 10 minutes. Remove it.

Break the eggs into the sauce.

PRESENTATION

Eat immediately—the eggs *will* be cooked.

TREATS AND TREATMENTS WITH EGGS

Eggs Avocado

TIME: ½ hour   SERVES: 1 man or 2 women

Serve only to those who like eggs, and avocado, and cheese—and who doesn't?

COMPOSITION

3 thin 3-inch-square cheese slices
¼ cup grated Parmesan cheese
1 small avocado
½ tablespoon lemon juice
capers
3 tablespoons butter
salt
pepper
2 eggs
paprika

PREPARATION

Preheat oven to 450°.
Slice and grate the cheeses as necessary.
Peel and slice the avocado.
Toss the lemon juice, butter, a few capers, and some salt and pepper into a one-man casserole. Put it in the oven. Let the sauce come to a boil.
Poach the eggs briefly in salted water.
Place a layer of avocado slices in the casserole. Add the eggs. Top them with another avocado layer. Top with the sliced cheese, sprinkle with salt, paprika, and the Parmesan cheese.
Bake at 450° until the cheese is melted.

PRESENTATION

Serve directly from the casserole.

P.S. *Doubled, this makes a marvelous ladies' lunch for four.*

Quick Curried Eggs

TIME: 20 minutes SERVES: 1

COMPOSITION

3 *eggs*
2 *tablespoons butter*
1 *tablespoon grated onion*

1 *teaspoon (more or less) curry powder*
¾ *cup milk*
2 *slices toast*

PREPARATION

Hard-cook, shell, and slice the eggs.
Sauté the onion in butter. Stir in the curry and the milk. When well blended, add the eggs. Heat well.
Toast the bread.

PRESENTATION

On toast.

Ox-Eyes

TIME: Depends upon the number SERVES: 1 or any number

COMPOSITION

bread
sour cream
butter

eggs
salt
pepper

PREPARATION

Slice good bread into thick slabs. Make a 3-inch hole in the center of each slice.
Spread each side of the bread with sour cream. Sauté each slice in butter. When one side is well tanned, turn it and

TREATS AND TREATMENTS WITH EGGS

break an egg into each hole. Sprinkle with salt and pepper and continue cooking slowly until the eggs are set, adding butter to the pan as necessary.

Eggs Riviera

TIME: 10-15 minutes   SERVES: 1

COMPOSITION

2 tablespoons dry sherry
½ cup milk
½ can cream of mushroom soup
2 teaspoons butter
salt
pepper
2 eggs

PREPARATION

Stir sherry and milk into the soup to make a creamy mixture. Heat in a heat-proof serving dish. Stir in a generous lump of butter. Add salt and pepper to taste.

Break in 2 eggs and continue cooking until they satisfy your taste in eggs.

P.S. *Double this and sprinkle it with lots of fresh parsley and you've got company food.*

Eggs with Mushrooms

TIME: 15-25 minutes   SERVES: 1

COMPOSITION

1 large mushroom
2 tablespoons fine bread crumbs
1 teaspoon minced parsley
¼ teaspoon salt
cayenne
½ cup dry white wine
1 or 2 eggs

PREPARATION

Clean the mushroom. Remove and chop the stem.

Crumble some dry bread.

Mince the parsley.

Combine bread crumbs, parsley, and mushroom stem. Sprinkle with salt and cayenne and moisten the mixture with wine. Boil it for about 5 minutes.

Coat a ramekin with oil, place the mushroom cap in the bottom and break an egg or two over the mushroom. Cover with the sauce and bake briefly in a 350° oven.

Ham and Eggs, Baked

TIME: 15-25 minutes   SERVES: 1

COMPOSITION

½ cup finely chopped cooked ham

1 teaspoon minced parsley

pepper

butter

2 eggs

sharp cheese

PREPARATION

Chop ham. Combine it with the chopped parsley and some freshly ground pepper.

Butter 2 muffin tins or custard cups. Press the ham mixture on the sides and bottoms of the cups.

Break an egg into each. Sprinkle with grated cheese.

Bake for about 12 minutes at 350°.

TREATS AND TREATMENTS WITH EGGS

Eggs Mornay

TIME: 15 minutes   **SERVES**: 1

COMPOSITION

2 eggs   1 cup Mornay Sauce

PREPARATION

Prepare the sauce (p. 8).

Poach the eggs. (Or hard-cook them, deshell, and chop into chunks.) Place them in a buttered ramekin.

Cover with sauce and slip under the broiler until the cheese is hot and browned.

P.S. *If you're going to make the recipe for Mornay Sauce, you might as well invite two or three guests.*

Swiss Eggs

TIME: About 25 minutes   **SERVES**: 1 (or 2)

COMPOSITION

1 cup grated Swiss cheese
½ teaspoon chopped chervil
½ teaspoon chopped parsley
½ teaspoon chopped chives
½ teaspoon chopped scallions
3 eggs

⅛ pound butter
¾ cup dry white wine
nutmeg
salt
pepper

PREPARATION

Grate the cheese.
Chop the herbs and onions.
Separate the eggs.

64

Put the cheese, the butter, the wine, and the seasonings into a buttered casserole. Mix well.

Cook gently on top of the stove until the cheese melts and bubbles. Stir constantly. Lower the heat. Beat in the egg yolks, one at a time. Add the egg whites, beaten stiff.

Continue cooking and stirring until the mixture is well scrambled but still moist.

P.S. *This is good for breakfast, brunch, or lunch; with the addition of one egg it would serve two.*

Eggs Orsini

TIME: About 15 minutes   SERVES: 2

COMPOSITION

4 eggs	2 tablespoons butter
½ cup grated Parmesan cheese	salt
	pepper

PREPARATION

Separate the eggs. Drop each yolk into its own individual cup or glass.

Butter a small pie tin liberally.

Beat the egg whites thoroughly. Spread the stiff froth in the pie pan. Level it. Make indentations in the surface of the white plane with a tablespoon.

Drop an unbroken yolk into each hole.

Sprinkle lavishly with grated cheese. Dust with salt and coarse pepper.

Bake at 350° until the egg yolks are set.

THE TREATMENTS

Eggs Obstaculos

TIME: 10 minutes   SERVES: 1

COMPOSITION

2 tablespoons oil
½ cup tomato sauce
Tabasco

2 eggs
3 ounces beer

PREPARATION

Heat the oil. Pour in the tomato sauce. Add Tabasco according to taste.

Break the eggs into the sauce and cook them slowly until set to your taste. Pour in the beer and let it heat thoroughly.

The Prairie Oyster, A Reminder

TIME: 3 minutes   SERVES: 1 hung-over man

COMPOSITION

1 egg, fresh and raw
1 dash Worcestershire sauce

1 dash of Tabasco
1 splash of liquor

PREPARATION

None

PRESENTATION

Take it like a man.

Eggs in Beer

TIME: 10 minutes   SERVES: 1

COMPOSITION

1 12-ounce can of beer
⅛ teaspoon celery salt

pepper
Tabasco
2 or more eggs

PREPARATION

Pour 1 full bottle or can of beer into a saucepan. Add the seasonings. Bring to a boil.
Add the eggs. Poach them for 5-6 minutes.
Conserve your energy; don't stir.

Egg-in-Your-Beer Soup

TIME: 10 minutes   SERVES: 4

This is tops for parched throats and throbbing heads on certain bleary mornings!

COMPOSITION

4 slabs French bread
4 egg yolks
3 tablespoons sour cream
1 quart beer

1 teaspoon sugar
salt
pepper
cinnamon

PREPARATION

Toast the bread.
Separate the eggs. Stir the yolks into the sour cream.
Bring the beer and the sugar to a boil. Add a small amount of

TREATS AND TREATMENTS WITH EGGS

the hot beer to the egg yolks, then stir them gradually into the pot of beer.

Season to taste with the salt, pepper, and cinnamon.

PRESENTATION

Pour the soup over the bread.

P.S. *This is also good on nonbleary, cool evenings.*

UNDERWATER EXPOSÉ: FISH, MOLLUSKS, AND CRUSTACEANS

MAN's culinary adventures with fish are far too limited; the chief reason is that sometimes he doesn't know a good fish when he sees one, unless he has caught it himself. In that case any fish looks good.

Good fish *must* be fresh fish. The signs are simple: the fish must smell sweet and not *too* fishy, the flesh should be firm to touch, and the skin tight but elastic. If the head is on, look at the eye. It should stare brightly back at you. If the fish passes the test, you have a fresh fish on your hands. If such inspection is beyond you, deal only with the best fish dealer in the area.

Cleaning a whole fresh fish is admittedly a chore, but it can be done very quickly. To remove the scales, dip the fish quickly in boiling water and scrape them off with the dull

UNDERWATER EXPOSÉ: FISH, MOLLUSKS, AND CRUSTACEANS

edge of a knife. Jab each side of the fins with a sharp pointed knife and jerk them out. Slash the belly from the tail upwards and expose the guts. Remove them completely and wash out with cold water. You and the recipe will decide whether the head and tail are to be removed.

If the fish available is not strictly fresh, buy the frozen variety. Let it thaw in the refrigerator shortly before cooking. Thawing at room temperature tends to make the fish flaccid and flat.

Fish cooks quickly. Never let it overcook. The final result should be moist and tender, with a delicate flaky texture. There are proven methods of baking, broiling and poaching fish that can be found in any standard cook book, but for new pleasures, try some of these recipes. Still more will be found in the Casserole chapter.

Court Bouillon for Fish and Shellfish

TIME: 40 minutes

To poach a fish in the best possible way, one must have a court bouillon, and the best is made with fish heads and bones. They are free for the asking from any fish dealer. If the idea of the heads is repulsive, they may be eliminated, but the bones and trimmings are a must.

COMPOSITION

- *1 pound fish trimmings and bones*
- *1 cup dry white wine*
- *1 quart water*
- *2 parsley sprigs*
- *½ celery stalk with leaves*
- *1 onion stuck with 2 cloves*
- *1 bay leaf*
- *1 teaspoon salt*
- *4-6 peppercorns*
- *¼ teaspoon thyme*
- *½ lemon*

PREPARATION

Put all ingredients together in a large kettle.
Bring to a boil.
Simmer for 30 minutes.
Strain before using to poach any fish.

FISH

Stuffed Fish

TIME: 45-60 minutes   SERVES: 6-8

COMPOSITION

3 dozen shucked oysters
1 pound shrimp
½ pound fresh mushrooms
8-9 green onions (scallions)
1 medium white onion
½ pound butter
1 cup flour
4 cups court bouillon (see preceding recipe)
cayenne
1 6-pound fish or 6 1-pound fishes
olive oil
parsley

PREPARATION

Scald, but do not boil, the oysters. Chop them fine.

Peel and cook the shrimp. Chop them fine.

Chop the mushrooms—fine. Chop the green and white onions, also fine.

Melt the butter. Sauté the onions. Stir in the flour. Add the court bouillon slowly. Stir thoroughly. Boil about 5 minutes. Add the oysters, the shrimp, and the mushrooms.

Remove the backbone(s) and stuff the fish, using as much of the stuffing as possible. Keep the rest hot, to be used as a sauce.

Brush the fish with oil and bake in a hot oven (400°-450°). Do not overcook. The time varies with the size and thickness of the fish or fishes. Test with a fork—the fish-flesh flakes easily when it is done; 30 to 40 minutes should be the maximum time.

Poached Trout

PRESENTATION

Arrange the fish or fishes on a large platter, cover with the remaining sauce, and garnish with parsley sprigs.

Poached Trout

TIME: 25-30 minutes   SERVES: 4

COMPOSITION

4 trout fillets, about ½ pound each
1 cup dry white wine
salt
1 cup chopped green onions (scallions) and chives, mixed

¼ pound butter
3 tablespoons flour
2 cups milk
¼ teaspoon cayenne
2 egg yolks
paprika

PREPARATION

Poach the trout in ⅔ cup of wine and enough lightly salted water to cover for about 6 minutes.

Meanwhile, chop the onions and chives. Sauté them in heated butter briefly. Stir in the flour. Cook slowly for 5-6 minutes.

Add the milk and ⅓ cup of wine. Cook and stir for about 10 minutes. Season with salt and cayenne. Stir in the egg yolks. Do not let the sauce boil.

PRESENTATION

Remove the trout to a flame-proof serving platter. Spoon the sauce over them. Sprinkle lightly with paprika. Place under the broiler until piping hot.

UNDERWATER EXPOSÉ: FISH, MOLLUSKS, AND CRUSTACEANS

Fish Fillets Marguéry

TIME: 30-40 minutes   SERVES: 4-6

COMPOSITION

1½ pounds whitefish fillets	1 cup milk
1 cup cooked shrimp	½ cup cream
1 cup sauterne	paprika
1 cup water	salt
⅛ pound butter	pepper
4 tablespoons flour	2 tablespoons sherry
½ cup fish liquid	1 dozen raw oysters

PREPARATION

Clean and fillet the fish. Cook and clean the shrimp.

Bring the sauterne and water to a boil in a large skillet. Add the fish. Cover. Simmer gently for about 5 minutes, only until the fish is white.

Drain off the liquid, reserving ½ cup for present needs. Use the rest the next time you prepare court bouillon (p. 73).

Melt the butter. Stir in the flour until well blended and light brown. Add the fish juice, the milk, and the cream. Continue cooking and stirring until the sauce is thick. Give it a dash each of paprika, salt, and pepper. Add the sherry.

Taste. Adjust the seasonings if necessary.

Place the fillets in a well-buttered shallow baking dish. Add the oysters and the shrimp. Cover with the sauce.

Broil until bubbly and delicately browned.

Sole Véronique

TIME: 25 minutes   SERVES: 6

COMPOSITION

1½ pounds sole fillets
1 small onion
1 garlic clove
4-6 peppercorns
2 parsley sprigs
juice of ½ lemon
1 bay leaf
1 cup dry white wine
¼ teaspoon thyme
¼ cup water

5 tablespoons butter
1½ tablespoons flour
salt
pepper
¼ cup milk
2 tablespoons cream
½ pound white grapes, preferably seedless
⅛ cup minced parsley

PREPARATION

Place the fillets in a well-buttered shallow baking dish. Add the onion (quartered), the garlic (pressed), the peppercorns, the parsley, the lemon juice, the bay leaf (crushed), the wine, the thyme, and the water.

Poach in a 350° oven for 15 minutes.

Melt 3 tablespoons of the butter. Stir in the flour until well blended. Season to taste with salt and pepper. Add ¾ cup of the liquid from the sole. Stir until thickened.

Add the milk, the cream, and 2 tablespoons of butter.

Add the grapes, peeled or not as you prefer but definitely seeded, and the parsley.

PRESENTATION

Pour the sauce over the fish and serve immediately.

UNDERWATER EXPOSÉ: FISH, MOLLUSKS, AND CRUSTACEANS

Kazia's Fish Steaks

TIME: 45-60 minutes   SERVES: 4

COMPOSITION

2 pounds fish steaks (salmon, halibut, tuna, yellowtail, or *swordfish*)
2-3 green onions (scallions)
½ cup dry bread crumbs
½ cup grated Parmesan cheese
¼ cup olive oil

salt
pepper
1 teaspoon oregano
1 garlic clove
¾ cup sauterne
¾ cup water
1 lemon
⅛ cup minced fresh dill

PREPARATION

Obtain the steaks at least one-inch thick.
Chop the onions very fine.
Grate the bread and cheese. Mix them together thoroughly.
Rub each fish steak with olive oil. Sprinkle each liberally with salt, pepper, and oregano. Sprinkle with pressed garlic. (This is an art but it can be done.)
Place the steaks side by side in a shallow baking dish. Mix the wine and water and pour it around but not over the fish. Cover them with the chopped onion and the bread-cheese mixture.
Bake uncovered in a 400° oven for 25-30 minutes.

PRESENTATION

Serve with thinly sliced lemon and the minced fresh dill.

Broiled Tuna or Swordfish Steaks

TIME: About 30 minutes   SERVES: 4

COMPOSITION

2 pounds fresh tuna or swordfish sliced about 1½ inch thick
4 tablespoons oil
salt
pepper

1 teaspoon chopped fresh mint
1 tablespoon minced parsley
1 garlic clove
1½ cups dry bread crumbs
1 lemon

PREPARATION

Lave the steaks with oil. Sprinkle them lightly with salt and pepper. Chop mint, parsley and garlic. Mix these with the bread crumbs.

Roll the fish in the crumb mixture. Pour additional oil over each steak and place in the broiler, about 4 inches below the flames.

Broil about 7 minutes on each side.

PRESENTATION

Serve hot, with thin lemon slices.

Curried Fish Steaks

TIME: 25 minutes   SERVES: 6

COMPOSITION

6 fish steaks (salmon, tuna, halibut, swordfish, or yellowtail)
juice of 1 lemon
3 tablespoons melted butter
½ cup dry vermouth
3 green onions (scallions), minced
salt
pepper
½ cup fine dry bread crumbs
½ cup grated Parmesan cheese
1 teaspoon curry powder

PREPARATION

Place the steaks on a broiling pan. Sprinkle them with lemon juice.

Combine the melted butter with the vermouth. Heat, but do not boil. Pour over the fish.

Mince the green onions and sprinkle half over the steaks.

Season with salt and pepper. Broil for about 8 minutes, basting carefully once or twice with the vermouth-butter.

Turn the fish. Sprinkle with the remaining onions. Season as before. Broil and baste as before for another 8 minutes.

Mix together the bread crumbs, the cheese, and the curry. Spread it on the steaks. Return them to the broiler for 2-3 minutes. Serve quickly.

Broiled Fish Steak with Olive Sauce

TIME: 25 minutes   SERVES: 6

COMPOSITION

2 pounds halibut or swordfish steaks
½ cup melted butter
1 teaspoon salt
1 teaspoon paprika
½ teaspoon pepper
¼ cup sliced ripe olives
1 tablespoon minced parsley
2 teaspoons lemon juice
1 garlic clove

PREPARATION

Have the steaks cut in pieces to serve 6.

Combine ¼ cup of the melted butter with the salt, the paprika, and the pepper.

Place the steaks on a broiler pan about 3 inches from the flame. Brush them with some of the seasoned butter. Broil for 6-8 minutes. Baste with more of the butter.

Turn carefully, brush with the butter sauce and broil for another 6-8 minutes or until the fish flakes easily with a fork.

Crush the garlic. In a small saucepan combine garlic and the remaining ingredients with ¼ cup of melted butter. Heat well.

PRESENTATION

Place the fish on a heated platter. Pour the hot sauce over it and serve immediately.

UNDERWATER EXPOSÉ: FISH, MOLLUSKS, AND CRUSTACEANS

Fish in Wine Sauce

TIME: 1½ hours   SERVES: 6-8

COMPOSITION

THE FISH:

1 small salmon or *whitefish* (or fillets, steaks, or center cuts, allowing ½ pound per serving)
salt
pepper
oregano

1 *large onion*
3 *lemons*
2 *celery stalks*
1 *carrot*
1 *bay leaf*
6-8 *peppercorns*

THE SAUCE:

2 *cups dry white wine*
8 *egg yolks*
1 *cup sugar*

1 *tablespoon vinegar*
1 *pound blanched almonds* (*chopped and slivered*)

PREPARATION

Season the cleaned fish with salt, pepper, and oregano. Let it relax in the kitchen for a few hours—at least for one. It will be cooked just before serving.

Chop the onion, 1 lemon, the celery, and the carrot. Toss them, together with the crushed bay leaf, the peppercorns, and about 1 teaspoon of salt into 2 quarts of water in a kettle that will accommodate the fish. Let it boil for about 10 minutes.

Start the sauce by heating the wine in a double boiler.

Squeeze the remaining lemons and separate 8 eggs.

Beat together the egg yolks, sugar, vinegar, and lemon juice. Season with salt to taste. Blend slowly into the hot (never boiling) wine. Keep stirring until the sauce is thick. Add the nuts. Set aside, keeping the sauce hot until you have poached the fish.

Allow approximately 7-10 minutes per pound for a whole fish (depending upon its thickness), and less for slices. Place the fish in the seasoned water. Let it cook gently until firm. Watch closely. Minutes count.

PRESENTATION

Remove the fish or fillets gently to your best and largest platter and cover with the sauce.

P.S. *If you live on the East Coast, a whole bluefish, halibut steaks, or flounder fillets would all be wonderful with this recipe. For those near Florida, pompano would love this treatment. Some shops carry the French fish kettles designed for cooking whole fish. They are worth the investment!*

Barbecued Fish Hawaii

TIME: 15 minutes (preparation)   SERVES: 4
60 minutes (marination)
10-12 minutes to barbecue

This is *luau* fare. Increase quantities in direct proportion to the number of hungry mouths surrounding you.

COMPOSITION

2 pounds fish fillets or steaks (tuna, salmon or halibut)
1 teaspoon marjoram
½ cup soy sauce
½ cup sherry

2 tablespoons fresh lime juice
2 garlic cloves
4 tablespoons olive oil
½ teaspoon salt
¼ teaspoon coarse pepper

PREPARATION

Rub the fish with marjoram. Crush the garlic and combine with the other ingredients to prepare a marinade. Soak the fish in the marinade for at least an hour.

Broil in the oven or over charcoal.

Salmon Soufflé

TIME: About 1 hour   SERVES: 4-6

COMPOSITION

1½ pound (or 1 7-ounce can plus 1 1-pound can) salmon
½ cup finely chopped onion
½ cup finely chopped green pepper
½ pint cream
salt
pepper
6 eggs
2-3 cups Shrimp Sauce or Almond Sauce for Fish

PREPARATION

Poach the fish in court bouillon (p. 73) for about 12 minutes. Clean, skin, bone, and mash it into a grainy mass. If canned salmon is used, empty the contents into a strainer and dunk it in boiling water for a few minutes to remove some of the strongness. Flake the meat.

Chop the onions and the green peppers.

Butter a casserole or soufflé dish liberally.

Separate the eggs.

Mix onions, green peppers, cream, salt, and pepper to taste, egg yolks and fish pulp.

Beat the egg whites until stiff. Fold them into the fish mix.

Bake for 45 minutes in a 400° oven.

PRESENTATION

Serve immediately with Shrimp Sauce (p. 14) or Almond Sauce for Fish (p. 11).

Salmon Aspic

TIME: 1 hour (plus overnight to chill) SERVES: 8-10

Use the best canned salmon you can find to make the best salmon aspic you can have.

COMPOSITION

4 eggs
*1 small bottle pimiento-
    stuffed olives*
1 7-ounce can pimientos
1 large green pepper
1 small cucumber
*2-3 celery stalks
    (including some leaves)*

1 lemon
1 bottle capers
*3 packages unflavored
    gelatin*
½ cup tarragon vinegar
½ cup sugar
1 teaspoon salt
2 1-pound cans salmon

PREPARATION

Hard-cook the eggs. Mince olives, pimientos, green pepper, cucumber, and celery. Drain the capers.

Squeeze the lemon. Peel and slice the eggs.

Soften the gelatin in ½ cup of cold water. Mix it with 2 cups of boiling water, the vinegar, the lemon juice, the sugar, and the salt.

Drain and flake the salmon, then mix together with the chopped fruits and vegetables.

Place the egg slices in a pattern of your own design on the

UNDERWATER EXPOSÉ: FISH, MOLLUSKS, AND CRUSTACEANS

bottom and sides of a plain or fancy mold. Add the salmon mixture. Pour on the now-flavored gelatin. Refrigerate overnight.

PRESENTATION

Unmold and serve forth with homemade mayonnaise (p. 21).

Tuna Terrific

TIME: 30 minutes   SERVES: 6

COMPOSITION

3 cups cooked rice
1 cup diced celery
½ cup chopped onion
1 cup diced green pepper
¼ pound sliced mushrooms
¼ cup minced pimiento
⅓ cup slivered toasted almonds

2 7-ounce cans tuna in oil
¼ cup dry sherry
1 teaspoon salt
½ teaspoon monosodium glutamate
½ teaspoon rosemary
½ teaspoon marjoram
¼ teaspoon pepper

PREPARATION

Cook the rice (p. 374).
Chop, dice, mince, and slice the vegetables.
Toast and sliver the almonds.
Drain the tuna oil into a skillet. Heat it.
Add the celery, the onion, and the green pepper. Cook and stir for 3-4 minutes.
Add the tuna, the mushrooms, the sherry, the almonds, and the seasonings. Heat well. Stir occasionally.

PRESENTATION

Combine with the rice and serve.

Caviar Mousse

TIME: 15 minutes to mix
5-6 hours to chill

SERVES: 6, presumably;
less, probably

COMPOSITION

1 tablespoon unflavored gelatin
2 tablespoons cold water
½ cup boiling water
1 tablespoon lemon juice
1 teaspoon Worcestershire sauce

2 tablespoons mayonnaise
1 pint sour cream
¼ teaspoon dry mustard
1 4½-ounce jar of red caviar (minimum quantity, this)

PREPARATION

Soften the gelatin in the cold water. Dissolve it in the hot water. Add the lemon juice and the Worcestershire sauce. Blend well.
In another bowl, combine the mayonnaise and the sour cream. Add the gelatin. Flavor with the mustard.
Stir in the caviar. Pour the mixture into a mold. Chill well.

I' A Maka
(Raw Fish)

TIME: 8-10 hours to marinate
20 minutes to prepare
1 hour to refrigerate

SERVES: 4-6

Don't be afraid—share this with your fearless friends. By the time you finish, the fish is really cooked, but in a fireless manner.

87

UNDERWATER EXPOSÉ: FISH, MOLLUSKS, AND CRUSTACEANS

COMPOSITION

6-8 green onions (scallions)
½ cup fresh lime juice
4 thin sole (or haddock) fillets weighing about 2 pounds
salt
pepper
1 cup (approximately) coconut milk
2 eggs
½ cup minced parsley and chives, mixed
½ pint sour cream

PREPARATION

Chop the onions. Squeeze the limes.

Cut the fish into bit-size pieces. Cover them with onions and juice. Sprinkle heavily with salt and pepper. Marinate for about 10 hours.

Meanwhile, obtain some coconut milk by fair means (wrestling with a coconut), or foul—which entails soaking a package of coconut in milk to cover for 20-30 minutes, then straining and squeezing out the milk.

Hard-cook the eggs. Mince the whites and eat the yolks.

Chop parsley and chives.

Mix together the coconut milk, the parsley and chives, and the sour cream.

About an hour before serving time, remove the fish from the marinade. Discard the marinade.

Cover the fish with the coconut-sour cream dressing and let it chill.

PRESENTATION

Serve very cold, with drinks or as a fish course.

MOLLUSKS AND CRUSTACEANS

Mollusks and crustaceans are among nature's most adaptable edible creatures. They can be served up as an impressive main dish or as a toothsome cocktail tidbit. Be it crab, shrimp, oyster, lobster, or even octopus, it deserves all the tender attention a cook can give. The rewards are great. When it comes to liquid accompaniment, let them keep company with white wine or beer, and you'll never go wrong.

Lobster Marsala

TIME: 25 minutes   SERVES: 4

COMPOSITION

1-2 *parsley sprigs*
2 *garlic cloves*
4 *tablespoons olive oil*
1½ *pounds cooked lobster meat*
salt
pepper
½ *cup Marsala wine*

PREPARATION

Chop the parsley. Peel the garlic. Heat the oil. Brown the garlic and remove the used cloves.

Add the lobster and season to taste. Add the chopped parsley. Stir gently and briefly then cover the pan. Simmer for about 20 minutes, add the Marsala, cook for 3-4 minutes and serve.

UNDERWATER EXPOSÉ: FISH, MOLLUSKS, AND CRUSTACEANS

PRESENTATION

This is very good served on or with crisp Melba toast points.

Quick Luncheon Crab

TIME: 15-20 minutes SERVES: 4 ladies or 2 men

COMPOSITION

½ cup grated Parmesan cheese
¼ cup grated bread crumbs
2 cans chicken gumbo soup
1 pint light cream
1 pound crab meat
1 tablespoon curry powder
½ cup sherry

PREPARATION

Grate cheese and bread.

Empty the soup into a saucepan. Stir in the cream. Heat. Add the crab meat. Heat further.

Mix together the curry and sherry. Stir into the hot mixture.

Ladle into individual ramekins, top with crumbs and cheese, and place under the broiler briefly.

Balls of Shrimp

TIME: About 20 minutes after shrimps are cleaned. About 10 minutes after balls are made. SERVES: 4-6

COMPOSITION

1 pound raw shrimp
10 water chestnuts
cooking oil
1 egg
1 tablespoon cornstarch
½ teaspoon salt
1 teaspoon sherry

PREPARATION

Shell, clean, and chop (do not mash) the shrimp. Chop the water chestnuts. Mix these together.

Fill a deep pot half full of cooking oil and heat to 375°.

Beat the egg. Stir the cornstarch, salt, and sherry into it. Stir this into the shrimp mix.

Wash your hands. Oil them.

Form the mixture into small balls. Drop them into the hot oil. Fry until golden. If your cooking oil supply is low, flatten the balls into small cakes and sauté them in oil or butter until golden.

PRESENTATION

Serve as hot hors d'oeuvres or a simple entrée.

P.S. *Make the shrimp balls as far ahead of time as you please and keep them in the refrigerator. Fry them in sight of your guests or behind closed doors, if you prefer, but serve them right away.*

Shrimp Butter

TIME: 20 to 60 minutes to produce SERVES: 6-8, possibly
1-2 hours to chill

COMPOSITION

1 quart cooked shrimp   nutmeg
⅛ pound butter   *salt*
mace   *pepper*

PREPARATION

Cook and clean the shrimp. Macerate it into a paste by hand or save trouble and use a blender.

UNDERWATER EXPOSÉ: FISH, MOLLUSKS, AND CRUSTACEANS

Melt the butter. Add it to the shrimp. Season to taste with mace, nutmeg, salt, and pepper.

Heat the paste until it just begins to bubble.

Pack it into a well-buttered mold and chill very thoroughly before serving.

PRESENTATION

With crackers at cocktails or bread at lunch.

Shrimp in Beer

TIME: 20 minutes SERVES: 4 friends, for dinner or cocktails

COMPOSITION

1 small onion	2 (or more) 12-ounce packages
thyme	quick-frozen shrimp
1 bay leaf	(or 1½ pounds cleaned
1 lemon	fresh shrimp)
1 12-ounce can beer	¼ pound butter
parsley	pepper
	paper napkins

PREPARATION

Toss the onion, sliced thin, a pinch of thyme, a crushed bay leaf, and 1 tablespoon of lemon juice into a pot containing 1 can of beer. Let it come to a boil.

Chop the parsley.

Add the shrimp and simmer for about 6 minutes.

Melt the butter. Add lemon juice to taste and chopped parsley to color. Powder with coarse pepper.

PRESENTATION

Serve the shrimp in a community bowl. Provide individual bowls of lemon butter for dunking.

Napkins are essential: have plenty on hand.

Shrimp Pâté

TIME: 15 minutes with a blender, or 45 minutes by hand. Chilling time: overnight

SERVES: At least 4, possibly more

COMPOSITION

2 pounds cooked shrimp
2 medium onions
¼ pound butter
3 tablespoons lemon juice
½ cup mayonnaise

salt
pepper
dry mustard
½ cup brandy

PREPARATION

Cook and clean (or clean, then cook) the shrimp. Drop them into your blender along with the sliced onions. Blend into a paste. (The alternative? Chop both ingredients as fine as possible, then mash as long as possible.)

Melt the butter. Pour it into the paste. Add the lemon juice and mayonnaise. Stir thoroughly.

Season the paste to taste with salt, pepper, and mustard. Add the brandy.

Pack the *pâté* into a mold and chill overnight.

PRESENTATION

Unmold. Slice thinly with a hot sharp knife.

P.S. *This has many reasons for special commendation, not the least of which is that it's done a day ahead of time.*

UNDERWATER EXPOSÉ: FISH, MOLLUSKS, AND CRUSTACEANS

Shrimp with Wild Rice

TIME: 40 minutes to an hour   SERVES: 6-8

COMPOSITION

- 2 pounds cooked shrimp
- 2 cups raw wild rice
- 1 large onion
- 1 green pepper
- ¼ pound butter
- 1 cup chili sauce
- 1½ cups cream
- ½ cup sherry
- salt
- pepper

PREPARATION

Prepare the shrimp.

Wash the wild rice several times. Drop it into 6 cups of boiling salted (2 teaspoons of salt) water. Cook for 30-40 minutes. Drain well.

While the rice is cooking, sauté the onion and the green pepper, chopped fine, in butter. When soft, add the chili sauce, the cream, and the sherry. Season with salt and pepper.

Add the rice and the shrimp to the sauce, heat well and serve immediately.

Cajun Shrimp

TIME: Shrimp cleaning: 20 minutes   SERVES: 2-3-4, but never more
        Shrimp cooking: 5 minutes

COMPOSITION

- 1½ to 2 pounds plump raw shrimp
- ½ cup flour
- 2 teaspoons salt
- 1 12-ounce can beer
- ¼ pound butter
- juice of 2 lemons
- 1 tablespoon tarragon vinegar
- 2 tablespoons Worcestershire sauce
- 2 tablespoons soy sauce
- ½ teaspoon Tabasco

PREPARATION

Clean the shrimp.

Make a thin batter of flour, 1 teaspoon of salt, and beer. Add the shrimp and stir to coat each thinly but completely.

Melt half of the butter in a skillet. Do not let it burn.

In another pan, melt the rest of the butter, adding the lemon juice, the vinegar, the Worcestershire, the soysauce, and the Tabasco (by the squirt, as you sample). Stir in a teaspoon of salt and let the sauce simmer, stirring occasionally, while you attend to the shrimp.

Fish the shrimp from the batter separately with a fork and sauté lightly in the skillet. This may require several operations, depending upon the size of the shrimp and the size of your skillet.

PRESENTATION

Serve as you see fit, for cocktails or dinner.

The shrimp are to be dipped into the butter sauce, preferably with fingers, then popped into the mouth.

Scallops St. Jacques

TIME: About 45 minutes   SERVES: 4-6

COMPOSITION

2 pounds scallops (sea or bay)
3 tablespoons chopped scallions (green onions)
2 tablespoons chopped parsley
½ pound mushrooms
¼ pound butter
½ cup dry white wine
1 bay leaf
¼ teaspoon thyme

juice of 1 lemon
½ teaspoon salt
½ teaspoon white pepper
2 tablespoons flour
4 egg yolks
½ pint heavy cream
¾ cup grated Parmesan cheese
¾ cup buttered crumbs

UNDERWATER EXPOSÉ: FISH, MOLLUSKS, AND CRUSTACEANS

PREPARATION

Rinse the scallops. If sea scallops are used, slice each one lengthwise.

Chop the onions, parsley, and mushrooms.

Place 2 tablespoons of the butter, the wine, ½ cup of water, the onions, the parsley, and the crumbled bay leaf in a shallow pan. Bring the mixture to a boil.

Add the scallops. Simmer gently for 5 minutes or until tender. Remove scallops from the pan, strain the broth, and set it aside.

Melt 3 tablespoons of butter. Add the mushrooms, ⅓ cup of water, and the salt and pepper. Cook and stir for 5 minutes. Drain the mushrooms and save the liquid.

Mix the mushroom liquid with the scallop broth and 3 tablespoons of butter. Slowly stir in the flour. Cook and stir until the mixture is thickened. Re-season if necessary, then add the scallops and mushrooms. Set aside to cool.

Beat together egg yolks and cream and stir into the cooled sauce. Place over simmering water and continue cooking and stirring until thoroughly smooth.

PRESENTATION

Divide the mixture into individual scallop shells or ramekins, top each with grated cheese and crumbs and place under the broiler.

Serve as soon as the cheese is lightly browned.

Oysters Poulette

TIME: 45 minutes   SERVES: 6

COMPOSITION

¼ pound mushrooms
2 dozen oysters, shucked
3 tablespoons butter
1 tablespoon lemon juice
½ teaspoon salt
¼ teaspoon coarse pepper
1 garlic clove
2 tablespoons flour

½ cup mushroom liquor
½ cup oyster liquor
nutmeg
2 egg yolks
½ cup heavy cream
12 slices Melba toast
2 tablespoons minced parsley

PREPARATION

Remove the mushroom caps. Slice and save them. Cook the stems in ¾ cup of water for 20 minutes.

Drain the oysters. Save the liquor.

Heat 1 tablespoon of the butter. Add the lemon juice, the salt, the pepper, and the oysters. Simmer until the oyster-edges curl. Remove from the heat and set aside.

Melt the rest of the butter in the top of a double boiler. Sauté the minced garlic very briefly. Stir in the flour until smooth.

Add the liquors. Cook and stir constantly until thickened.

Add the oysters and their sauce, the mushroom caps and the nutmeg. Simmer for 5 minutes, stirring occasionally.

Beat the egg yolks into the cream. Stir slowly into the oysters. Cook over hot water for 10 minutes. Stir from time to time.

PRESENTATION

Serve over Melba toast. Sprinkle with parsley.

UNDERWATER EXPOSÉ: FISH, MOLLUSKS, AND CRUSTACEANS

Oysters Roffignac

TIME: An hour or more SERVES: 4

You will need to find four shiny pie tins and some rock salt for this. Everything else is easy.

COMPOSITION

½ cup minced cooked shrimp
½ cup chopped mushrooms
⅓ cup chopped green onions (scallions)
1 fat garlic clove
2 dozen oysters in shells

1¼ cups butter
2 tablespoons flour
salt
pepper
cayenne
½ cup red wine

PREPARATION

Cook the shrimp. Mince them. Chop the mushrooms and the onions extremely fine. Open and drain the oysters, saving the juice. You will need 1 cupful.

Fill 4 pie tins with rock salt. Put them into the oven to heat.

Heat the butter. Sauté the pressed garlic, the onions, the mushrooms, and the shrimp. When the onions are golden, stir in the flour, salt, pepper, and cayenne. Amalgamate well. Simmer for 10 minutes.

Blend in the oyster juice and the wine. Simmer for 20 minutes.

Place 6 half shells on each plate of hot salt. Place 1 oyster in each half shell. Cover each oyster with sauce.

Bake at 400° for 10 minutes.

Octopus in Wine

TIME: God only knows if you don't have the animals; otherwise about 2 hours

SERVES: 6

Don't be alarmed and don't turn up your nose. Here is an opportunity to enjoy one of the real delicacies of the sea. To some people octopus is reminiscent of lobster. Try it and make your own conclusions.

COMPOSITION

6 baby octopuses
2 medium onions
1-2 celery stalks
½ cup olive oil

2 cups red wine
pepper
1 bay leaf

PREPARATION

Clean the octopuses. Remove the beak, the spine, the intestines, and the ink bag. Prune the tips of the tentacles slightly. Wash the octopuses well and set aside. (Of course you have had the fish man do this for you.)

Chop the onions and the celery. Sauté the onion in hot oil until transparent and golden.

Add the octopuses, the wine, ¼ teaspoon of coarse pepper, the celery, and the crumbled bay leaf.

Cover the pot and cook slowly for about 1½ hours. Move the creatures around occasionally so they won't stick.

PRESENTATION

Serve with rice for a main course, alone (with a parsley garnish) for a fish course, or cut up for hors d'oeuvres.

HOW TO EAT MEAT LIKE A MILLION (INSTEAD OF MILLIONS OF OTHERS)

THE HUMAN CRAVING for good red meat needs acknowledgment from time to time. From a popular point of view, the urge is most often for steak. With the desire upon us, we set off in the appropriate direction—usually toward the most expensive steak house. We end up (too often) by complaining about the service, by criticizing the parentage of the steak (and the cook), and by raging over the bill. With the desire still, or again, upon us, we might better do-it-ourself and get what we want for less.

You can't go far wrong in buying raw beef. (Let the sleeping dogs lie: prepackaged cuts will be dried out and lack flavor.) Any reputable butcher will provide the cut of your choice if you let *him* know that *you* know meat. A real beef-lover will demand it well aged. This is a tip-off. The butcher will eye you with respect and reward you with service—and meat. An occasional complaint on general principles will let him know that you are on your toes and will keep him on his.

Far be it from me to enter into a discussion over the best cooking methods for steak. There are a thousand ways. Steak should be what, and how, *you* like it. And so should any cut of meat. The trouble is that some Americans forget that there is any good meat other than steak.

The following suggestions are not ways and means for glorifying poor meat. Far from it! They are just glorious ways of eating all cuts and kinds of meat.

BEEF

Brandied Sirloin Steak

TIME: 12-15 minutes   SERVES: 2

COMPOSITION

⅛ pound butter
Tabasco
juice of 1 lemon
a sirloin steak (amout 1½ pounds)

Worcestershire sauce
1 teaspoon oregano
½ cup brandy

PREPARATION

Melt the butter in a heavy skillet. Add about ½ teaspoon of Tabasco and the lemon juice. Brown the steak on both sides over high heat.

Cover and continue cooking to your own standard of doneness. Just before serving, pour on a couple of tablespoons of Worcestershire, sprinkle with the oregano and the brandy.

P.S. *This doesn't have to be limited to a sirloin steak. It's marvelous with any good cut.*

Filets aux Champignons

TIME: 20 minutes   SERVES: 4

COMPOSITION

½ pound mushrooms
¼ cup cream
1 teaspoon flour
1 tablespoon dry mustard
⅛ pound butter

salt
pepper
1 jigger sherry
1 jigger brandy
4 1-inch thick beef tenderloins

PREPARATION

Slice the cleaned and trimmed mushrooms, using both stems and caps.

Stir together the cream, the flour, and the mustard until well blended.

Sauté the mushrooms in half of the butter. Season lightly with salt and pepper.

Add the sherry, the brandy, and then the cream. Cook for about 10 minutes.

Sear the steaks in the rest of the butter for about 3 minutes on each side.

PRESENTATION

Remove them to a hot platter and cover with the sauce.

Filet Flambé

TIME: 12-15 minutes   SERVES: 4

This calls for two skillets and a certain amount of showmanship. Let your guests see you do it and take a bow!

COMPOSITION

4 filets (tenderloin) steaks cut 1½ inches thick	*pepper*
	¼ pound (minimum) butter
2 (or more) garlic cloves	*4 slices French bread*
salt	*¼ cup brandy*

PREPARATION

Rub the steaks with pressed garlic.

Season them well with salt and coarse pepper.

Heat 2 skillets. Divide the butter between them. In one, sauté the bread on both sides, using more butter if needed.

In the other, simultaneously, sauté the steaks over high heat. Sear them quickly on the bottom, lower the heat and cook for 4-5 minutes. Repeat the process on the reverse side. Add butter when, as, and if it is necessary. When blood seeps from the meat, it should be ready to eat.

Souse the steaks with brandy, touch it with a flame, and start a fire. Shake the skillet briskly and let the flames die naturally.

PRESENTATION

Slip a slice of bread under each filet. Pour some of the pan juices over each. Serve immediately.

Beef Filet in a Crust

TIME: 45-60 minutes   SERVES: 2

COMPOSITION

pastry crust sufficient for a 2-crust 9-inch pie
1½ pounds beef tenderloin
salt
pepper

garlic
½ pound mushrooms
butter (approximately ⅓ pound)
½ cup (or more) sherry

PREPARATION

Make the pastry (p. 517). Divide it into two parts and roll each about ¼ inch thick. Place on cookie sheet.

Season the steak with salt, pepper, and pressed garlic.

Clean and slice the mushrooms.

Sauté the meat in some of the butter over a very high flame, on both sides. Remove it from the pan.

Add more butter and sauté the mushrooms. Remove them from the pan.

Add more butter and the wine. Reduce it by half by cooking rapidly.

Place the meat on one pastry round. Top with the mushrooms and the sauce. Cover with the other round. Fold and seal the seam tightly.

Bake 25-30 minutes at 375°.

PRESENTATION

Equally delicious hot or cold.

Stuffed Steak

TIME: 15-20 minutes, no more   SERVES: 4

Purchase steaks at least 1½ inches thick for this gem. If your friendly butcher does not object to maltreating meat, ask him to make a deep pocket in each. Otherwise, slit a pocket in each steak yourself with your sharpest knife.

COMPOSITION

4 thick club steaks	Tabasco
1 medium onion	chives
½ pound mushrooms	parsley
⅛ pound (or more) butter	salt
1 garlic clove	1 cup red wine
Worcestershire sauce	

PREPARATION

Chop the onion and the mushrooms, that have been trimmed and cleaned.

Melt the butter. Sauté the pressed garlic and the onion until both are limp. Toss in the mushrooms. Cook and stir for a few minutes.

Steak with Cheese

Add a dash of Worcestershire, the same of Tabasco, a few chopped chives, some chopped parsley if you have it, and salt to taste.

Pour in the wine and boil the mixture to reduce the sauce by half. Strain it, retaining the solids for stuffing and the liquid for basting.

Stuff the steaks, fastening the open slits with toothpicks.

Broil the meat over charcoal or in the oven, allowing 4-5 minutes per side. Baste often, using all the liquid.

Steak with Cheese

TIME: It's your steak   SERVES: 2

COMPOSITION

1 3-ounce package Roquefort cheese	1 garlic clove
2 tablespoons sour cream	1 sirloin steak (1½-2 pounds)
2 tablespoons fresh horse-radish	salt
	pepper

PREPARATION

Mix the cheese with the sour cream and the horse-radish.

Smear pressed garlic on both sides of the steak. Sprinkle liberally with salt and coarse pepper.

Broil the steak as you see fit, but briefly.

Transfer the steak to a metal steak platter.

Spread the cheese mixture over the steak. Return it to the broiler until the cheese bubbles.

Flank Steak—Three Ways

TIME: About 1 hour, each way   SERVES: 4

Don't overlook this section of the beast. It may not be your idea of a steak, but there are those (among them, me) who insist that it has the best flavor of all.

Flank steaks should be treated gently. They can be completely wrecked by overcooking. Let them be rare inside and crusty on the surface. Slice the cooked meat thinly, on the diagonal and at right angles to the grain.

I

COMPOSITION

1 3-pound flank steak   butter
meat tenderizer

PREPARATION

Jab holes into the steak. Sprinkle it with *un*flavored meat tenderizer. Let it rest for an hour or so. Broil or pan-fry it quickly in butter, allowing 5-6 minutes per side, no more.

Slice and serve with the pan juices.

II

COMPOSITION

1 garlic clove   3 tablespoons wine vinegar
1 teaspoon salt   1 cup water
¼ cup chili sauce   1 3-pound flank steak
½ teaspoon oregano

PREPARATION

Mash the garlic and prepare a marinade by combining all ingredients.

Marinate the meat for at least 1 hour.
Broil or grill the steak to your own taste while basting with the marinade.

III

COMPOSITION

1 3-pound flank steak
2 parts soy sauce
1 part sugar

1 garlic clove, pressed fresh or powdered ginger to taste

PREPARATION

Let the steak swim in the marinade, then proceed as above.

P.S. *One hour is the minimum for preparing the steak—or letting the steak prepare itself—in these three ways, so relax and take as long as you want over your drink. The final cooking is a matter of moments; the result, a matter of moment!*

Chopped Steak

TIME: About 15 minutes   SERVES: 2

This is the solution for men with T-bone tastes on a hamburger wallet.

COMPOSITION

1½ pounds chopped (or ground) chuck
1 cup mixed chopped onions, parsley, capers, green pepper, chives, and herbs of your own choice

1 cup good red wine
¼ pound butter
3-4 tablespoons A-1 sauce (oyster sauce or Worcestershire sauce or some of each)

HOW TO EAT MEAT LIKE A MILLION

PREPARATION

Purchase meat—not merely "hamburger" but good chuck or better. If possible, have it chopped fine (or very coarsely ground).

Chop and mix vegetables and herbs.

Shape the meat into 1½-inch thick rounds.

Get a heavy iron skillet very hot. Quickly sear the steaks on both sides. Remove them to a hot platter and deposit the platter in a hot oven. (The meat will continue to cook. Allow for this when searing.)

Pour a cup of red wine into the skillet. Swirl the pan to cleanse the sides, then add the butter and the herb-vegetable mixture. Cover and cook for 2-3 minutes. Uncover and boil rapidly for a couple of minutes to reduce the sauce. Add the A-1 sauce or whatever.

PRESENTATION

Pour the final amalgamation over the meat.

Serve immediately with plenty of French bread for sopping.

Garlic Steak—Swiss Style

TIME: 1¼ hours   SERVES: 4

COMPOSITION

1 flank steak (at least 2½ to 3 pounds)	2 tablespoons wine vinegar
flour	1 teaspoon dry mustard
¼ pound butter	6 garlic cloves (at least)
1 12-ounce can beer	salt
	pepper

PREPARATION

With a very sharp knife remove the tough membrane covering the steak. Pound all the flour possible into it. Brown quickly in butter. Cover with beer.

Add the vinegar, the mustard, and the chopped garlic and simmer, covered, for about 1 hour.

PRESENTATION

Add salt and pepper at the table.

Hamburgers Big Sur

TIME: ½-¾ hour to prepare; cooking time is your own   SERVES: 4

These man-size hamburgers require a man-size cookie cutter. I recommend mine: a ½-pound coffee tin with the bottom removed. No matter what brand of coffee you prefer, use it and keep the can. It will become a very useful kitchen tool.

COMPOSITION

2 pounds lean chuck
1 medium-size tomato
½ celery stalk
¼ green pepper
¼ medium onion
4-6 slices bread-and-butter pickles

6-8 pimiento-stuffed olives
Spice Parisienne
pepper
Parmesan cheese
8 bacon slices

PREPARATION

On wax paper, roll or pat out the ground meat to ¼ inch thick. With your new cutter, make 8 rounds. Place them side by side in pairs on sheets of wax paper. Roll or pat them to an even thickness of ⅛ inch.

Slice the tomato—4 thick slices please.

Mince the celery, the green pepper, the onion, the pickles, and the olives. Mix them together. (The final quantity must total 4 heaping tablespoons. Don't fret if you have chopped too much, just toss it into a salad.)

Sprinkle one of each pair of rounds with the spice, the pepper, and grated cheese. Place a tomato slice in the center. Top with a heaping spoonful of the vegetables.

Flip the undecorated meat round on top of the other by folding over the wax paper. Press the edges together.

Pick up the double round and, using both hands, work it into a fat, compact ball. The idea is to work out the air contained inside. (You will both hear and feel it escaping.)

This accomplished, stretch and wrap two bacon slices around each hamburger. Repeat the process with each pair of rounds.

They are now ready to be pan-fried, broiled, or charcoal-broiled to your own taste. These are large hamburgers; they require 6-10 minutes on each side.

Wrapped in foil, they can be transported later to your favorite picnic spot or frozen, to be used next week or next month.

Beef Stroganov

TIME: Approximately 1¼ hours   SERVES: 4-6

COMPOSITION

2 pounds lean beef (absolutely no fat or gristle) in thin slices	⅛ pound butter
salt	1 tablespoon flour
pepper	1 pint rich beef stock
paprika	½ pint sour cream
1 medium onion	1 tablespoon tomato paste
	parsley

PREPARATION

Sprinkle the meat with salt, pepper, and paprika. Permit it to relax for an hour or so.

Grate the onion.

Heat half of the butter. Sauté the meat and the onion.

In another pan heat the rest of the butter. Stir in the flour. Add the stock slowly. Bring it to a boil, stirring steadily. Add the sour cream and the tomato paste.

Transfer the meat (and onion and pan juices) from one pan to the other. Let it simmer for about 15 minutes, stirring frequently.

PRESENTATION

Top with chopped parsley and fresh coarse black pepper. Serve with rice.

Ground Beef Pie

TIME: 1 hour, depending where you start with the pastry
SERVES: 2-4

COMPOSITION

pastry for a 2-crust 9-inch pie
2-3 eggs
1 onion
1 green pepper

⅛ pound butter
1 pound fat-free ground beef
salt
pepper

PREPARATION

Make the pastry. (See your shelf, your grocer's shelf, or pp. 516–518.)

Line a square or rectangular tin with about three-quarters of the pastry. Roll out the rest for a top crust.

Hard-cook the eggs. Chop them.

Chop the vegetables. Sauté them in some of the butter. Add more butter and then the meat. Cook and stir until the meat is well browned. Please do not let it dry out.

Remove the pan from the fire. Mix in the chopped eggs. Season with salt and pepper.

Spread the mixture in the baking pan. Cover with the pastry lid, seal the edges, slash the top, and bake. About 35 minutes in a 375° oven should do nicely.

Pot Roast in Beer

TIME: 3-4 hours to marinate SERVES: 6-8
About 3 hours to cook

COMPOSITION

1 pot roast of beef, at least 4 pounds
1 cup Witch's Brew or Barbecue Sauce
salt
pepper
4 tablespoons olive oil
1 12-ounce can beer

PRELIMINARY PREPARATION

Marinate the roast in a cup or so of Witch's Brew (p. 13) or Barbecue Sauce (p. 11) for 3-4 hours. Turn it from time to time.

PREPARATION

Drain off the liquid. Season the meat thoroughly with salt and pepper.

Brown the roast in oil on all sides.

Add the marinade and a can of beer to the roasting pan. Cover. Simmer the meat for about 3 hours.

PRESENTATION

Arrange boiled potatoes and onions around the meat on a platter. Provide quantities of French bread for sopping up sauce.

Smothered Beef

TIME: 6½ hours   SERVES: 6

COMPOSITION

3 pounds beef round
3 garlic cloves
salt
pepper
1 bacon slice
4 shallots or green onions
2 parsley sprigs
6-8 boiling onions
2 small carrots
1 bay leaf
1 piece of ham rind about 4 inches square
thyme
3 whole cloves
¼ cup brandy
2 cups red wine
½ cup rich beef stock
1 cup strong coffee

PREPARATION

Jab holes in the meat. Insert garlic slivers in the holes. Sprinkle it well with salt and pepper.

Dice the bacon. Halve the shallots. Chop the parsley. Peel the onions. Cut up the carrots. Crush the bay leaf.

Heat the oven to 250°.

Place the ham rind in a casserole. Add the meat and all other ingredients. Add enough water to almost (but not quite) cover the meat. Put the lid on the casserole. Seal it with a flour-and-water paste.

Go to mass. Let the meat cook for about 6 hours.

PRESENTATION

Serve it forth: meat surrounded by vegetables and covered with sauce.

P.S. *This slow-cooked, delicious concoction is started early in the evening to be ready and waiting at midnight for church-*

goers on Christmas Eve. It should not be kept from the heathen. It's conversion material.

Tamara's Beef Stroganov

TIME: Overnight, plus 1 hour   SERVES: 4-6

COMPOSITION

2 pounds lean beef (tenderloin or sirloin)	2 tomatoes or 2 tablespoons tomato sauce
salt	1 teaspoon chopped fresh dill
pepper	½ pound mushrooms
dry red wine	10 tablespoons butter
1 small onion	1 tablespoon flour
1 garlic clove	2 cups rich beef stock
	½ pint sour cream

PREPARATION

Cut strips of meat ¼ in. wide. (Use a very sharp knife: this is not an easy job.) Season the strips with salt and pepper. Marinate overnight in red wine to cover.

Chop the onion. Mince the garlic. Peel the tomatoes. Chop the dill. Clean and slice mushrooms.

Sauté the onion and garlic in a walnut-size lump of butter. When they are golden, stir in the flour. Continue to cook and stir until the flour is golden.

Add the tomatoes, the stock, and the meat marinade. Simmer the sauce for about 15 minutes. Toss in the mushrooms which have been sautéed briefly in 2 tablespoons of the butter.

Sauté the meat in the rest of the butter until brown. Add the meat to the sauce.

Marinated Short Ribs

Transfer the whole works to a casserole. Bake at 250°-300° for about 30 minutes.

Cool the stroganov slightly. Blend in the sour cream. Sprinkle with dill.

PRESENTATION

Serve immediately. (If this is impossible, turn off the oven and let the casserole reside inside until serving time.)

Marinated Short Ribs

TIME: For preliminary preparation:
15 minutes to 2 days
For cooking: 1¾ hours

SERVES: 6

COMPOSITION

3 pounds short ribs
3-4 onions
2 garlic cloves
2 tablespoons dry mustard
½ teaspoon pepper
½ teaspoon chili powder

½ teaspoon sugar
1 tablespoon lemon juice
⅓ cup olive oil
2 tablespoons soy sauce
½ cup red wine or
2 cups Barbecue Sauce

PRELIMINARY PREPARATION

Have meaty short ribs cut into serving pieces. Slice the onions. Press the garlic.

Prepare a marinade using all ingredients. (For variety, refer to p. 11, and make the Barbecue Sauce.)

Let the meat soak in marinade for two days if possible.

PREPARATION

Place the meat in a roasting pan. Brown in a hot oven (450°) for 15 minutes.

Add the onions and the marinade. Reduce the heat to 350°.

Bake the ribs (covered) for an hour. Uncover and continue cooking until the onions are brown and the fat crisp.

Short Ribs in Burgundy

TIME: 2¼ hours   SERVES: 6

COMPOSITION

6 large short ribs
3 medium onions
¼ cup chopped parsley
2 garlic cloves
oil
butter
½ cup strong coffee

1 bottle red Burgundy
1 teaspoon salt
½ teaspoon marjoram
½ teaspoon basil
1 bay leaf
5-6 peppercorns

PREPARATION

For 6 people, obtain 6 meaty short ribs.
Slice the onions. Chop the parsley. Press the garlic.
Brown the ribs in equal amounts of oil and butter.
Add the coffee and sufficient wine to cover the meat. Throw in the other ingredients.
Cover the pot. Let it simmer for 2 hours on top of the stove or in a slow oven.
Skim off the fat. Serve now, or preferably, let the meat cool in its juice overnight, add another dash of wine, reheat and serve.

P.S. *If you let the meat cool overnight, postpone the fat removal until it forms on the surface—so easy!*

VEAL

Roast Veal

TIME: 2½ hours   SERVES: 6

COMPOSITION

1 4-pound boneless roast (rolled and tied)
rosemary, tarragon, or thyme
pepper
3 garlic cloves

1 2-ounce can anchovy fillets
½ pound bacon
1 cup dry vermouth or white wine

PREPARATION

Ask the butcher to bone, roll, and tie a roast cut from a leg of veal.

Insert the herb of your choice under the strings. Use plenty. Sprinkle the meat lavishly with fresh ground black pepper. Rub it with garlic pressings.

Lay the roast in a roasting pan. Turn on the oven to 325°.

Open the anchovies. Pour the oil over the meat and place the fillets on top of it. Cover them with thin bacon slices. Add the wine.

Roast the roast for about 2 hours. Baste it with pan juices every 15-20 minutes.

Les Oiseaux sans Têtes

TIME: Less than 2½ hours   SERVES: 6

COMPOSITION

12 pieces (about 3 pounds) veal, preferably from the leg
1½ cups fine bread crumbs
1 medium onion
12 medium mushrooms
2-3 parsley sprigs
¾ cup (plus) butter
½ teaspoon thyme
1 teaspoon salt
1 teaspoon pepper
1 garlic clove
1 egg
12 anchovy fillets
12 slices bacon
flour
½ cup rich stock
½ cup red wine
½ cup strong coffee
1 pint sour cream

PREPARATION

Order the veal cut in pieces 5 to 6 inches square and ¼ to ⅜ inch thick. Pound them until thin between two sheets of wax paper.

Chop the onion, the mushrooms, and the parsley. Sauté them in ½ cup of butter together with the thyme, the salt, the pepper, and the pressed garlic. Remove the pan from the fire.

Melt ¼ cup of butter in another pan. Beat the egg. Stir the butter into the egg. Add it to the vegetable mixture. Mix well.

Lay one or two anchovy fillets on each piece of veal. Cover with the stuffing. Roll the meat into *oiseaux* (birds, to you). Wrap each with a slice of bacon. Tie up with string. Sprinkle with flour.

Heat the rest of the butter in a large skillet. Sear the birds-without-heads on all sides. Add the wine, the stock, and the coffee.

Cover the pot. Let the birds simmer slowly for 1¾ hours. Turn them occasionally and add more liquid if necessary. Thicken the sauce with sour cream just before serving.

Veal Parmigiana

TIME: 30-40 minutes   SERVES: 6

COMPOSITION

6 boned veal cutlets, weighing at least ¾-1 pound each
¾ cup fine bread crumbs
¼ cup grated Parmesan cheese
2 eggs
⅛ pound butter
salt
pepper
6 slices Mozzarella cheese
1 6-ounce can tomato sauce (or ¾ cup homemade)

PREPARATION

Pound the boned cutlets as thin as your energy permits.
Make fine bread crumbs. Grate the Parmesan cheese. Beat the eggs.
Dip the meat into egg, then bread crumbs, then cheese.
Sauté on both sides in the butter. Season generously with salt and coarse pepper.
Place the browned meat in a casserole. Place a slice of Mozzarella cheese on each cutlet. Dilute the tomato sauce with an equal amount of water and pour it over the meat.
Bake for about 20 minutes at 350°.

Veal St. Marcoux

TIME: 45 minutes   SERVES: 3-6

COMPOSITION

6 thick rib chops cut with a pocket in each
6 slices bacon
6 slices Gruyère cheese
salt
pepper
¼ cup olive oil
⅛ pound butter
¾ cup Madeira

PREPARATION

Stuff the chops with the chopped bacon and the cheese which has been cut into strips. Season them with salt and pepper. Brown on both sides in equal amounts of hot oil and butter.

Cover the pan. Lower the heat. Continue cooking for about 10 minutes. Remove the meat to a hot dish.

Rinse the pan with wine. Boil it briskly to reduce the quantity by half. Pour it over the chops.

Veal Marsala

TIME: 20-30 minutes   SERVES: 4

COMPOSITION

1½ pounds veal
¾ cup grated Parmesan cheese
1 cup chopped mushrooms
8 tablespoons butter
salt
cayenne
¼ cup stock
1 teaspoon meat glaze (p. 5)
¼ cup Marsala wine

Salpicon of Veal

PREPARATION

Have the veal cut into *scaloppine*-type bits. Pound them flat.

Grate cheese.

Clean and chop mushrooms.

Melt half of the butter. Dip the meat into grated cheese, then sauté it on both sides. If you have beaten it hard and well, this should cook it. Remove it to a hot platter and let it rest in a warm oven.

In another pan, melt the rest of the butter. Sauté the mushrooms. Season them lightly with salt and cayenne.

Heat the stock. Dissolve the meat glaze in it. Add to the mushrooms. After 2-3 minutes, add the wine.

PRESENTATION

Heat the sauce well, pour it over the meat and serve.

Salpicon of Veal

TIME: Less than 45 minutes   SERVES: 4-6

COMPOSITION

2 cups Béchamel Sauce	1 8-ounce can beets
¼ pound mushrooms	1 small cucumber
¼ pound butter	½ cup chopped almonds
1 cup peas	or *cashews*
2 tablespoons chopped candied ginger	1 garlic clove
	½ cup seedless raisins
1 small carrot	6 veal scallops, pounded flat
½ green pepper	and thin

PREPARATION

Prepare the sauce (see p. 8).

Clean and chop the mushrooms. Sauté them quickly in 2 tablespoons of butter.

Cook the peas very briefly, not more than 2 minutes.

Chop ginger, carrot, pepper, beets (saving the juice), cucumber, and almonds.

Melt the remaining butter. Add the pressed garlic. Sauté the meat for a few minutes until it is well browned. Set it aside and keep warm.

Add the beet juice to the white sauce. Blend well. Fold in the vegetables, the raisins, and the meat. Avoid violence. Simmer over low heat for 10-12 minutes. The vegetables should be crunchy in texture.

P.S. *This is equally delicious made with thin beef steaks.*

Vitello Tonnato

TIME: 4 hours or so   SERVES: 6

COMPOSITION

1 medium size sour pickle
2 garlic cloves
3-4 celery stalks
1 carrot
1 large onion
3-4 parsley sprigs
2 7-ounce cans tuna (in oil)
1 2-ounce can anchovy fillets

salt
pepper
1 teaspoon thyme
2 cups dry white wine
1 cup olive oil
3½-4 pound boned and rolled leg of veal

PREPARATION

Slice the pickle. Peel and chop the garlic. Chop the celery and the carrot. Mince the onion and the parsley. Open cans.

Put all the ingredients, including the veal, into a large kettle. Bring it to a boil. Reduce the heat. Cover the pot. Let it simmer for 2 hours.

Permit the meat to remain submerged in the sauce until it is cool. Place the meat on a platter and sieve the sauce into a saucepan. Chill the meat.

PRESENTATION

Warm the sauce and pour it over the sliced cold meat.

Osso Buco

TIME: Just over 3¼ hours   SERVES: 4

The number of ingredients in this recipe is deceptively discouraging. It looks so complicated when in fact it's a very easy recipe and will give you a dish rarely found in the home.

COMPOSITION

4 meaty chunks of veal shank (sawed about 2 inches thick and with plenty of marrow in the bones)
salt
pepper
4 tablespoons flour
⅛ pound butter
1 large onion
2 garlic cloves
1 carrot
1 celery stalk (including leaves)
1 large tomato
1 cup dry white wine
1 tablespoon rosemary
oregano
marjoram
basil
1 bay leaf
½ teaspoon (or less) cayenne
1-2 parsley sprigs
grated peel of ¼ lemon

PREPARATION

Salt and pepper the meat. Roll it in half of the flour. Brown it in some of the butter. Remove it from the pan.
In the remaining butter, using more as necessary, brown the

onion (chopped), one garlic clove (pressed), the carrot (shredded or very thinly sliced), and the celery (chopped). Cook slowly for about 10 minutes.

Sprinkle with the remaining flour and cook and stir for another 5 minutes.

Peel the tomato. Add it, the wine, the herbs, and the seasonings (except for the parsley, grated lemon peel, and the remaining garlic clove).

Taste, after simmering for about 5 minutes. Adjust the seasonings.

Add the meat. Pour in enough hot water to cover it. Cover the pot. Let the meat cook slowly for 3 hours.

Chop the parsley, grate the lemon peel, and mince one garlic clove. Scatter them over the top of the meat just before serving.

INNARDS

Braised Sweetbreads

TIME: 50 minutes   SERVES: 2

COMPOSITION

2 pairs sweetbreads
1 lemon
4 teaspoons flour
   (potato, preferably)
salt
pepper
1 tablespoon minced onion
1 garlic clove
1 bay leaf

2 tablespoons butter
1 pony brandy
1 teaspoon tomato paste
1 teaspoon meat glaze
   (p. 5)
1 cup rich beef stock
1 jigger sherry
1-2 tablespoons red currant
   jelly

PRELIMINARY PREPARATION

Drop the sweetbreads in enough cold water to cover. Add the juice of a lemon. Bring the water to a brisk boil.

Remove the sweetbreads immediately. Plunge them into ice water. Skin them. Split in half. Dust with 2 teaspoons of flour and season with salt and pepper.

PREPARATION

Mince the onion and the garlic. Crush the bay leaf.

Melt the butter in a skillet. Brown the sweetbreads on all sides.

Warm the brandy. Pour it over the meat. Touch with a lighted match. When the flames have died down, remove the meat and keep it hot.

Cook the garlic and the onion in the same pan, for not more than 2 minutes. Stir in the tomato paste, the meat glaze, and 2 teaspoons of flour. Blend well. Add the stock and

HOW TO EAT MEAT LIKE A MILLION

the sherry. Stir the sauce until it comes to a boil. Add the bay leaf and a gob of red current jelly.

Taste. Adjust the seasonings if necessary.

Place the sweetbreads in the sauce and simmer very gently for 15-20 minutes.

PRESENTATION

With rice or on toast.

Brains à la Parisienne

TIME: 1 hour, if you work fast   SERVES: 4

COMPOSITION

2 calf's brains
1 medium onion
1 tablespoon wine vinegar
parsley
½ teaspoon salt
⅓ cup grated Gruyère cheese
⅔ cup chopped cooked ham

2-3 green onions
½ cup chopped mushrooms
6-8 tablespoons butter
⅓ cup rich veal or chicken stock
2 tablespoons olive oil

PREPARATION

Soak the brains in cold water for ½ hour. Remove the membrane carefully.

Chop the onion.

Starting with enough cold water to cover, together with the vinegar, onion, parsley, and salt, bring the brains to a boil, then remove the pan from the fire. Permit the brains to remain in the water until it cools. Fish them out and slice them in half.

Grate the cheese and chop the ham.

Chop the mushrooms and the green onions. Sauté them in a

walnut-size lump of butter until the onions are soft but not colored. Cook and stir until most of the juice is gone.
Add the stock. Cook for 7-8 minutes.
Add the ham. After a minute or two, remove the pan from the fire. Keep it and its contents hot.
Heat the oil and an equal amount of butter in a skillet.
Sauté the halved brains for 5 minutes. Place them on a hot serving platter.
Cover with the sauce. Top with the cheese. Put under the broiler until the cheese melts. Serve now.

Empty Brains

TIME: an hour, all told and done   SERVES: 4

COMPOSITION

2 calf's brains
1 medium onion
1 tablespoon wine vinegar
parsley
½ teaspoon salt
2 eggs

2 tablespoons flour
2 tablespoons water
1 tablespoon brandy
plenty of oil for deep-fat frying

PREPARATION

Soak, poach, and treat the brains according to the preceding recipe.
Cut the cooled meat into cubes.
Separate the eggs.
Mix the flour and water. Add the brandy and the egg yolks. (If the paste is very thin, add more flour. If too thick, add brandy.)
Beat the egg whites until stiff. Fold them into the mixture.

Heat the oil. Dip the meat into the batter and drop the pieces into boiling oil. Fry until golden, drain, and serve.

Herbed Liver

TIME: about 20 minutes   SERVES: 3-6

COMPOSITION

1 teaspoon chervil	¼ cup flour
1 teaspoon tarragon	6 thin liver slices
1 teaspoon rosemary	6 tablespoons butter
1 teaspoon parsley	½ cup dry white wine

PREPARATION

Crush and mince the herbs. Cast them into a paper bag with the flour. Add the liver. Shake the bag.

Heat the butter. Sauté the meat quickly and lightly. Arrange the slices on a serving platter. Keep them hot.

Add the wine and the herbed flour to the pan. Stir. Heat. Pour the sauce over the liver.

Liver and Onions

TIME: 12-15 minutes   SERVES: 4

Savor this combination mentally for a moment and give my method a quick try. You might like it better than the usual overcooked liver with fried onions.

It's your liver, your onions, and your house, but in my home liver is always sautéed very quickly. It is always served with crisp French-fried onions. No fuss, no muss, and no overpowering odor to fight.

Chanfaïna of Liver

COMPOSITION

1-2 packages frozen French-fried onions
3 tablespoons butter
3 tablespoons oil
1½ pounds calf's liver, thinly sliced
flour
salt
pepper
½ cup minced scallions (green onions) and parsley, mixed

PREPARATION

Turn on the oven and heat the frozen onions.
Heat the oil and butter together.
Sprinkle the liver slices with flour and sauté them quickly, allowing less than 1½ minutes per side. They should be nicely browned on the outside with a pinkish interior.
Sprinkle with salt, pepper, and the minced scallions and parsley after flipping sides.
Serve with crisp onions and pan juices.

Chanfaïna of Liver

TIME: 20 minutes   SERVES: 4-6

COMPOSITION

1 pound calf's liver
4 medium onions
3-4 mint leaves
3-4 parsley sprigs
2 pimientos (or a few bits of dried pimiento)
a heaping handful of bread crumbs (about ½ cup)
¼ teaspoon each: camin, saffron, cinnamon
freshly ground pepper
¼ cup oil

PREPARATION

Chop the liver coarsely. Drop it into a small pot of salted boiling water. Remove it immediately but do not discard the water.

HOW TO EAT MEAT LIKE A MILLION

Chop the vegetables and herbs. Make bread crumbs.
Heat the oil. Toss in everything, excluding bread crumbs.
Add a small amount of the liver water. Simmer and stir for about 5 minutes.
Stir in the bread crumbs.

PRESENTATION

Serve immediately. Or try it cold for tomorrow's lunch.

Liver in Sour Cream

TIME: 25-30 minutes   SERVES: 3-4 liver-lovers

COMPOSITION

⅛ pound butter
5 tablespoons flour
½ cup chicken stock
2 parsley sprigs
1 pint sour cream

1½ pounds calf's liver (sliced thin)
salt
pepper

PREPARATION

Melt half of the butter. Stir in 3 tablespoons of the flour. Cook and stir until the flour is tawny colored.
Add the chicken stock and simmer for about 15 minutes. Agitate from time to time.
Mince the parsley. Add it and the sour cream to the sauce. Keep it warm, but don't let it boil.
Dust the liver with salt, pepper, and 2 tablespoons of flour.
Sauté the thin slices in butter for 1-2 minutes per side. If they are properly thin, they should be done.

PRESENTATION

Place the meat on a warmed platter. Cover it with sauce.

LAMB

Stuffed Leg of Lamb

TIME: Several hours—worth every hour
SERVES: At least 8

COMPOSITION

1 large leg of lamb (7-8 pounds)	salt
½ pound smoked ham	1 small onion
¼ pound veal	juice of 1 lemon
¼ pound lean pork	grated rind of ½ lemon
12 bacon slices	3 bay leaves
½ cup dry bread crumbs	2 cups red wine
4 garlic cloves	¾ can tomato paste
½ pound mushrooms	¼ cup catsup
2 tablespoons butter	2 tablespoons Worcestershire sauce
⅛ teaspoon cayenne	1 tablespoon vinegar
½ teaspoon marjoram	1 tablespoon sugar
⅛ teaspoon nutmeg	1½ cups water
2 eggs	coarse pepper
¼ cup cream	

PRELIMINARY PREPARATION

Ask a butcher who favors you to skin and bone the leg of lamb, leaving a few inches of the shank bone to hold the meat together.

Order the smoked ham, the veal, and the pork. Have your man grind them together, using a coarse blade. (If you hesitate to ask, chop them yourself. It's not too much work.)

PREPARATION

Make the bread crumbs. Press the garlic. Clean and chop the mushrooms. Sauté them briefly in butter.

Mix together the following: chopped meats, cayenne, marjoram, nutmeg, bread crumbs, mushrooms, with the butter, garlic, eggs, and cream. Salt the mixture to taste.

Cram the stuffing into the leg cavity. (If any is left over, cook it separately, basting with some of the sauce.)

Lace up the leg with twine. Lay it in a roasting pan. Cover it with half of the bacon. Set it aside for the moment.

Chop the onion. Squeeze and grate the lemon. Crush the bay leaves.

Get out the wine jug. Have a sip. (You probably need it by now.)

Blend together all remaining ingredients, using only 1 cup of the wine. Sample the blend. It should be good. If not, adjust the seasonings. Simmer for 15 minutes.

Preheat the oven to 300°.

Spoon the sauce over the lamb, reserving some for basting. Add the rest of the bacon and cover the pan. Roast the meat until tender, allowing 30 minutes per pound. When done, remove it to a serving platter and keep hot.

Add any unused basting sauce to the pan juices. Pour in a second cup of wine. Cook the sauce down over high heat until reduced by about one half.

PRESENTATION

Pour the sauce over the lamb and serve forth in glory.

Roast Shoulder of Lamb

TIME: 4-12 hours to marinate
    2½-3 hours to complete
SERVES: 4

COMPOSITION

¼ cup chopped parsley
1 teaspoon rosemary (pulverized)
2 cups red wine
2 tablespoons olive oil
1 garlic clove
2-3 pound boned shoulder of lamb
3 tablespoons butter

¼ cup finely chopped walnuts
4-5 chicken livers
¼ pound mushrooms
1 tablespoon arrowroot or cornstarch
salt
pepper
Mei Yen seasoning

Prepare a marinade by combining the parsley, the rosemary, the wine, the oil, and the pressed garlic. Let the lamb rest in it for 4-5 hours or overnight.

PRELIMINARY PREPARATION

Roast the lamb, in a 325° oven for 35-40 minutes per pound. Baste it occasionally with the marinade.

Melt 1 tablespoon of the butter in a small skillet. Sauté the chopped walnuts. Remove them from the pan.

Melt another tablespoon of butter. Sauté the chicken livers, then chop them fine.

Melt the rest of the butter. Add the sliced mushrooms. Sauté them briefly.

Add the marinade. Simmer for 5 minutes.

Remove the roast to a serving platter.

Skim the fat from the pan juices. Stir in 1½ cups of hot water. Cook and stir for 5 minutes. Add the mushrooms and their juice, the chicken livers, and the walnuts.

Combine the arrowroot with 1 tablespoon of cold water. Stir it into the sauce. Season with salt, pepper and Mei Yen. Continue cooking and stirring until the sauce is thickened.

PRESENTATION

Let each guest pour sauce over his own portion of lamb.

Anchovy Stuffed Lamb

TIME: 3 hours   SERVES: 4

COMPOSITION

4-pound breast of lamb, prepared for stuffing
3 cups soft bread crumbs
2 2-ounce cans anchovies
1 large onion
2 garlic cloves
½ cup chopped parsley
2 eggs
1½ teaspoons pepper
¼ teaspoon rosemary
dry sherry

PREPARATION

Have the butcher prepare the lamb for stuffing.
Make bread crumbs.
Chop anchovies.
Chop the onion, the garlic, and the parsley.
Beat the eggs.
Prepare the dressing by combining all ingredients, using enough dry sherry to moisten.
Stuff the lamb.
Bake at 350° for 2-2½ hours.

Lamb Chops Diable

TIME: 25-30 minutes (provided Sauce Espagnole is on hand) SERVES: 3-6

COMPOSITION

2-3 green onions (scallions)
juice of 1 lemon
1 teaspoon dry mustard
1 teaspoon Worcestershire sauce

Tabasco
2 cups Sauce Espagnole (p. 6)
6 loin or shoulder lamb chops
⅛ pound butter

PREPARATION

Create a sauce: chop the onions and mix with the other ingredients (except the meat and butter). Cook and stir until smooth.

Remove all fat from the chops. Sauté them in butter until edible.

Pour the sauce over them.

Serve.

Cora's Lamb Shanks

TIME: 2 hours   SERVES: 4

COMPOSITION

4 lamb shanks
2 garlic cloves
1 lemon
¼ teaspoon tarragon
½ teaspoon monosodium glutamate
¼ teaspoon dry mustard
salt

pepper
¼ cup olive oil
1½ cups strong black coffee
2 beef bouillon cubes
1 cup dry red wine
¼ cup red currant jelly
3-4 mint sprigs

HOW TO EAT MEAT LIKE A MILLION

~~~~~~

PREPARATION

Rub the shanks with crushed garlic and lemon juice. Sprinkle them with tarragon, monosodium glutamate, dry mustard, salt, and pepper.

Brown them in the oil. Place tenderly in a large casserole.

Heat the coffee. Dissolve the bouillon cubes in it. Pour both over the meat. Add the wine.

Cover the casserole. Bake for an hour at 350°.

Brush the shanks with the jelly.

Bake, uncovered, for another 45 minutes. If they are pale and anemic, glaze them under the broiler before serving.

Skim all fat from the sauce. Serve it (sauce, not fat) on the side.

Sprinkle the meat with chopped mint.

P.S. *Serve this with rice (boiled or baked). It makes a very special repast.*

Shashlik

TIME: Short, sweet, and dramatic   SERVES: You decide

Live dangerously; get out your best swords or fencing foils. Use skewers only in a pinch. The quantites in this recipe depend upon both available skewers and hungry guests. The sauce ingredients given here will make sufficient delicious *shashlik* for two.

COMPOSITION

1 cup minced onion and parsley, mixed	cayenne
2 tablespoons butter	½ cup brandy or vodka
½ pint sour cream	lean lamb in 1½-inch cubes
1 full teaspoon caraway seeds	chicken livers
salt	fat mushroom caps
pepper	slab bacon cut in squares
	brandy

Shashlik

PREPARATION

Chop and mince enough onion and parsley to fill a cup. Melt butter.

Prepare a sauce of onion and parsley, sour cream, butter, caraway seeds, seasonings, and liquor. Simmer it for about 10 minutes.

Plunge the skewers (or swords, if you can) through the lamb, the livers and the mushrooms caps. Interlace with bacon squares as you pierce.

Swish the laden skewers through the sauce. Broil (over charcoal if possible) until the meat is well charred. Run the skewers through the sauce every few minutes.

PRESENTATION

Dip the tip of each sword in warmed brandy. Set it afire and make a mad dash to the table.

P.S. *If the meat is already cubed, this can all be done in 20-30 minutes.*

PORK

Stuffed Pork Chops

TIME: 1¼-1½ hours   SERVES: 6

Choose your stuffing from the following recipes and fill the chops. These are party fare.

COMPOSITION

6 thick pork chops   stuffing

PREPARATION

Ask the butcher to cut chops at least 1½-2 inches thick with pockets slit in them.
Trim off the excess fat and stuff them.
Rub a hot skillet with pork fat and sear the chops on both sides.
Place them in a baking dish and bake at 350° for an hour.

Pork Stuffing

TIME: 20 minutes   SERVES: 6

COMPOSITION

½ cup ground pork   ½ teaspoon oregano
½ cup chopped onion   salt
⅛ pound butter   pepper
½ cup fine bread crumbs   1 cup dry white wine

PREPARATION

Grind the pork and chop the onion. Sauté them in the butter.
Make crumbs and add to the stuffing.
Season. Stuff. Sear.
When the chops are in their baking dish, pour the wine around them.

Mushroom Stuffing

TIME: 15-20 minutes   SERVES: 6

COMPOSITION

1 pound mushrooms
6 tablespoons butter
2 tablespoons flour

salt
pepper

PREPARATION

Clean and chop the mushrooms very fine. Sauté them in butter. Thicken with the flour. Season lightly with salt and pepper.
Stuff the chops.

Pork Chops with Almonds

TIME: Just over an hour   SERVES: 6

COMPOSITION

6 thick chops, 1 to 1½ inches thick
1 can mushroom soup

1 soup-can evaporated milk
1 cup Almond Sauce for Meat

PREPARATION

Brown the chops in fat trimmings. Place them in a casserole. Add the soup.
Bake for 40 minutes at 350°
Add the milk. Bake for another 15-20 minutes.
Meanwhile, prepare the sauce (p. 10).

PRESENTATION

Remove the chops to a warmed platter. Cover with sauce and serve.

Marinated Pork Chops

TIME: 1½ hours   SERVES: 4

COMPOSITION

4 thick chops	salt
1 cup wine vinegar or 1 cup Barbecue Sauce	pepper
	1 egg
1 cup fine bread crumbs	1 tablespoon water
1 parsley sprig	½ cup flour
1 garlic clove	¼ cup oil

PREPARATION

Marinate the meat in the vinegar (or Barbecue Sauce, p. 11) for an hour.

Make the bread crumbs. Chop the parsley. Mix the two together. Add garlic pressings. Season to taste with salt and pepper.

Beat the egg with the water.

Fish the chops out of the vinegar. Sprinkle them with salt and pepper. Roll in flour, dip into the egg and then into the crumbs.

Heat the oil. Sauté the chops for about 5 minutes on each side. Lower the heat, cover the pan, and continue cooking until the meat is tender (20-25 minutes).

Wined Pork Chops

TIME: 1½ hours   SERVES: 6

COMPOSITION

1 large onion
1 green pepper
3 celery stalks
2-3 tomatoes
6 thick (at least 1 inch) loin chops
1½ cups raw rice
6 tablespoons butter
salt
pepper
1 cup sweet vermouth
1 cup water

PREPARATION

Chop the vegetables. Trim the chops.

Render the pork fat in a skillet. Brown the chops in the fat.

Sauté the rice in 3 tablespoons of butter until transparent. Put it in a casserole. Add the chops.

Sauté the vegetables in the remaining pork fat plus the rest of the butter. Add them to the casserole. Season to taste with salt and pepper.

Deglaze the skillet with the vermouth. Pour it into the casserole. Add 1 cup of boiling water.

Cover and bake the chops at 350° for 1 hour.

Glazed Spareribs

TIME: 2 hours marinating   SERVES: 2
        1 hour cooking

COMPOSITION

4 garlic cloves
½ cup chopped parsley
juice of 3 lemons
1¼ cups soy sauce
½ cup honey
2 teaspoons basil
1½ teaspoons pepper
2-3 pounds spareribs

PRELIMINARY PREPARATION

Mince the garlic and the parsley. Squeeze the lemons. Concoct a marinade with these and the rest of the ingredients.
Soak the spareribs in the marinade for at least 2 hours.

PREPARATION

Place the ribs on a rack in a roasting pan.
Roast them for an hour at 350° Baste occasionally with the marinade.

PRESENTATION

Cut the ribs into 3-4 rib sections before serving with plenty of garlic bread and wine.

Spareribs in Wine

TIME: 1½ hours   SERVES: 2

COMPOSITION

2-3 pounds meaty spareribs	*1 small onion*
salt	*½ cup chili sauce*
pepper	*1 cup red wine*
3 apples	*¼ cup brown sugar*

PREPARATION

Wipe the ribs with a damp cloth. Sprinkle them with salt and pepper. Deposit in a roasting pan.
Peel, core, and slice the apples.
Peel and slice the onion. Place all slices on the spareribs.
Mix the chili sauce with half of the wine. Drizzle it over the meat. Spread brown sugar over all.
Cover the pan. Roast the ribs at 450° for an hour. Uncover

the pan, add the rest of the wine and continue roasting for 15-20 minutes.

PRESENTATION

Remove the ribs to a hot serving platter. Skim the fat from the sauce. Boil it down to half its quantity. Pour the sauce over the ribs and serve.

Fresh Ham with Capers

TIME: 10-12 hours preliminary SERVES: 6
2½ hours final preparation

COMPOSITION

½ medium onion
½ carrot
1 clove garlic
½ teaspoon salt
½ teaspoon pepper
½ teaspoon dry mustard
½ bay leaf
½ teaspoon thyme

1 teaspoon minced parsley
2 cups dry red wine
2-pound fresh ham
⅛ pound butter
½ tablespoon flour
2 cups beef stock or water
3 tablespoons capers

PRELIMINARY PREPARATION

Peel and chop the onion and the carrot; crush the garlic.
Make a marinade of onion, carrot, garlic, salt, pepper, dry mustard, crumbled bay leaf, thyme, parsley, and wine. Let the meat stand in this for 10-12 hours, turning occasionally.

PREPARATION

Melt the butter in a large pan. Remove the meat from the marinade. Dry it well. Brown it thoroughly on all sides. Remove it from the pan.

Add the flour to the pan, blend well, and add the marinade. Bring to a boil, stirring constantly.

Return the meat, add the stock (or water), cover the pan, lower the flame, and cook for 2 hours.

Add capers just before serving.

Ham Calvados

TIME: 4 hours or so   SERVES: 4-6

COMPOSITION

- 2 oranges
- 1 lemon
- 1 teaspoon ginger
- 1 teaspoon nutmeg
- 1 cup dark brown sugar
- 16-ounce can pitted black cherries
- ½ cup dry sherry
- 1 6-pound fresh ham
- ¼ cup Calvados (or other good apple brandy)

PREPARATION

Squeeze the oranges and the lemon. Grate the rinds.

Combine the juice, the gratings, the ginger, the nutmeg, the brown sugar, the cherry juice, and the sherry. Cook over a low flame for 3-4 minutes.

Wipe the ham with a damp cloth. Score it into diamonds. Place it in a roasting pan. Pour over the prepared syrup.

Roast in a 325° oven for 40 minutes per pound, uncovered. (If you use a thermometer, insert it, bypassing the bone.) It should register 175° when the meat is done.) Baste every 20 minutes or so with the pan drippings.

About 15 minutes before the ham is ready, pour over the Calvados and baste several times.

Remove the ham from the pan and let set for at least 10 minutes before carving.

Pour the pan juices into a saucepan, add the cherries and simmer 5 minutes before serving over the ham slices.

Ham Nivernaise

TIME: 20 minutes SERVES: 4

COMPOSITION

4 slices baked ham
⅛ pound sweet butter
1 cup dry white wine
1 teaspoon flour

1 teaspoon dry mustard
1 cup chicken consommé
½ cup heavy cream

PREPARATION

Sauté the ham in butter without burning.
Add the wine. Permit it to boil down by half, turning the ham once during the process.
Remove the meat to a warm platter. Keep it hot.
Stir the flour into the pan juices. Add the dry mustard and the consommé. Simmer for 5 minutes.
Add the cream. Heat without boiling.
Pour the sauce over the ham.

Ham with Bananas

TIME: 25-30 minutes SERVES: 6

COMPOSITION

6 ripe bananas
paprika
dry mustard
monosodium glutamate
black pepper

6 thin slices boiled ham (preferably Prosciutto), totaling ¾ pound
½ pint heavy cream
6 tablespoons grated Parmesan cheese

PREPARATION

Peel the bananas. Sprinkle them lightly with paprika, dry mustard, monosodium glutamate, and coarsely ground pepper.

Preheat the oven to 450°

Butter a shallow baking dish.

Roll each banana in a ham slice. Place them side by side in the baking dish.

Add the heavy cream. Sprinkle with the grated cheese.

Bake for 15-20 minutes, basting occasionally.

P.S. *Don't count the calories. Just revel in them!*

Ham and Beans Steffy

TIME: 20-25 minutes   SERVES: 4

COMPOSITION

1½-2 cups chopped ham (fresh or cooked), including fat

2 large onions

¾ cup (minimum) grated Parmesan cheese

2 1-pound-1-ounce cans red kidney beans

6 tablespoons butter

1 cup (plus or minus) consommé

1 cup (plus or minus) red wine

2 tablespoons flour

½ teaspoon oregano

2 tablespoons chopped parsley

salt

pepper

PREPARATION

Chop the ham coarsely. Chop the onions as well.

Grate the cheese. Drain the beans.

Get out a heavy skillet. Melt half of the butter. Sauté the ham and the onions until the fat is nicely browned.

Add the drained beans.

Ham and Beans Steffy

Pour in the consommé and the wine. (The *liquid* must come up to the level of the solids.) Let everything heat thoroughly, stirring from time to time.

Toss in the rest of the butter and all the flour. Stir the mélange as it cooks to thicken the sauce. If more butter and flour are necessary, add them. If more liquid is necessary, concentrate on wine. The final sauce should be runny but not thin.

Add the seasonings, using great care with the salt.

Cook for 5-10 minutes before serving.

PRESENTATION

Provide copious quantities of Parmesan cheese, French bread and red wine, and Hot Sweet-Sour Cabbage (p. 334). You won't want dessert.

VENISON

Roast Haunch of Venison

TIME: 24 hours marinating
4 hours cooking

SERVES: 10-12

COMPOSITION

1 6-pound haunch of venison (or any part that can be roasted)
6 garlic cloves
1 quart olive oil
1 bottle dry white wine
1 large onion
1 tablespoon sage
12 cloves
1 bay leaf
1 teaspoon salt
½ teaspoon pepper
2 dashes Tabasco
½ cup flour
1 cup beef bouillon

PRELIMINARY PREPARATION

Jab the meat deeply on all sides. Insert peeled garlic slivers.

Mix together the oil and the wine in a roasting pan. Add the meat. Ladle the mixture over it.

Peel and quarter the onion. Add it.

Add the sage, the cloves, the bay leaf, the salt, the pepper, and the Tabasco.

Cover and let stand for 24 hours at room temperature. Turn occasionally.

PREPARATION

Roast at 450° for 4 hours, covered.

Remove the roast and excess fat from the pan.

Add the flour. Cook and smooth until it is well browned. Add the bouillon. Simmer until thick.

PRESENTATION

Serve the roast with noodles, with the gravy in its own boat.

Venison Stew

TIME: 1½-2 hours   SERVES: 4

COMPOSITION

1 *pound venison*	2 *teaspoons salt*
1 *medium carrot*	⅛ *teaspoon coarse pepper*
6 *dried prunes*	¼ *teaspoon monosodium*
1 *lemon*	*glutamate*
1 *dozen boiling onions*	1 *cup water*
½ *cup olive oil*	1 *cup red wine*

PREPARATION

Cut the venison into ½-inch cubes.
Dice the carrot. Pit and dice the prunes.
Halve the lemon. Squeeze one half. Quarter the other half. Peel onions.
Brown the meat lightly in oil. Add all other ingredients.
Simmer over low heat for 2-3 hours until the meat is tender.

PÂTÉ

Liver Pâté

TIME: ½ hour to chop and blend
2 hours to bake
3-4 hours to cool
1-2 hours to chill

SERVES: 6-8-10

COMPOSITION

- 1 pound lean pork
- 1 pound liver (calf, beef, pig, lamb, or chicken)
- 1 small onion
- ¼ cup chopped parsley
- 1 tablespoon brandy
- 1 tablespoon sherry
- 1 garlic clove
- 1 teaspoon salt
- ¼ teaspoon powdered ginger
- ¼ teaspoon black pepper
- cayenne (a dash)
- ⅛ teaspoon cloves
- ⅛ teaspoon cinnamon
- ⅛ teaspoon nutmeg
- 6 bacon slices

PREPARATION

Grind the pork. Chop the liver and the onion. Mince the parsley. Take as long as you like at this. The ingredients must be very small.

Mash and mix everything together, add the remaining ingredients except for the bacon. Use the latter to line a deep rectangular baking dish.

Turn on the oven, set at 350°.

Put the *pâté* mixture into the baking dish and cover it tightly. Let it bake for 2 hours.

Cool the *pâté* under a weight. (Use this cook book or a brick if necessary.) It must be firm and well packed. Chill it well before serving in very thin slices.

Pâté Maison

TIME: 25 minutes plus aging time (minimum 2 hours)
SERVES: 6-8-10-12

COMPOSITION

1 pound liverwurst or braunschweiger
3-4 (or more) chicken livers
2 tablespoons butter
6 bacon slices
1 tablespoon minced chives
1 tablespoon minced parsley
¼ cup chopped pistachio nuts
1 garlic clove
¼ cup sour cream
1 jigger (or more) brandy or whisky

PREPARATION

Go all out on the liverwurst. Buy the best. In times of emergency, the chicken livers may be skipped.

Sauté the chicken livers in butter. Chop and mash them.

Broil the bacon until very crisp. Drain and crumble.

Mince some parsley and chives.

Mash the liverwurst. Get into it with both hands and squeeze —a messy but efficient procedure.

Mix together all the ingredients. Place in an attractive serving bowl and cover.

Refrigerate the *pâté* for a few hours to permit the booze to permeate. Add more liquor before serving if you like.

PRESENTATION

Serve as a do-it-yourself paste for canapés. Don't permit your guests to eat it all at once. It ripens beautifully with age.

155

THE PROMISE OF A GOOD MEAT LOAF

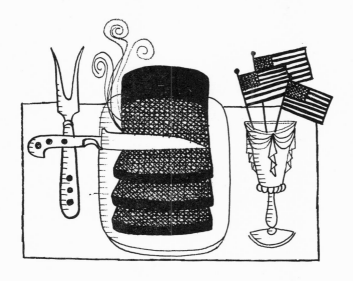

ONE Chinese ancient says that "the care of the cow brings good fortune." The prophet was probably not thinking of meat loaf, but his statement does apply. Too many sins have been perpetrated in the form of greasy meat combinations obscured in a haze of sage.

Meat loaf *can* be superb and liable to make any man feel fortunate. On the promise that you will buy good cow (and pig) and treat them carefully, I promise the best possible loaf.

Plain (More or Less) Meat Loaf

TIME: Just over 2 hours   SERVES: 4-6-8

Various combinations of meat are possible. Here are two that meet my taste along with the sauces that finish them off.

COMPOSITION

2 pounds ground beef	or	1½ pounds ground beef	or	1 pound ground beef
		¼ pound ground pork		½ pound ground pork
		¼ pound ground veal		½ pound liverwurst

1 cup red wine
⅔ cup bread crumbs
2 medium onions
1 garlic clove
1 small green pepper
2 celery stalks
4 tablespoons butter or bacon fat

½ cup chopped parsley
1½ teaspoons salt
freshly ground black pepper
nutmeg
thyme
ground cloves
cayenne
1½ teaspoons mustard
2 eggs

Sauce for topping (pp. 161, 162)

PREPARATION

Marinate the meats in the wine as long as possible, at least 1 hour.
Make bread crumbs.
Chop vegetables and sauté in butter or bacon fat until limp. Add them and the fat to the meats.
Season with the herbs and spices.
Stir in the eggs and mix very thoroughly.

Sauce for the Loaf

Place in a baking dish.

Choose from the following sauces and make one. Spread over the top of the loaf. Place the pan in a 350° oven, 45-60 minutes will do it up brown.

P.S. *Don't be too hospitable. The fewer the guests, the more there'll be to eat next day. Either hot or cold, it's mighty tasty.*

Sauce for the Loaf

I

TIME: 5 minutes

COMPOSITION

½ cup catsup
¼ cup wine vinegar
2 teaspoons Worcestershire sauce
1 garlic clove

1 tablespoon grated onion
½ teaspoon chili powder
1 teaspoon prepared mustard
salt

PREPARATION

Combine the ingredients. Spread or pour over the meat loaf before baking.

II

TIME: 3 minutes

COMPOSITION

¼ cup catsup
3 teaspoons brown sugar

1 teaspoon dry mustard
½ teaspoon nutmeg

THE PROMISE OF A GOOD MEAT LOAF

PREPARATION

Combine, mix, and use.

III

TIME: 8 minutes

COMPOSITION

1 cup chopped onions
1 cup chopped nuts
3-4 tablespoons butter

2 tablespoons tomato paste
1½ cups water

PREPARATION

Mince the onions. Chop nuts. Sauté both in butter. Simmer all ingredients for about 5 minutes. Spread on the loaf.

Pain de Boeuf

TIME: { Cooking: under 3 hours
{ Marinating: ½-12 hours

SERVES: 4-6 (or more, but don't count on it)

This has to be made to be believed. It still comes under the heading of meat loaf, but the lily is gilded so magnificently that it takes on a French flavor and a French title. If you don't like to meddle with pastry, read the next page for variations. If, by any remote chance, you have some of this loaf left over, don't bother to reheat. It may possibly be even better served cold.

Pain de Boeuf

COMPOSITION

Pastry for a 2-crust 9-inch pie

TO MAKE THE LOAF

2 pounds ground beef
1 cup red wine
2 cups bread crumbs
1 garlic clove
2-3 medium onions
3 tablespoons butter
2 teaspoons salt
2 teaspoons paprika
1½ teaspoons allspice
2 eggs

TO GILD THE LILY

2-3 parsley sprigs
1 small onion
a few celery tops
8 mushrooms
8 ripe olives
3-4 anchovy fillets
3-4 chicken livers
2 tablespoons butter
½ teaspoon salt
tarragon
nutmeg
ground cloves
coarsely ground black pepper
small bay leaf, powdered
sherry

PREPARATION

Work up the pastry. Let it rest in the refrigerator until the meat is cooked and the gilding prepared.

Marinate the meat in the wine for as long a time as possible—long meaning up to 12 hours. Anything over ½ hour is permissible.

Make the bread crumbs.

Chop the garlic and onions. Sauté them briefly in butter.

Mix together the meat, the wine, the garlic, the onions, the bread crumbs, the seasonings, and the eggs.

Preheat the oven to 350°.

Pour the meat mixture into a French loaf pan. (If you don't own one, any large rectangular pan will suffice.)

Bake it for about 1½ hours. Turn it out on a rack to cool slightly before gilding.

THE PROMISE OF A GOOD MEAT LOAF

Chop, mash, mince, and mix the ingredients for gilding. Sauté them in butter for a few minutes. Season with the various spices. Add enough sherry to make a spreadable mixture, then let it cool.

Roll out the pastry into a rectangle large enough to completely envelop the meat loaf.

Spread the gilding mixture over the sheet of pastry.

Place the loaf of meat in the center of the sheet. Wrap it up. Moisten and seal the seams. Slash the top in several places. Brush it with butter. Return it to the same (or a slightly larger) pan.

Bake at 400° for about 12 minutes. Lower the heat to 350° and continue baking for another 12 minutes. The crust should become beautifully tanned.

PRESENTATION

Remove the *pain* from the oven. Make a small hole in the top crust. Pour sherry—as much as possible—into the hole.

Now, and not until now, serve it forth.

Variations on the Preceding Theme

I

TIME: About 2 hours   SERVES: 4-6

COMPOSITION

Refer to the *Pain de Boeuf* recipe. Follow it exactly, excluding the pastry. Arm yourself with a large (Pullman size) unsliced loaf of bread, a quantity of soft butter, 1 egg, and 1 tablespoon of milk.

Pain de Boeuf (Cold)

PREPARATION

Cook the meat loaf ingredients on top of the stove for 20-25 minutes. Prepare the gilding mix.

Slice a ½-inch slab from the top of the loaf of bread. Scoop out the interior, leaving a ½-inch thick unbroken and unpierced shell. Smear the interior (all surfaces) with the gilding. Do not forget the bottom of the top.

Fill the hollow loaf with the meat mixture.

Slather the exterior with butter.

Glue on the lid with egg-milk paste (1 egg beaten with 1 tablespoon of milk). Use any extra paste to glaze the top of the loaf.

Place the loaf on a buttered baking sheet.

Bake it at 400° for 30-40 minutes.

Inject sherry just before serving.

II

Does the idea of wrapping meat in either pastry or bread throw you?

Skip it then. Pour about ½ cup of sherry or warmed brandy over the meat just before serving.

III

Pain de Boeuf (Cold)

TIME: Approximately 4½ hours, including chilling   SERVES: 4-6 hot people

COMPOSITION

meat loaf mixture (p. 162)	¾ *cup beef stock*
gilding mixture (p. 163)	*salt*
⅛ *pound butter*	*pepper*
3 tablespoons flour	*1 tablespoon unflavored*
¾ *cup heavy cream*	*gelatin*

THE PROMISE OF A GOOD MEAT LOAF

PREPARATION

Make the meat loaf and the gilding mixture.

Place the loaf in a long loaf pan. Spread the gilding mixture over the top.

Bake it at 350° for 1½-2 hours. Cool. Remove from the pan. Chill.

Melt the butter. Stir in the flour. Add the cream and the stock. Stir steadily.

Season.

Add the gelatin softened in ¼ cup cold water. Continue stirring until the gelatin has dissolved and the sauce is smooth and well blended.

Coat the top and sides of the cold loaf.

Chill again.

An Italian Meat Loaf

TIME: About 1 hour   SERVES: 4

COMPOSITION

½ pound chopped beef
½ pound chopped lean pork
½ cup grated Romano cheese
3 eggs
1 tablespoon chopped parsley

salt
pepper
¼ cup olive oil
¼ pound (or more) Mozzarella cheese

PREPARATION

Mix together the meats, the grated cheese, 2 eggs, the parsley and salt and pepper to your own good taste.

Hard-cook 1 egg. Slice it.

Pour half of the oil into a baking dish. Add half of the meat mixture.

Ham Loaf

Make a layer of sliced Mozzarella. Cover it with egg slices.
Add the rest of the meat. Pour on the rest of the oil.
Bake at 350° for 30-40 minutes or until golden but not dried out.

PRESENTATION

Let the loaf cool slightly before turning out on a warm platter. Serve with a salad or save it for superb sandwiches.

Ham Loaf

TIME: 1¾ hours   SERVES: 6-8

COMPOSITION

½ pound ground beef
½ pound ground pork
¼ pound ground lean ham
¼ cup dry bread crumbs
1 egg
¼ cup milk
¼ teaspoon paprika
¼ teaspoon Worcestershire sauce

½ teaspoon dry mustard
½ cup crushed pineapple
¾ cup brown sugar
1½ teaspoons prepared mustard
¼ cup vinegar
¼ cup dry white wine

PREPARATION

Combine the meats with the crumbs, the beaten egg, the milk, the paprika, the Worcestershire sauce, and ¼ teaspoon of the dry mustard.
Drain the pineapple. Spread it in the bottom of a loaf pan. Sprinkle with ¼ teaspoon of dry mustard.
Add the meat mixture.
Bake for 1¼ hours at 350°

THE PROMISE OF A GOOD MEAT LOAF

Combine the brown sugar, the prepared mustard, the vinegar, and the wine. Use the sauce for basting.

Wined Meat Loaf

TIME: 5-6 hours   SERVES: 6-8

COMPOSITION

1 pound veal
1 pound ham
1 pound lean pork
¼ pound round steak
½ pound liver (calf or baby beef)
1 small onion
2 tablespoons chopped parsley
2 tablespoons minced chives
½ bay leaf
cayenne
⅛ teaspoon coarse black pepper
⅛ teaspoon ground mace
⅛ teaspoon pulverized sage
⅛ teaspoon thyme
⅛ teaspoon allspice
salt
½ cup sherry
¾ cup beef stock
2 teaspoons Worcestershire sauce
½ cup port

PREPARATION

Have the meats ground up together. If your butcher refuses, and some of them will, have them finely chopped even if you have to do it yourself.

Add the seasonings.

Mix together the sherry, the stock, and the Worcestershire. Add it to the meats.

Let everything stand at room temperature for 4-5 hours.

Bake the loaf (in a loaf pan) at 450° for an hour.

Remove it from the oven.

PRESENTATION

Douse it with the port and serve.

P.S. *This deserves a fancier title. You cook it and then name it.*

Jellied Meat Loaf

TIME: 25 minutes to produce   SERVES: 6-8
1½ hours to chill and set

Almost any variety of cooked meats can go into this as long as it measures 4 cups. Clean out the refrigerator or start from scratch. It is always good.

COMPOSITION

2 cups chopped ham
2 cups chopped chicken (veal, pork, or what-have-you, already cooked)
3 eggs
2 packages unflavored gelatin
½ cup sherry
2 cups rich beef stock or *consommé*
salt
pepper
dry mustard
cayenne
½ cup chopped parsley and chives, mixed

PREPARATION

Chop the meat smaller than bite-size.
Hard-cook the eggs.
Soften the gelatin in the sherry.
Bring the stock to a boil. Pour it over the gelatin. Stir until the gelatin is dissolved. Season to taste with salt, pepper, dry mustard, and cayenne. Let it cool.
Chop parsley and chives. Mix them with the chicken.
Shell the eggs.

THE PROMISE OF A GOOD MEAT LOAF

Butter a rectangular mold or baking dish. Spread the chopped ham in the bottom of the mold. Add the eggs, running them east to west (lengthwise). Scatter the chicken meat around and over the eggs. Pour the gelatin mixture over all.

Put the loaf to rest in the refrigerator until it is firm.

PRESENTATION

Place the mold upside down on a platter. Wipe it with a hot towel. The meat loaf *should* drop out intact, to be sliced with a hot sharp knife.

CAPITAL GAINS
WITH LEFTOVERS

LEFT-OVER meat deserves better treatment than it usually receives. Too often it is relegated to the back of the refrigerator, eventually to be consigned to the garbage can.

Properly appreciated and pampered, left-overs can give you capital gains that you'll never have to pay taxes on. Be kind to your *restes de viande* and they will be more than kind to you. Their potentials as the basis for curries, hash, chili con carne, or salads is enormous.

Cold Veal Salad

TIME: 1¼ hours   SERVES: 4

COMPOSITION

4-6 thin slices cooked veal (or 2-3 cups chopped)
½ cup olive oil
¼ cup wine vinegar
½ teaspoon salt
⅛ teaspoon pepper
¼ teaspoon dry mustard
6-8 anchovy fillets
a few capers

PREPARATION

Slice or chop the meat.

Make a marinade using half of the oil, half of the vinegar, and all the salt and pepper. Pour it over the meat and let it marinate for an hour or so.

Prepare a sauce by mixing the rest of the oil, the vinegar, the mustard, the anchovies (washed and chopped), and the capers.

PRESENTATION

Drain the meat. Lay it on a serving platter. Cover it with the sauce.

Left-over Roast Beef in Wine Sauce I

TIME: 15 minutes   SERVES: 2-4

COMPOSITION

4 generous slices cold roast beef
juice of ½ lemon
2 tablespoons butter
2 tablespoons flour
¾ cup beef stock or consommé

1 jigger red wine
1 tablespoon Worcestershire sauce
salt
pepper

PREPARATION

Squeeze lemon juice over the beef slices.

Melt the butter. Stir in the flour. When it is browned but not burned, add the stock. Stir until thickened. Add the wine and seasonings to taste. Add the meat, heat through, and serve.

Left-over Roast Beef in Wine Sauce II

TIME: About 25 minutes   SERVES: 4

COMPOSITION

1 small onion
3 tablespoons chopped parsley
½ cup bread crumbs
3 tablespoons butter
2 tablespoons flour
1 cup beef stock

½ cup dry white wine
1 tablespoon tomato purée (or catsup, in a pinch)
salt
pepper
4 slices of cold roast

PREPARATION

Chop onion, parsley, and bread.

Use a tablespoon of butter to grease a shallow baking dish.

CAPITAL GAINS WITH LEFTOVERS

Heat the remaining butter and sauté the onion until it is limp. Stir in the flour. Add the stock, the wine, and the puree. Season to taste with salt and pepper. Simmer for about 10 minutes uncovered.

PRESENTATION

Place the beef in the baking dish. Cover it with bread crumbs. Add the sauce. Top with parsley. Brown under the broiler for 8-10 minutes.

Chestnut Beef Hash

TIME: About 1 hour   SERVES: 4-6

COMPOSITION

10-12 chestnuts
2-3 cups diced cooked beef
1 small onion
2 parsley sprigs
2 tablespoons butter
1 tablespoon flour
1 cup beef stock
¾ tablespoon tomato sauce
salt
pepper

PREPARATION

Cook the chestnuts. Cover them with boiling water and boil for 8-10 minutes. Remove the shell and inner skin immediately, keeping the chestnuts in the hot water while peeling. When peeled, cook the blanched chestnuts in lightly salted water for about 15 minutes or until they are tender.

Chop the onion and the parsley. Sauté them in the butter. Stir in the flour. Add the stock and the tomato sauce. Cook and stir until the sauce is thick.

Continue cooking for about 20 minutes. Add the beef. Bring

to a boil. Season to taste. Add the chestnuts. Heat and serve.

Beef in Sour Cream

TIME: 30 minutes   SERVES: 4

COMPOSITION

2-3 cups cubed cooked beef	1 tablespoon flour
1 small onion	1 tablespoon water
½ pound mushrooms	salt
⅛ pound butter	pepper
1 tablespoon paprika	½ pint sour cream
1 cup stock or bouillon	

PREPARATION

Dice the meat. Chop the onion. Slice the mushrooms.

Melt the butter. Sauté the onions and mushrooms briefly. Add the meat, the paprika, and the stock or bouillon. Simmer for about 20 minutes.

Make a paste of flour and water. Stir it into the sauce. Season to taste. Simmer for another 5 minutes.

Stir in the sour cream. Serve before it comes to a boil.

Sukiyaki for Six

TIME: 7-10 minutes to cook
1 hour (or less) for preliminaries
SERVES: 6

COMPOSITION

plenty of rice
2 medium yellow onions sliced
2 bunches green onions (scallions), sliced
½ can water chestnuts, sliced
½ can bamboo shoots, sliced
1½ pounds spinach, coarsely chopped
1 large Chinese cabbage, chopped
½ pound fresh mushrooms, sliced, or better, 2 8-ounce packages dried mushrooms soaked in water until unshriveled
¼ pound beef suet
1½ pounds beef fillets, sliced very thin
1 tablespoon sugar
soy sauce
½ cup beef stock (canned consommé can be used)
¼ pound soy bean curd
6 eggs

PREPARATION

Boil the rice (p. 374).

Chop, cut, dice, or slice all ingredients. Arrange them in separate piles on one or more large platters.

Assemble your guests at the table.

Heat a large iron skillet or your best chafing dish.

Sauté the diced suet to get fat.

Sauté the yellow onions briefly. Add the cabbage. Add sugar, soy sauce, and some of the stock. Stir gently.

Add the green onions, the mushrooms, the bamboo shoots, and the chunks of bean curd. Stir.

Add the water chestnuts, the spinach, and, finally, the beef.

Stir and toss the ingredients frequently with chopsticks—which no well-supplied kitchen should lack.

Keep the mixture moist with beef broth and soy sauce, added as necessary.

Break the eggs into the sukiyaki about 3-4 minutes before serving.

When done, the beef should be tender but not stewed. The vegetables should be crisp. The eggs should be set and not too runny. Everything should retain its own individuality.

PRESENTATION

Serve immediately in rice-laden bowls, giving each guest his fair share plus an egg.

Never attempt more than 6 servings at one time. If seconds are needed, start again from scratch.

Corned Beef Hash

TIME: 45-50 minutes   SERVES: 4

COMPOSITION

2 cups cooked corned beef
4 medium potatoes, cooked
1 small green pepper
1 small celery stalk
1 small onion
1 garlic clove
2-3 parsley sprigs
salt
pepper

PREPARATION

Preheat the oven to 425°

Chop all ingredients very fine (or use a food grinder).

Mix thoroughly.

Place in a buttered shallow baking dish.

Bake 20-25 minutes.

P.S. *If you're hungry—or you think your guests are—crown with 4 poached eggs—cooked but runny.*

Baked Beef Hash

TIME: 50 minutes　　SERVES: 6

COMPOSITION

4 cups diced left-over beef
6 boiled potatoes
¼ cup chopped onion
2 tablespoons chopped parsley
⅛ pound butter

1 garlic clove
½ cup dry red wine
2 tablespoons soy sauce
¼ teaspoon marjoram
¼ teaspoon thyme
paprika

PREPARATION

Dice the meat and the potatoes.
Chop the onion and the parsley.
Melt the butter. Sauté the onion and the pressed garlic until soft.
Combine all ingredients except paprika. Place in a shallow baking dish. Sprinkle liberally with paprika.
Bake at 350° for 30 minutes.

Beef Vinaigrette

TIME: About 20 minutes, plus time to marinate and chill　　SERVES: 4

COMPOSITION

6 medium onions
milk
6 cups lean roast beef
¼ cup chopped chives
2 tablespoons lemon juice
¼ cup wine vinegar
½ cup olive oil

½ teaspoon dry mustard
3 teaspoons summer savory
2-3 squirts Tabasco
few capers
salt
pepper

Cold Veal with Tuna Sauce

PREPARATION

Slice the onions thinly. Cover them with milk and let them stand for as long as possible—from 15 minutes to an hour. This removes excessive sting and some of the after-effects.

Cut the meat into thin narrow strips.

Chop chives. Squeeze a lemon.

Drain the onions.

Combine all ingredients. (Save the onion-flavored milk for sauce on another day.)

Let the meat marinate in the sauce for several hours at room temperature. Chill it briefly before serving.

Cold Veal with Tuna Sauce

TIME: 45 minutes   SERVES: 6

COMPOSITION

cold sliced veal for 6   *3-4 anchovies*
1 8-ounce can tuna   *½ pint sour cream*
juice of 1 lemon   *salt*
¾ cup mayonnaise   *pepper*

PREPARATION

Drain the tuna. Mash it. Combine with the lemon juice, the mayonnaise, and the minced anchovies, by hand or in a blender.

Add the sour cream.

Season to taste.

Chill well before serving the sauce over the sliced veal.

CAPITAL GAINS WITH LEFTOVERS

Chicken Hash Parmesan

TIME: 45 minutes   SERVES: 4

COMPOSITION

1½ cups cooked chicken	½ pint cream
½ cup cooked potatoes	1½ cup milk
1 small green pepper	Tabasco
½ cup grated Parmesan cheese	Worcestershire sauce
¼ pound butter	Maggi Seasoning
2 tablespoons flour	salt

PREPARATION

Dice the chicken and the potatoes.

Chop the green pepper.

Grate cheese.

Make a sauce: melt 4 tablespoons of the butter. Stir in the flour until well blended. Add the cream, the milk, and the seasonings. Salt to taste. Cook and stir for 3-4 minutes.

Sauté the green pepper in 4 tablespoons of butter. Add the chicken, the potatoes, and the sauce. Blend and stir gently. Adjust the seasonings.

Top with the grated cheese just before serving.

Casserole for Left-over Fowl
(M-in-I)

TIME: 1 hour (or more if you are serious about noodles)   SERVES: 4

COMPOSITION

3 cups cooked egg noodles
1 cup cooked poultry meat, cubed
½ cup fresh or canned chopped mushrooms
⅛ pound butter
½ cup grated sharp cheese
milk
salt

PREPARATION

First, make noodles (p. 293). If you are weak in that department, purchase the best and freshest available.

Cook the noodles in boiling salted water until tender yet bitey.

Cube the meat.

Clean mushrooms (or open a can) and chop them coarsely.

Grate cheese.

Butter a casserole.

Light the oven.

Sauté the mushrooms in butter. Combine mushrooms, meat, cheese, and drained noodles. Add enough milk to mix well. Salt to taste. Pour into the casserole and bake at 300° for about ¾ hour.

PRESENTATION

Serve this with Marinated Zucchini and invite your gourmet friends.

Turkey Soufflé, Mushroom Sauce

TIME: 2¾ hours   SERVES: 6

COMPOSITION

1 cup raw rice
1 cup soft bread crumbs
1 tablespoon grated onion
2 cups finely diced turkey
1 cup turkey stock or consommé
1½ teaspoons poultry seasoning
⅛ teaspoon ground coriander
1 teaspoon salt
¼ teaspoon pepper
4 eggs
¼ pound mushrooms
2 tablespoons butter
2 cups Béchamel Sauce

PREPARATION

Cook the rice (p. 374).
Make bread crumbs.
Grate onion.
Dice turkey.
Preheat the oven to 325°.
Combine the turkey, the rice, the bread crumbs, the onion, and the stock. Season.
Separate the eggs.
Beat the egg yolks until lemony. Add them.
Beat the egg whites until stiff. Fold them in.
Turn the mixture into a buttered soufflé dish.
Place the dish in a shallow pan of hot water.
Bake for 1¼ hours.
Meanwhile clean and slice the mushrooms. Sauté them briefly in butter.
Prepare Béchamel Sauce (p. 8). Add the mushrooms.

PRESENTATION

Serve the soufflé at once with the sauce on the side.

Lamb Hash

TIME: 30 minutes, including rice cookery   SERVES: 4-6

COMPOSITION

3 cups diced or cubed cooked lamb
2-3 tablespoons olive oil
⅔ cup peanut butter or 1 small can peanuts
2¾ cups water
2 teaspoons salt
¼ teaspoon pepper
½ teaspoon paprika
¼ teaspoon nutmeg
cayenne

PREPARATION

Chop the cooked lamb.

Heat the oil. Add all ingredients, the meat last. Stir thoroughly. Cover the pan and cook the conglomeration for 8-10 minutes. Reseason if necessary.

PRESENTATION

Serve with rice and chutney.

THE STATUS OF STEWS AND RAGOUTS

GENERALLY SPEAKING (if you like to speak generally), tastes for food are similar. And there are few things in such good taste as stews. If you object to the plebeian name, call them ragouts.

Stews make only three basic demands—good ingredients, time, and healthy appetites. Actual preparation time is short. Long slow cooking is necessary for the substances to blend and amalgamate. Escaping odors will invariably engender the appetites. The stew pot need not and should not be watched. Often the cooking stretch can be broken into short intervals, accomplished at the convenience of the cook. Most stews are improved by cooling and reheating. Like people, they mellow and improve with age.

One word of caution: when the time comes to make a stimulating stew, make plenty—more than plenty. The leftovers will be all the better tomorrow or the day after.

Boeuf Bourguignon

Boeuf Bourguignon fits into many categories, including stews, but it will appear in the guise of a casserole, so please turn to page 232.

Lamb Ragout

TIME: ¾ hour for preliminaries
8-10 hours for marinating
½ hour for final production
4-5 hours to cook

SERVES: 6-8

COMPOSITION

5 pounds lean shoulder or *breast of lamb*
½ pound chopped lean ham
¾ pound diced salt pork
1 cup finely chopped onion
2 garlic cloves, pressed
1 medium carrot, chopped
½ orange, sliced
¼ cup minced parsley
bay leaf
salt
pepper
¼ cup olive oil
½-¾ bottle red wine
¾ to 1 pound sliced bacon
½ cup (more or less) rich stock
flour
water

PREPARATION

Find a friendly butcher. Have him cube the lamb. If he is very friendly, ask him to chop (not grind) the ham and the salt pork.

That done, prepare the vegetables.

Make a marinade, using the vegetables, seasonings, oil, and wine.

Add the lamb cubes. Stir to coat each one. Let them marinate overnight.

Line the bottom and sides of a large casserole with bacon.

Make a layer of half the lamb-vegetable mixture. Add a layer of ham. Top with a layer of salt pork.
Repeat the layers and cap with a few bacon slices. Add the marinade and enough rich stock to cover.
Seal the casserole lid with a flour-water paste.
Bake the stew in a 200° oven for 4-5 hours.

P.S. *It's cooking like this that transforms an Irish stew into a Lamb Ragout.*

Son-of-a-Bitch Stew

TIME: 2-2½ hours   SERVES: 8-10

My favorite Grandma was five feet high. She made every effort to adjust her width to her height and came close to succeeding. She loved to eat.

Grandma ran a cattle ranch. As a widow somewhat beyond the age of fifty, she gave up civilization and pushed off to the wilds of Montana. There she not only worked cattle with the cowhands, but was their cook and bottle-washer. This suited her just fine. She loved to cook.

Grandma's "boys" were strictly carnivorous. They loved stew. Grandma fed them stew. If beef was lacking or a change of menu desired, she mounted her pony and tracked down a deer. No matter what the ingredients, the boys would demand more "son-of-a-bitchin' stew."

COMPOSITION

1 large iron pot
4 pounds red meat
  (bought or caught)
1 1-pound hunk of salt pork
8-10 onions, peeled
8-10 potatoes

a bottle of drinking liquor
  (corn, rye, rotgut)
salt
pepper
water

THE STATUS OF STEWS AND RAGOUTS

PREPARATION

Throw everything into the pot.
Lace liberally with any (or all) liquor.
Add water to cover.
Cook for at least 2 hours.

P.S. *Grandma was quite a gal!*

Wine Stewed Veal

TIME: Under 2 hours   SERVES: 4-6

COMPOSITION

2 pounds shoulder or breast of veal	⅓ cup dry vermouth
10-12 boiling onions	salt
½ pound mushrooms	pepper
¼ pound butter	herbs to taste
⅓ cup flour	1 egg yolk
½ cup dry white wine	1 teaspoon lemon juice
	½ cup cream

PREPARATION

Hew the meat into 1½-inch cubes or order it that way.
Peel onions. Clean and chop mushrooms.
Brown the veal in the butter. Add the onions. Stir until they are browned on all sides.
Stir in the flour. Blend it well.
Add the wine and the vermouth, slowly.
Season to taste as usual. Throw in a pinch or two of your favorite herbs.
Add about 4 cups of warm water.
Let the stew simmer for at least 1¼ hours.
Add the mushrooms. Simmer for 10-12 minutes.

Mix together the egg yolk and the lemon juice. Stir this into the mélange.

Add the cream. Stir. Serve immediately.

P.S. *New potatoes boiled in their jackets go well with this dish.*

Rabbit Stew

TIME: 2 hours   SERVES: 6

COMPOSITION

1 4-5-pound rabbit
4 tablespoons bacon fat or butter
3 tablespoons flour
2 cups chicken stock
2 cups dry white wine
1 garlic clove
2½ tablespoons tomato paste
salt
pepper
1 teaspoon tarragon
1 bay leaf, crushed
½ teaspoon thyme
3 tablespoons sour cream

PREPARATION

Have the butcher cut the rabbit into serving pieces.

Heat the fat. Brown the pieces on all sides. Sprinkle them with the flour. Blend well.

Add the stock, the wine, the crushed garlic, the tomato paste, and the seasonings.

Simmer, covered, over low heat for 1½ hours.

Transfer the meat to a warm serving platter.

Reduce the sauce if necessary. Stir in the sour cream. Let it warm but not boil. Pour it over the rabbit.

P.S. *If your butcher doesn't have a rabbit, look in the frozen-food department.*

THE STATUS OF STEWS AND RAGOUTS

Oyster Stew for Two

TIME: 10-12 minutes   SERVES: 2

COMPOSITION

2 cups milk	butter
1 pint cream	salt
1½ dozen shucked oysters	pepper

PREPARATION

Heat the milk and the cream.

In another pan cook the oysters in their own juice over a very low fire. When they have curled slightly, add them to the milk.

Toss in a large lump of butter.

Season to taste and eat with satisfaction.

Fish Stew

TIME: About 1 hour   SERVES: 4-6

COMPOSITION

3 pound assorted fresh fish (whiting, mullet, cod, etc.)	2 teaspoons salt
2 bacon slices	¼ teaspoon pepper
3 tablespoons butter	1 bay leaf
3 tablespoons oil	¼ teaspoon thyme
3 tablespoons flour	⅛ teaspoon nutmeg
1 bottle dry white wine	½ cup chopped parsley
1 garlic clove, pressed	½ cup brandy

PREPARATION

Cut the fish into serving pieces.

Chop the bacon. Brown it in the butter and oil. Stir in the

flour. Cook and stir until the mélange is a rich brown color.

Add the wine and the seasonings. Cover and cook for about 15 minutes over low heat.

Add the fish. Cook for 20-25 minutes.

Add the heated brandy, kindle a flame, and serve immediately.

PRESENTATION

White wine, French bread, and man-size napkins are necessary accompaniments.

CHICKENS AND THEIR BARNYARD BRETHREN

CHICKEN

CHICKENS are versatile creatures. There are types to suit every taste and pocketbook. If you are going to take the trouble to cook one, provide yourself with the very best of its kind. There is a use for every one, no matter what its sex or age.

Squabs are very young chickens—and should be. One squab serves one person, roasted or broiled. *Broilers* are somewhat larger. They should weigh up to 2½ pounds with very little fat showing. *Fryers* should also be well padded but not fat. They will tip the scales around 3½ pounds. *Roasting chickens* run 3-5 pounds. For larger roasts, try *capons*. They will weigh between 8-9 pounds and are always tender and tasty. *Tough old hens and roosters* weighing between 5-8 pounds can be recognized by their aged, yellow, and hairy skin. Sacrifice them only for stewing and fricaseeing.

For most things, a tender, plump chicken with thin moist skin is what you want. You'll get it if you look for it. Claim it, fresh, cleaned, and split or cut up as necessary, allowing at least 1 pound per serving. Hurry home and enjoy one of the following recipes—chicken at its very best.

Charcoaled Chicken

TIME: 1-24 hours for marinating
About 1 hour for cooking
SERVES: 2-4

COMPOSITION

1 broiler
2 tablespoons tarragon
2-3 parsley sprigs
basil
oregano
2 tablespoons sugar
2 teaspoons salt
1 teaspoon coarsely ground pepper
1½ cups salad oil
¼ cup white wine vinegar
⅓ bottle catsup

PREPARATION

Cut the chicken into quarters.
Chop the herbs.
Mix and blend together all ingredients. Marinate the chicken for 1 to 24 hours, preferably the latter.
Simmer the bird in the marinade for 30 minutes.
Broil over charcoal to your own degree of doneness. Baste often with the marinade.

Chicken Breasts with Mushrooms

TIME: 1 hour SERVES: 4

COMPOSITION

1 pound mushrooms
4 chicken breasts
salt
pepper
1 heaping teaspoon paprika
¼ cup flour
6 tablespoons butter
1 pint cream
½ cup Madeira

CHICKENS AND THEIR BARNYARD BRETHREN

PREPARATION

Clean and slice the mushrooms.

Season the breasts with salt, pepper, paprika, and flour.

Brown them in 4 tablespoons of the butter. Remove from the pan for a moment.

Stir in the cream and the wine. Return the breasts.

Cover the pan. Let the chicken cook slowly for ½-¾ hour or until the meat is tender.

Sauté the mushrooms in 2 tablespoons of butter. Add them to the chicken about 5 minutes before serving.

Chicken Cacciatora

TIME: Almost 2 hours   SERVES: 6

COMPOSITION

2 broilers
¾ cup flour
1-2 onions
1-2 green peppers
⅔ cup olive oil
2 garlic cloves
1 No. 2 can Italian-style tomatoes
1 8-ounce can tomato paste

1 cup dry red wine
1 teaspoon salt
½ teaspoon each allspice
½ teaspoon oregano
½ teaspoon black pepper
½ teaspoon thyme
3 pulverized bay leaves
¼ teaspoon cayenne
spaghetti for 6

PREPARATION

Purchase dismembered chicken or do it yourself. (If you dislike the skin, remove it.) Dry the parts.

Dredge the chicken in the flour, using a brown paper bag. (Better still, use a plastic bag. Keep it on hand at all times for this purpose, adding flour as needed.)

Chop onions to obtain a full cupful.
Chop green peppers to obtain ¾ cup.
Brown the chicken in the oil. Remove it from the pan.
Sauté the onions, the peppers, and the crushed garlic cloves in the remaining oil until they are soft. Add all other ingredients. Bring to a boil and cook for 4-5 minutes.
Add the chicken. Cover the pot. Simmer for about 1½ hours.

PRESENTATION

Serve with spaghetti. Let the wine flow freely.

Chicken Tarragon

TIME: 30-40 minutes SERVES: 2

COMPOSITION

1 tablespoon dried tarragon	*⅛ pound butter*
¾ cup dry white wine	*¾ teaspoon salt*
1 fryer	*⅛ teaspoon black pepper*

PREPARATION

Put the tarragon in the wine. Soak for an hour.
Cut up the chicken (or use parts). Sear it in butter. Season with salt and pepper. Cover the pan. Let chicken cook at low heat for 20 minutes.
Uncover the pan. Raise the heat. Add the herbed wine and let it boil. Stir the sauce and turn the chicken. Serve when only a few tablespoons of sauce remain.

Chicken with Lemon Sauce

TIME: 1½ hours   SERVES: 4

COMPOSITION

2 2-pound fryers (or 1 4-pound chicken)
¼ pound (plus) butter
1 orange
1½ lemons
¾-1 cup grated Gruyère cheese
1 jigger sherry
1 jigger dry white wine
salt
pepper
1½ cups cream

PREPARATION

Hack up the chicken. Sauté it in the butter. Cover the pan. Let it cook slowly for 40-50 minutes.

Grate the peel of the orange. Do the same to one lemon. Squeeze 2 tablespoons of lemon juice. Cut the half-lemon into thin slices.

Grate cheese.

Remove the chicken to a flat, shallow oven-proof dish.

Add the sherry and the white wine to the butter remaining in the skillet. If none is there, add some.

Stir in the grated peelings and the lemon juice. Season the sauce to taste.

Turn up the flame. Stir in the cream. Pour the sauce over the chicken, sprinkle with cheese, and top with several thin lemon slices.

Shove under the broiler until beautifully browned.

Coq au Vin

TIME: 2 to 2½ hours   SERVES: 4

COMPOSITION

1 roasting chicken
salt
pepper
½ lemon
¼ pound butter
1 jigger brandy
1 bottle dry red wine

15-20 small boiling onions
1 tablespoon sugar
1 jigger port
3-4 drops wine vinegar
1 pound mushrooms
2 garlic cloves

PREPARATION

Clean and cut up the chicken. Rub it with salt, pepper, and the cut lemon.

Melt half of the butter. Brown the chicken. Pour on the brandy. Light it. When the flames die down, add the red wine.

Cover the pan. Simmer the bird slowly for an hour or so until it is tender.

Peel the onions.

Clean and slice the mushrooms.

Brown the onions in 2 tablespoons (or more) of butter. Glaze them with the sugar, the port, and the vinegar.

In another pan, sauté the mushrooms in the rest of the butter.

Add the vegetables and the squeezed garlic to the chicken shortly before serving. If a thick sauce is desired, thicken it with a *roux* of butter and flour or merely cook it down to reduce the quantity.

Oven-Fried Chicken

TIME: Just over 1 hour   SERVES: Up to you—normally, 2 persons per chicken

COMPOSITION

1 or more fryers
flour
salt

pepper
butter

PREPARATION

Cut up the fryers.

Put about ½ cup of flour per chicken into a paper bag. Add what appears to be enough salt and pepper. Toss in the chicken. Shake vigorously.

Melt at least ¼ pound butter per chicken.

Set the oven to 350°. Light it.

Place the chicken parts on a rimmed cookie sheet (or in a shallow pan). Pour half of the butter over chicken. Let each part get its fair share.

Bake for 30 minutes, turn the parts upside down, add the rest of the butter, and bake for another 30 minutes.

Chicken in Marsala

TIME: 1 hour   SERVES: 2-4

COMPOSITION

1 roasting chicken (1 pound per person)
salt
pepper

4-6 tablespoons butter
1 onion
¼ cup water
½ cup Marsala

Cold Chicken with Tuna

PREPARATION

Quarter the chicken. Sprinkle it with salt and pepper.

Melt the butter in a skillet. Brown the chicken parts for about 5 minutes on each side. Add the sliced onion and cook for about 3 minutes.

Reduce the fire. Add the water. Cover the pan. Simmer the chicken until it is tender (about 45 minutes).

Add the wine. Simmer for another 10 minutes. If the sauce gets too low and thick, add more wine and water.

P.S. *Delicious with noodles and a green salad.*

Cold Chicken with Tuna

TIME: 1½-2 hours to stew the bird
      1 hour to chill it
      15 minutes to prepare sauce

SERVES: 4

COMPOSITION

1 stewing chicken	*½ lemon*
1 onion	*36 capers*
¾ cup celery leaves	*½ cup canned tuna*
¼ teaspoon nutmeg	*3-4 anchovies*
1 teaspoon salt	*olive oil*
3 eggs	*pepper*
2 parsley sprigs	

PRELIMINARY PREPARATION

Cut up the chicken.

Chop the onion.

Cook the chicken in a quart of water with the onion, the celery leaves, the nutmeg, and the salt. When tender (1½-2 hours), discard the bones. Chop the meat. Let it cool. Refrigerate until serving time.

CHICKENS AND THEIR BARNYARD BRETHREN

PREPARATION

Hard-cook the eggs. Chop the yolks. (You may eat the whites.)
Mince the parsley. Squeeze the lemon. Drain the capers. Flake the tuna. Mash the anchovies.
Blend these ingredients, adding enough oil to make a paste. Add more oil to make a thin paste.

PRESENTATION

Pour the paste over the cold chicken.

Chicken Brazil

TIME: Up to 4 hours   SERVES: 8-10

COMPOSITION

1 *stewing chicken*	¼ *cup pimiento*
1 *onion*	¼ *cup minced green pepper*
½ *lemon*	⅛ *pound butter*
3 *celery stalks*	½ *cup flour*
2-3 *parsley sprigs*	2 *cups cream*
1 *bay leaf*	*cayenne*
1 *tablespoon salt*	*saffron*
1 *cup raisins*	*allspice*
½ *cup white wine*	*rice*
1 *cup almonds*	

PREPARATION

Cut up the chicken. Cover it with water. Chop the onion, the lemon, the celery, and the parsley. Toss them into the pot. Add the bay leaf and the salt. Let the pot simmer until the chicken is tender—from 1½ to 2 hours.
Marinate the raisins in the wine.
Blanch and chop the almonds.

Chicken Brazil

Mince the pimiento and the green pepper.

Remove the chicken from the pot. Dice the meat. Return the bones to the broth. Cook until the juice is reduced to about 3 cups. Strain it. Skim off the fat, saving both fat and broth.

Heat the butter and about 2 tablespoons of chicken fat. Blend in the flour. Add 2 cups of broth and the cream. Stir steadily and cook slowly until the mixture thickens and comes to a boil.

Season with salt, cayenne, allspice, and saffron.

Add the raisins and the wine.

Add the chicken and the almonds.

Add the pimiento and the green pepper.

Heat well and serve forth. Better yet, set it aside to mellow for a few hours, then heat and serve.

PRESENTATION

Over rice, of course.

P.S. *If skimming fat off broth throws you, time the recipe so the broth can be chilled beforehand.*

CHICKENS AND THEIR BARNYARD BRETHREN

The Chicken for Every Pot
(Poule au Pot Henri IV)

TIME: 2-3 hours   SERVES: 6

COMPOSITION

1 plump middle-aged chicken	2 carrots
5-6 slices French bread	2 turnips
½ cup milk	2 onions
2-3 bacon slices	2-3 whole cloves
2 garlic cloves	2 leeks
2-3 parsley sprigs	1 celery stalk (with leaves)
2 green onions or shallots	1 bay leaf
nutmeg	½ dozen peppercorns
salt	1 teaspoon salt
pepper	about 3 quarts water
rosemary	grated Gruyère cheese
thyme	coarse salt
1 egg	

PREPARATION

Crumble the bread. Soak it in the milk.

Grind (or chop fine) the bacon and the heart, liver, and giblets of the chicken.

Press the garlic. Mince the parsley. Chop the green onions.

Combine these ingredients with the seasonings.

Stir in the egg.

Stuff the hen and sew her up. Toss her into a large pot.

Clean and quarter the carrots, turnips, onions, leeks, and celery. Add the remaining ingredients (excluding cheese and coarse salt) to the pot.

Let everything simmer for 2 or more hours until the chicken is tender.

Sieve the broth and remove the fat.

Almond Chicken

PRESENTATION

Carve the chicken. Arrange the meat, the stuffing, and vegetables on a platter. Sprinkle with grated cheese. Serve the broth as soup. Supply coarse salt on the side.

Almond Chicken

TIME: About 2 hours, depending upon the chicken   SERVES: 6

COMPOSITION

- 1 stewing chicken
- ½ tablespoon fresh or dried ginger
- ⅛ cup soy sauce
- 1 teaspoon sugar
- 1½ cups chopped almonds
- ½ cup chopped bamboo shoots
- ½ cup chopped water chestnuts
- ¾ cup chopped mushrooms
- ⅓ cup chopped cucumber
- 2-3 green onions (scallions)
- ⅛ pound butter
- 1½ cups dry white wine
- 2 teaspoons salt
- 1½ tablespoons cornstarch

PREPARATION

Stew the chicken according to any good recipe (pp. 207–210). Dice the meat.

Peel and mince the ginger. Let it marinate in the soy sauce and the sugar for at least 15 minutes. Squeeze it out, saving the juice. Discard the used pulp.

Blanch and chop the almonds.

Chop bamboo shoots, water chestnuts, mushrooms, cucumber, and onions.

Sauté the almonds in 2 tablespoons of butter. When tanned, remove from the fire. Stir in ½ teaspoon of the salt.

Sauté 2 cups of chicken meat in the rest of the butter for 4-5 minutes. Add the chopped vegetables. Stir in the wine and the ginger-flavored soy sauce. Season with the rest of the salt. Simmer for 15 minutes.

Make a thin paste of cornstarch and water. Add it.

Simmer for another 5 minutes.

Stir in the almonds just before serving.

Chicken Livers and Mushrooms

TIME: 45 minutes SERVES: 4

COMPOSITION

½ pound mushrooms
2 tablespoons minced green pepper
1 small onion
1 tablespoon minced parsley
1 pound chicken livers
⅛ pound butter (or more)
1 tablespoon flour

½ cup dry white wine
½ cup chicken stock
1 small bay leaf
salt
pepper
thyme
nutmeg

PREPARATION

Clean and chop the vegetables.

Sauté the livers, the vegetables, and parsley in butter for 2-3 minutes. Stir steadily.

Add the flour. Continue stirring until it is well blended and browned.

Add the wine and the stock. Continue stirring.

Pulverize the bay leaf. Add it and the seasonings.

Simmer for about 10 minutes. Recheck the seasoning before serving.

Chicken Liver Risotto

TIME: Almost 45 minutes   SERVES: 4

COMPOSITION

¼ pound mushrooms
1 small onion
¾ cup grated Premesan cheese
1 cup rice
¼ cup olive oil
2 cups chicken stock
1 garlic clove

salt
saffron
powdered ginger
dry white wine
½ pound chicken livers
4 tablespoons butter
coarse black pepper

PREPARATION

Clean and slice the mushrooms.
Chop the onion.
Grate cheese.
Sauté the rice in oil until it is well tanned. Stir constantly. Add the onion. Pour in the stock. Press in the garlic. Season with a pinch each of salt, saffron, and powdered ginger.
Cover the pan tightly. Steam for 20-25 minutes until the rice is tender. Moisten with wine if the stock is absorbed before the rice is done.
Meanwhile, sauté the mushrooms and livers in butter, quickly and briefly. Add them (and their juice) to the rice. Mix thoroughly.
Sprinkle liberally with pepper and the cheese.

CHICKENS AND THEIR BARNYARD BRETHREN

Chicken Liver Pâté

TIME: 1 hour plus 3 days   SERVES: 4-6 more or less dainty eaters

COMPOSITION

½ cup chopped chives
1 pound chicken livers
6 tablespoons butter
1 tablespoon curry powder
salt
pepper
thyme
basil
marjoram
allspice
½ cup dry vermouth
¼ cup sour cream

PREPARATION

Chop the chives. Cut up the livers.

Sauté the latter in butter for 12-15 minutes. Mash them. Stir in the seasonings and the chives. Add the wine. Mash again to make a paste. Taste. Adjust the seasonings.

Blend in the sour cream.

Cover the bowl and refrigerate the *pâté* for 3 days before serving.

THE BRETHREN

Roast Duckling with Oranges

TIME: 2¼ hours   SERVES: 4-6

COMPOSITION

1½ cups duck stock
2 Long Island ducklings
2 small onions
2 celery stalks, with leaves
1 bay leaf
2 tablespoons butter
2 tablespoons flour
minced rind of 1 orange
minced rind of 1 lemon

juice of 2 oranges
½ cup currant jelly
salt
pepper
1 cup orange peel strips
preserved kumquats
peeled orange sections
watercress

PREPARATION

Start the duck stock by simmering giblets and neck in 2 cups of water. Continue slow cooking until duck is done.

Stuff 1 onion, 1 celery stalk and one-half of the bay leaf in the cavity of each duckling. Place them in a roasting pan in a 325° oven.

Roast for 1½ hours, removing all fat from the pan as it collects.

Raise the heat to 425°. Roast the ducklings for another 30 minutes. The skin should be crisp and brown and the birds should be tender. Place them on a warmed serving platter and keep warm.

Remove all fat from the roasting pan. Add the stock. Bring it to a boil. Scrape off all rich brown scraps which have stuck to the pan.

In another pan, melt the butter. Stir in the flour. Add the stock, stirring constantly until smooth.

Add the orange and lemon rinds, the orange juice, and the currant jelly. Season to taste with salt and pepper. Simmer for 10 minutes.

Prepare and parboil the strips of orange peel for 3 minutes.

PRESENTATION

Pour the sauce over the ducklings. Garnish the platter with orange strips, kumquats, orange sections, and watercress.

Brandied Duck

TIME: 4 hours to overnight, plus 1¼ hours   SERVES: 4-6

COMPOSITION

1 duck (5-6 pounds)
2 large onions
¼ cup minced parsley
1 bay leaf
½ teaspoon thyme
2 garlic cloves

3 jiggers brandy
2 cups red wine
¼ cup olive oil or *butter*
¾ pound mushrooms
salt
pepper

PREPARATION

Clean, then cut the duck into serving pieces. Place in a deep dish.

Chop the onion and the parsley.

Add them, the bay leaf, thyme, crushed garlic cloves, brandy, and wine to the duck.

Marinate for at least 4 hours. Overnight is better by far.

Heat the oil. Brown the pieces of duck for about 15 minutes.
  Add the marinade and the sliced mushrooms.

Season.

Cover tightly and simmer over a low flame for at least 1 hour.

Rock Cornish Game Hens Vermouth

TIME: 2¾ hours   SERVES: 6

COMPOSITION

6 game hens
salt
2 jiggers vermouth
½ cup chopped celery
½ cup chopped mushrooms
¼ cup chopped nuts
¾ cup bread crumbs

⅓ cup sliced water chestnuts
3 tablespoons butter
¼ teaspoon rosemary
¼ teaspoon thyme
⅛ teaspoon pepper
6 bacon slices

PREPARATION

Wash and dry the hens and sprinkle them with salt inside and out. Sprinkle with vermouth and let stand during the stuffing-making process.

Chop celery, mushrooms, and nuts.

Make bread crumbs. Slice the water chestnuts.

Melt the butter. Add the celery, the mushrooms, the nuts, and the seasonings, including 1 teaspoon of salt. Sauté until the celery is tender.

Add the chestnuts and the bread crumbs. Mix.

Stuff the birds. Tie them up. Cut the bacon slices in half. Place two on each chicken breast.

Roast and baste for 1½ hours at 350°.

PRESENTATION

With immodest pride.

Rock Cornish Game Hens San Francisco

TIME: 2 hours   SERVES: 6

COMPOSITION

6 game hens
salt
½ cup cooked wild rice
½ cup grated onion
½ pound mushrooms
¼ cup pistachio nuts

½ cup diced cooked ham
6 tablespoons butter
½ teaspoon marjoram
½ teaspoon thyme
6 bacon slices
watercress

PREPARATION

Wipe the game hens. Sprinkle the cavities lightly with salt. Cook the wild rice.

Grate onions. Slice mushrooms. Chop pistachios. Dice ham.

Melt the butter. Sauté ham, nuts, mushrooms, and onion for 5 minutes.

Add the cooked rice. Season with the herbs and ½ teaspoon of salt. Combine thoroughly.

Stuff the birds loosely. Truss them.

Place them in a roasting pan. Lay 2 half-slices of bacon over each breast.

Roast uncovered for 1½ hours in a 350° oven, basting occasionally.

PRESENTATION

Place on a heated platter. Encircle with watercress.

TURKEY GABBLE
TO BUY—TO STUFF—TO ROAST

Why limit turkey to holidays? It is a reasonably priced meat for any dinner, with a greater percentage of good leftovers than almost any other. From beginning to end it can (and should) be delicious.

Turkeys now come in a variety of sizes, although the shape remains the same. Youngsters from 3-6 pounds are most often split for broiling and frying. If this is the final destination of your bird, be certain that it *is* a young one and not just a small one. Older hens and toms weigh between 7 and 20 pounds, while senior citizens of both sexes weigh up to 30 pounds. Both mature types should be reserved for roasting only. In any event, inspect your choice carefully. It should have a plump breast and plump legs and thighs. Its flesh should be firm and fresh. A long scrawny, wizened bird should be avoided like the poison it may well be.

How much to buy? Most cooks settle tentatively on a turkey affording a minimum of 1 pound (dressed weight) per person. I approach it differently. Knowing what future meals will be, I buy the largest bird my roasting pan (and oven and platter) will take. The larger the turkey, the greater proportion of edible meat it will contain. If refrigerator space is a problem, remember that the carcass need not be stored whole. It is really better to remove the meat in pieces and slices immediately after the first attack. Stored in foil or jars, it will not become dessicated and dried out.

What to buy? Fresh or frozen? The choice is yours. Needless to say, fresh-killed-and-dressed turkey is by far the better.

Turkey in hand—not forgetting the neck and giblets—it is now necessary to carry the poultry-man's work to its close. Seldom are all the stray pinfeathers removed. Use tweezers;

even pliers if necessary. With a rolled, flaming newspaper, singe the skin—without scorching, of course. Remove all remnants of interior viscera. Check to be sure the oil sac at the base of the tail has been removed. (If not, a V-shaped cut with a sharp knife will do it quickly.) Wash and dry the bird carefully both inside and out. Full immersion in a cold water bath does no harm at all, if the turkey is thoroughly dried off afterwards.

The stuffing is up to you. We offer several choices. (I am fed up with stuffings stuffed with sage and poultry seasoning. They are not included.) Your selection should be personal. It may be wet or dry, fluffy or solid, and as plain or fancy as you like. Try making it in advance, but be sure it is cool before stuffing the bird; then refrigerate immediately or freeze until ready to use. It is hard to tell how much is required for any given bird. Plan for 1 to 1¼ cups per pound. At this rate, there *will* be left-overs which you can cook separately and baste with turkey juice.

Actually, stuffing is *never* really stuffed. Fill the neck and body cavities loosely to allow for expansion. Sew or skewer the openings. Fold the wing tips back under and in toward the body. They will become a brace for the bird both in the pan and on the platter. Bring the legs together and tie them securely with cord.

Splurge on the butter. And absorb the advice on roasting in "Turkey Addenda."

A meat thermometer is probably the best way to determine the correct roasting time. Insert it in the thickest part of a thigh, avoiding the bone. When it registers 185°, the bird is done. Test by moving a leg joint. It should "give" readily, or even break. Juices should run clear, with no trace of pink showing.

Personally, I prefer moist turkey. If you agree, don't overcook. You lose flavor and the meat gets much too dry. I am more than convinced that the best moist turkey is achieved by roasting in a 325° (slow) oven for 20-25 minutes per stuffed pound. An 8-10 pound bird will take from 2 to 4 hours; 10-15 pounds will require 4-5 hours and 5 to 6½ hours will be needed for one weighing up to 30 pounds.

You are now on your own, but don't forget to read farther.

Turkey Gravy

TIME: 1½ hours, more or less   YIELD: 2 cups

COMPOSITION

turkey giblets	*¼ cup (or more) flour*
turkey neck	*salt*
2 tablespoons turkey fat	*pepper*

PREPARATION

Place the heart, gizzard, and neck in a large pot of salted water. Cook until tender. Add the liver. Cook until it has barely lost its pinkness.

Pull the meat from the neck.

Chop everything very fine. Return it to the pot of stock.

When the turkey is done, remove it to its platter.

Pour all but 2 tablespoons of surplus fat from the roasting pan. Scrape all crispings from the sides and bottom of the pan.

Add the flour. Cook and stir until it is well browned (¼ cup of flour should make a thick gravy with 2 cups of liquid).

Add 1 cup of water. Continue stirring and smoothing until thick.

Add 1 cup of the stock. Simmer until thickened to your own taste.

Season with salt and pepper.

Serve forth, unadulterated.

TURKEY ADDENDA

I

In most normal (and some abnormal) households, since everyone assumes—and rightly—that the turkey will be roasted, the entire turkey question revolves around the stuffing. It seems reasonable to conclude that two people—(or twelve)—could be satisfied with two stuffings.

So make two stuffings. Cram one into the neck. Use the other (cook's choice, therefore larger) in the body cavity.

II

After stuffing and trussing your turkey, deposit it in a roasting pan. Melt ¾ pound of butter. Pour most of it over the bird. Cover with a clean cloth—cheesecloth, an old sheet, or the back of an old shirt. Pour butter over the cloth.

Roast the turkey breast side down for tenderness. Start it in a cold oven set at 300°. If it is small, 20-25 minutes per pound will be good. Larger birds thrive if cooked for 15-20 minutes per pound.

Remove the butter-laden cloth about 20 minutes before the turkey is to be let out of the oven. (The rag will never be the same again. Throw it away.)

For carving ease, let the turkey cool off for about 15 minutes. Spend the time wetting your whistle and whetting your knife. These accomplished, bear the bird to the board and get down to business.

III

Truffles reputedly make women more loving and men more lovable. They are decidedly expensive, which seems reasonable if this is true. You won't be able (or want) to use them every day. On special occasions however, buy some. Two large ones will do.

Slice them. Sauté them for a moment in butter and a soupçon of sherry. Before roasting, slit the turkey skin here and there. Slide in a truffle-slice. *Voilà!*

Stuffing for a Turkey

TIME: 45-60 minutes   YIELD: For an 18-20 pound turkey

COMPOSITION

2 cups chopped onion
2 cups milk
¾ cup chopped parsley
1 cup chopped celery
1 cup chopped apples
2 cups chopped mushrooms
1 cup chopped water chest-nuts
1 cup chopped walnuts
3 chopped garlic cloves

3 cups sour-dough or *French bread crumbs*
2-3 tablespoons brown sugar
1 teaspoon salt
1 teaspoon pepper
1 tablespoon monosodium glutamate
1 tablespoon Spice Islands Beau Monde seasoning
¾ pound butter

PREPARATION

Chop the onions first. Let them swim in the milk. When ready to use, drain off the milk and reserve it for a sauce to serve with left-over turkey (see pp. 226, 227).
Chop everything else that has to be chopped.
Mix and blend and stir all ingredients together thoroughly and well.
Melt the butter. Pour it over the mélange. Stir to coat each morsel.
Stuff the turkey loosely.
Seal the openings with foil or bread crusts or skewers.
Bake any extra stuffing separately. Baste it with turkey juice.

Chestnut Stuffing à la Bourgeoise

TIME: About 1½ hours   YIELD: For an 18-20 pound turkey

COMPOSITION

2 pounds chestnuts
1 cup oil
1 small onion
4 celery stalks
consommé
salt
pepper
2 shallots or green onions
1 teaspoon minced parsley
1 teaspoon minced chives
1-2 truffles
sherry
½ cup bread crumbs
milk
2 tablespoons butter
½ pound sausage meat
¼ bay leaf
thyme

PRELIMINARY PREPARATION

Gash the chestnuts on the flat side.

Heat the oil in a skillet. Add the chestnuts. Shake or stir the pan for 2-3 minutes. Drain the chestnuts, let them cool, and remove the shells and inner skins with a sharp knife.

Slice the onion and one stalk of celery.

Cook the chestnuts until tender in half water and half consommé to barely cover, together with the onion, the celery, the salt, and the pepper.

Let them cool.

PREPARATION

Chop the shallots, the parsley, the chives, and 3 celery stalks.

Chop or slice the truffles. Let them soak in sherry to cover for a while.

Make bread crumbs. Let them soak in milk. Squeeze them, then separate the mass with a fork.

Sauté the shallots in butter. Add the sausage, the parsley, the

chives, the truffles and their juice, the bay leaf, and the thyme. Season to taste with salt and pepper.
Mix together with the cold chestnuts.
Stuff the turkey.

Wine Chestnut Stuffing

TIME: 50-60 minutes YIELD: 5 cups

COMPOSITION

2 pounds chestnuts
1 cup oil
2 cups consommé
6 green onions (scallions)
2 celery stalks
2 tablespoons chopped parsley
1 tablespoon chopped chives
2 cups soft bread crumbs
3 tablespoons butter
¾ pound sausage meat

½ teaspoon thyme
½ teaspoon marjoram
1 bay leaf
1 tablespoon monosodium glutamate
salt
pepper
¼ cup red wine
¼ cup brandy

PREPARATION

With a knife make an X cut on the flat side of each chestnut.
Heat the oil in a heavy skillet. Add the chestnuts. Cook them over high heat for about 3 minutes, stirring and shaking the pan constantly.
Remove the shells and inner skin as soon as possible.
Place the nuts in a pan with the consommé. Cook 15-20 minutes, until they are tender. Drain and chop coarsely.
Chop onion, celery, parsley, and chives.
Make bread crumbs.
Melt the butter. Add the celery and onions. Cook and stir for 3-4 minutes.

Add the sausage, the parsley, the chives, and the herbs. Season
    to taste with salt and pepper. Cook and stir with a fork,
    breaking up the meat.
Moisten the bread with the wine and the brandy. Add it to
    the skillet. Mix well.
Add the chestnuts. Mix again.
Stuff the bird.

P.S. *This makes a really elegant turkey.*

Turkey Florentine

TIME: 30 minutes   SERVES: 6

COMPOSITION

2 pounds spinach
cold turkey for 6
2 cups onion-flavored milk
    (left over, p. 223)
3 tablespoons butter
3 tablespoons flour

salt
pepper
¼ teaspoon nutmeg
grated Parmesan cheese (at
    least ½ cup)

PREPARATION

Clean and cook the spinach. Purée it.
Slice or dice the turkey.
Heat the left-over onion-flavored milk.
Melt the butter. Stir in the flour. When well blended, add the
    milk. Cook and stir until the sauce is thickened and
    smooth. Season with salt and pepper.
Combine the spinach, the nutmeg, and a third of the cream
    sauce. Heat well without boiling. Pour this onto a warmed
    oven-proof platter.

Arrange the turkey slices over all, sprinkle with half of the cheese and pour sauce on top. Add the rest of the cheese and brown lightly under the broiler.

Turkey and Ham with Chestnuts

TIME: 1¼ hours   SERVES: 6

COMPOSITION

1 cup cooked chestnuts	½ cup dry white wine
2 cups chopped cooked turkey	⅛ pound butter
1 cup chopped cooked ham	¼ cup flour
1 cup onion-flavored milk (p. 223)	salt
½ cup turkey stock	pepper

PREPARATION

Prepare the chestnuts (p. 224). Chop them coarsely.

Chop turkey and ham.

Combine the milk and the stock. Heat well. Add the wine. Continue heating without boiling.

Melt the butter. Stir in the flour. Season. Continue stirring until smooth. Add the hot liquid, stirring constantly until thickened.

Add the chestnuts, turkey, and ham.

PRESENTATION

Serve over rice (p. 374), or noodles (p. 293).

CASING THE CASSEROLE CIRCUIT

🎃🎃🎃🎃🎃🎃🎃🎃🎃🎃🎃🎃🎃🎃🎃🎃🎃🎃🎃🎃🎃🎃

A CASSEROLE is a covered cooking dish. Once filled, it can be left more or less to its own devices until it appears on the table. Some men, probably judging on painful experience, scorn a casserole as a king-size catch-all for left-over food. This does not have to be. A casserole is only as good as the ingredients that go into it. Marvelous things, including meat, chicken, fish and shellfish, vegetables—even desserts in the form of puddings or soufflés—can headline a meal cooked *en casserole*. Be my guest while I prove this point! Once I lead you into camp, you will revel in results all out of proportion to the comparatively small work and expense involved.

P.S. *One strong point in favor of this form of cooking is that there is no presentation problem and very few dishes. Same dish for everything—mixing, cooking, and serving.*

MEAT CASSEROLES

Boeuf Bourguignon
(M-in-I)

TIME: About 1 hour to prepare
About 3 hours to cook

SERVES: 4-6-8

COMPOSITION

4 pounds *chuck beef*
½ pound *salt pork*
4 dozen small *boiling onions*
parsley
1 pound *fresh mushrooms*
peel of 1 *orange*
croutons
sweet butter
2 tablespoons *flour*

1 bottle *red wine (Burgundy or Cabernet Sauvignon for choice)*
2 *garlic cloves*
1 *bay leaf*
mace
marjoram
thyme
basil
pepper

PREPARATION

Ask your butcher to cube the beef into 2-inch squares.

Chop the salt pork into small bits.

Peel the onions. Chop parsley. Clean and slice the mushrooms. Slash the orange peel into matchstick strips.

Make a liberal quantity (minimum 2 cups) of croutons by frying coarsely chopped bread in sweet butter until it is nicely tanned and crisp.

Brown the salt pork in a large skillet until it is crisp. Place the bits in a casserole and sauté the onions in the fat. When they are a rich gold color, set them aside for later use.

Brown the beef in the same fat. (If necessary, add bacon fat.)
Add the beef to the casserole. Sprinkle it with the flour.
Rinse out the skillet with wine and pour the wine over the meat. Season with minced garlic, crushed bay leaf, pulverized mace, marjoram, thyme, and basil. Add a generous grind of black pepper. Stir in the orange peel.
Cover the casserole. Place it in a 250° oven.
Relax for the next 3 hours. You have earned it.
About 15-20 minutes before serving time, melt a walnut-size lump of sweet butter. Sauté the mushrooms quickly.
Add them and the waiting onions to the casserole.

PRESENTATION

Serve from the casserole, with parsley and croutons tossed on top.
An Artichoke and Romaine Salad (p. 409) complements this dish to perfection and makes it a whole meal. Red Burgundy for your wine, please.

Boeuf à la Mode du Barry

TIME: 3 hours in all   SERVES: 4-6

COMPOSITION

1 pound carrots	salt
8-10 boiling onions	pepper
½ cup chopped parsley	1 garlic clove
1 bay leaf	thyme
4 tablespoons bacon fat or ⅛ pound butter	1 cup dry white wine
	1 jigger brandy
1½ pounds cubed chuck beef	beef stock
3 tablespoons flour	1 jigger sherry

PREPARATION

Slice the carrots. Peel the onions. Chop parsley. Crush the bay leaf. Keep each in a separate pile.

Melt half of the fat. Brown the meat.

In a casserole, melt the rest of the fat. Add the carrots and the onions. Sauté them briefly. Stir in the flour. Refuse to let it burn.

Add the meat. Season it with salt and pepper. Flavor it with pressed garlic, a pinch of thyme, the parsley, and the bay leaf.

Add the white wine, the brandy, and enough rich beef stock to cover the meat.

Cover the casserole. Place it in a slow oven (300°) for 2 to 2½ hours.

When done, remove the meat and the vegetable. Skim off the fat. Sieve the sauce. Return the meat and vegetables to the sauce, add the sherry, reheat quickly and serve.

Chateaubriand en Casserole

TIME: 3 hours   SERVES: 4

COMPOSITION

1 jigger brandy	butter
2 jiggers Madeira	1 2-pound fillet of beef
2 jiggers dry white wine	2 garlic cloves
5-6 fine carrots	salt
5-6 small onions	pepper
3-4 medium tomatoes	flour
1-2 shallots or scallions	water

PREPARATION

First of all, preheat oven at 250°.

Pour a jigger of brandy, the Madeira, and the white wine into a casserole. Shove it into the oven.

Clean and chop the vegetables. Sauté the carrots and the onions in a skillet in an ungrudging amount of melted butter—maybe even 6 tablespoons. Put them to one side.

Brown the fillet in the same pan, using more butter if necessary.

Place the meat in the casserole with the brandy and wine, and add the rest of the ingredients. Season with salt and pepper. Seal the casserole and its cover with a thick flour and water paste. Replace casserole in oven. Break the seal after 2½ hours.

Ground Beef Delight—also en Casserole (M-in-I)

TIME: 45-60 minutes   SERVES: 6-8-10

COMPOSITION

1 dozen small carrots, diced	⅛ teaspoon red pepper
1 dozen small onions, diced	3 pounds ground chuck
1 dozen medium potatoes, diced	1 cup soft bread crumbs
2 celery stalks, chopped	¼ cup heavy cream
4 leeks (white part, chopped)	nutmeg
salt	4 parsley sprigs
pepper	1 egg
1 bay leaf	½ cup red wine
1 thin lemon slice	1 package frozen peas
	chives

PREPARATION

Do what must be done to the vegetables in the way of cleaning and peeling and chopping as necessary.

Into a casserole toss the carrots, the onions, the potatoes, the celery, the leeks, a teaspoon of salt, a liberal grinding of black pepper, the bay leaf, the red pepper, and the lemon slice.

Add water to more than cover (by about 2 cups).

Bake at 350° until the vegetables are tender (about 20-25 minutes).

Mix the meat, the crumbs, the cream, a big pinch of nutmeg, half of the minced parsley, the beaten egg, and some salt and pepper. Form the mixture into ping-pong balls.

Retrieve the bay leaf and the lemon from the casserole. Add the wine. Toss in the meat balls.

Continue cooking for about 20 minutes.

Meanwhile cook the peas in very little water. Add them to the casserole just before serving.

P.S. *Serve with French bread to sop up the sauce and a tossed green salad.*

Lamb-Chops-in-Wine Casserole

TIME: About 40 minutes   SERVES: 3-6

COMPOSITION

6 lamb shoulder chops	1 small onion
3 garlic cloves	2 shallots
salt	2-3 parsley sprigs
pepper	1½ tablespoons flour
butter	1 cup dry white wine

PREPARATION

Smear the chops with garlic pressings. Salt and pepper them well. Brown in butter. Deposit in a casserole.

Chop the onion, the shallots, and the parsley. Sauté them in butter. When the onion is golden, add the flour. Blend in

Lamb and Eggplant Casserole

well. Pour in the wine. Cook and stir until the sauce is smooth and thick.

Pour the sauce over the chops. Cover the casserole. Cook in a 350° oven for about 20 minutes. Remove the cover and continue cooking for another 10 minutes.

Lamb and Eggplant Casserole

TIME: 1½ hours   SERVES: 4

COMPOSITION

1 large eggplant	*½ cup cream*
1 medium onion	*salt*
1 pound leg of lamb in 1-inch cubes	*pepper*
	2 medium tomatoes
6 tablespoons butter	*2-3 parsley sprigs*

PREPARATION

Bake the unpeeled eggplant at 450° for 45 minutes.

Chop the onion. Mix it with the meat and 2 tablespoons of the butter, which has been melted. Place the mixture in a casserole. Bake it at 450° for ½ hour.

Peel and mash the eggplant. Mix the pulp with the rest of the melted butter and the cream. Season with salt and pepper. Keep the mixture warm.

Peel, quarter, and drain the tomatoes. Stir them and the eggplant into the lamb.

Bake at 350° for 20-30 minutes.

Chop the parsley. Sprinkle on the casserole just before serving.

Cassoulet (One Version of) (M-in-I)

TIME: A night and a day   SERVES: 6-8 or more

COMPOSITION

1 quart white beans, dried
2 pounds pork fillet
salt
pepper
1 ham shank
1 carrot
2 medium onions
1 whole clove
2 garlic cloves
1 parsley sprig
1 bay leaf
1 celery stalk
thyme
2 pounds boned shoulder of lamb
butter
½ cup tomato purée
½ cup stock
½ pound Italian garlic sausage
bread crumbs

PRELIMINARY PREPARATION

Soak the beans in water overnight. Sprinkle the fillet wtih salt and pepper. Let it stand at room temperature overnight.

PREPARATION

On the following morning, roast the pork at 325° for an hour. Drain the beans. Cover with fresh water. Bring to a boil for about 10 minutes. Remove and discard any floaters. Drain again.

Place the beans in a large pot together with the ham shank, the carrot, one whole onion, the clove, one garlic clove, the bay leaf, the celery stalk, and a pinch or sprig of thyme. Add boiling water to cover. Boil, skim, and simmer for 1½ hours.

Cut the shoulder of lamb into bite-sizes. Brown in butter. Add a finely chopped onion and a well-pressed garlic clove. Brown them. Add the tomato purée and the stock. Bake the mixture for 1½ hours in the 325° oven.

In the afternoon, retrieve the seasoning vegetables from the bean pot. Discard them and the shank.

Chop the sausage coarsely. Add it to the beans. Cook them for another hour.

Chop the pork into bite-size pieces.

In a very large casserole, place a layer of pork. Add a layer of beans (with sausage), then a layer of the stewed lamb. Alternate the layers until all ingredients are used. Top with bread crumbs. Bake the cassoulet at 300° for 1 more hour.

PRESENTATION

Serve with French bread, and complete the meal with a good cheese and cool fruit.

Baked Ham en Casserole

TIME: 1½-2 hours   SERVES: 4-6

COMPOSITION

1 slice tenderized ham at least 1½ inches thick and weighing at least ½ pound per serving
milk
pepper
1 bay leaf

brown sugar
dry mustard
flour
butter
salt
monosodium glutamate

PREPARATION

Place the ham in a casserole. Cover it with milk. Season it with freshly ground pepper and a crushed bay leaf. Bake it, uncovered, at 350° for 1 to 1½ hours, depending on thickness of ham.

Thirty minutes before serving, strain off the milk and save it. Spread brown sugar and mustard on the ham. Return it to the oven to become glazed.

Using the usual method, make a sauce with the milk, butter and flour, allowing 2 tablespoons of flour and butter per cup of milk. Season with salt, pepper, and monosodium glutamate.

PRESENTATION

Pour the sauce over the ham. Serve from the casserole.

A Quick Ham Casserole for Two

TIME: 45 minutes   SERVES: 2

COMPOSITION

2 *yams* or *sweet potatoes*	*pepper*
1 *1-pound ham slice, precooked*	¾ *cup brown sugar*
	cinnamon
butter	*ground cloves*
salt	1 *small can sliced pineapple*

PREPARATION

Boil, peel, and slice the yams. Toss them neatly into a buttered casserole. Season lightly with salt, pepper, half the brown sugar, cinnamon, and cloves.

Add the ham slice.

Top with the pineapple. Sprinkle with the remaining sugar and additional butter.

Bake at 350° for ½ hour, more or less.

Ham Soufflé

TIME: 45 minutes   SERVES: 4

COMPOSITION

1 cup ground cooked ham
3 eggs
⅛ pound butter
4 tablespoons flour

1 cup milk
½ teaspoon salt
¼ teaspoon pepper

PREPARATION

Grind ham.

Separate eggs. Beat the yolks until lemon-colored. Beat the whites until stiff.

Butter a casserole.

Melt the butter. Add the flour, then the milk. Cook and stir until the sauce is thick. Remove from heat.

Add the ham, the seasonings, and the egg yolks.

Fold in the egg whites.

Bake for 30 minutes at 350°.

Ham and Eggs en Soufflé
(M-in-I)

TIME: 30 minutes   SERVES: 6

COMPOSITION

3 cups diced cooked ham
1½ tablespoons chopped chives
1½ cups bread crumbs
9 eggs
3 tablespoons butter

3 tablespoons flour
1½ cups dry white wine
salt
pepper
cayenne
nutmeg

PREPARATION

Dice the ham. Chop the chives. Crumb some dry bread. Mix the three together.

Separate 3 of the eggs. Beat the whites until stiff.

Melt the butter in a double boiler, and blend in the flour. Add the wine slowly, stirring steadily. Cook and stir for 4-5 minutes, until the sauce becomes thick and smooth.

Add the 3 egg yolks, one at a time. Stir after each addition.

Follow with the ham mixture. Season to taste.

Permit the concoction to cool for several minutes before folding in the egg whites.

Divide the sauce into 6 individual casseroles (or ramekins). Break an egg into each. (So you don't own six small casseroles? Use a single large one, spacing the eggs evenly.)

Bake at 350° for 15-20 minutes. The eggs should be set and the soufflé light and puffy.

P.S. *This may not be designed specifically for a brunch, but it's a natural. Add a salad and you have a supper.*

Ham Sandwiches in a Casserole (M-in-I)

TIME: To make: 30 minutes
To stand: 1-12 hours
To cook: 1 hour

SERVES: 4-6

COMPOSITION

¾ pound cooked ham
12 slices bread
butter
1 small onion
4 eggs
3 cups milk

½ teaspoon salt
pepper
¾ pound sharp cheese
mustard
Mushroom Sauce

Meat Jambalaya

PREPARATION

Grind the ham or chop it finely.
Trim the bread. Butter it liberally.
Grate the onion.
Beat together the eggs, the milk, the onion, and the salt. Add pepper to taste.
Place 6 slices of the bread in the bottom of a casserole. Add the sliced cheese. Slather them with mustard.
Add the ground ham. Top with more bread, buttered side up.
Pour in the milk mixture.
Refrigerate the casserole for 1 hour (or 4 hours or overnight).
Bake the casserole at 300° for 1 hour.
Make the Mushroom Sauce (p. 12).

PRESENTATION

Serve from the casserole with sauce on the side.

P.S. *This is ideal for a simple buffet supper on a cool autumn evening after a football game or the like. Make it a day or hour in advance, pop it in the oven, and reheat the sauce. Relax!*

Meat Jambalaya

TIME: Almost 2 hours   SERVES: 6

COMPOSITION

1 pound fresh pork	*thyme*
1 pound lean smoked ham	*1 teaspoon ground cloves*
1 dozen pork sausages	*1½ quarts beef stock*
2 medium onions	*1 cup raw rice*
3-4 parsley sprigs	*salt*
2 bay leaves	*pepper*
2 tablespoons butter	*½ teaspoon chili powder*
2 garlic cloves	*cayenne*

CASING THE CASSEROLE CIRCUIT

PREPARATION

Dice the meats. Cut up the sausages. Mince the onion. Chop the parsley. Crumble the bay leaves.

Brown the pork in melted butter for 10 minutes. Add the onions. Cook until they are golden. Add the ham, press in the garlic, and toss in the parsley, the bay leaves, a pinch of thyme, and the cloves.

Brown for another 10 minutes.

Add the sausage bits. Cook for another 10 minutes. Stir with a steady hand.

Skim off the grease, then place the entire mixture in a casserole. Add the beef stock and the rice. Stir.

Season with salt, pepper, chili powder, and cayenne.

Bake, covered, at 350° for 45 minutes to 1 hour, or until the rice is done.

Cool slightly, skim off excess grease, reheat, and serve.

Lasagna
(M-in-I)

TIME: Approximately 2½ hours   SERVES: 6

COMPOSITION

2 garlic cloves
1 fat onion
olive oil
1 can tomato paste plus 1 can water
1 1-pound can tomato purée
3-4 tablespoons sugar
½ teaspoon salt

1 large pinch basil
1 pound lasagna
½ pound ground beef
½ pound ground pork
½ pound pot cheese
½ pound Mozzarella cheese
½ cup grated Parmeson cheese

Baked Liver—Casserole Style

PREPARATION

Peel and chop the garlic and the onion. Brown them briefly in oil. Combine the tomato paste and water. Pour into the pan. Add the tomato purée, the sugar, the salt, the pepper, and the basil.

Permit the sauce to simmer for 2 hours over low heat. Stir from time to time.

Cook the lasagna until tender in a large pot of salted water. Drain thoroughly.

Brown the meats in oil. Add them to the sauce. Stir.

In a large casserole, well oiled, make layers of lasagna, sauce, pot cheese, Mozzarella, Parmesan, and more sauce.

Bake at 350° for about 20 minutes.

PRESENTATION

This plus a salad *or* a dessert meets all the requirements for a full meal, but don't forget the red wine.

Baked Liver—Casserole Style

TIME: 1¾ hours   SERVES: 4

COMPOSITION

1 small onion	*salt*
marjoram	*pepper*
1 2-pound slab of calf's liver	*1 cup bouillon*
4-6 bacon slices	*1 pint sour cream*

PREPARATION

Mince the onion. Mix it with a pinch of marjoram.

Wash the liver. Remove the tough strings. Dry it. Cut a horizontal pocket in it.

Lay 2 or 3 bacon slices in the pocket. Spread the onion mixture over the bacon. Season the exterior of the liver with salt and pepper.

Place the liver in a casserole. Lay the rest of the bacon over it. Add the stock. Cover the casserole. Bake for 1½ hours at 350°. Baste occasionally.

PRESENTATION

Remove the liver to a hot platter. Keep it warm. Blend the sour cream into the pot juices. Pour the resultant sauce over the meat.

Pastetseo

TIME: About 2 hours   SERVES: 4-6

COMPOSITION

½ pound macaroni
3 large onions
1 teaspoon cinnamon
salt
pepper
½ cup dry white wine
1½ pounds lean ground beef
¼ pound butter

1-2 tomatoes
½ teaspoon nutmeg
6 eggs
¼ pound grated Parmesan cheese
3 tablespoons olive oil
1 tablespoon cornstarch
2 cups milk

PREPARATION

Cook the macaroni in salted water until soft but firm. Drain.

Peel and slice the onions. Simmer them for ½ hour with the cinnamon, 1 teaspoon of salt, freshly ground pepper, and the wine plus ½ cup of water.

Add the ground beef and the butter. Cook and stir until both meat and onions are browned.

Peel the tomatoes. Add them to the mixture. Cook and stir until it becomes dry. Sprinkle with nutmeg and add more salt and pepper if necessary.

Beat 3 eggs. Add them, the macaroni and 90 per cent of the grated cheese. Churn everything together. Deposit it in a casserole, preferably shallow, and sprinkle with half of the oil.

Beat 3 more eggs.

Warm the rest of the oil. Stir in the cornstarch. Add the milk. Simmer and stir until it is thick. Add the eggs slowly. Cook and stir until the sauce is smooth.

Pour the sauce over the meat. Sprinkle with remaining grated cheese. Bake for ½ hour at 350°.

A Pork Chop Casserole

TIME: 2 hours   SERVES: 8

COMPOSITION

4-5 yams
4-5 tart apples
1 medium onion
4 bacon slices
8 pork chops, ½ inch thick
1 teaspoon salt

⅛ teaspoon pepper
1 tablespon Worcestershire sauce
Tabasco
1 cup water

PREPARATION

Boil, peel, and slice the yams. Core, peel, and slice the apples. Chop the onion.

Sauté the bacon. Remove it and brown the onion in the bacon fat. Remove the onion and sear the chops.

Place the meat in a casserole, sprinkle with salt and pepper, then build up layers of yam and apple.

CASING THE CASSEROLE CIRCUIT

Blend the Worcestershire sauce and a dash of Tabasco into the water. Pour this into the casserole.
Add the onions and top with the bacon.
Bake at 350° for 1½ hours.

Casserole Pot Roast in Beer

TIME: 2½ hours   SERVES: 4-6

COMPOSITION

4 bacon slices
1 4-pound pot roast
1 12-ounce can beer
12 boiling onions
2 carrots
1 cup beef stock
1 tablespoon wine vinegar

2 tablespoons sugar
1 garlic clove (or 2)
1 tablespoon salt
1 teaspoon thyme
6 whole cloves
6 crushed peppercorns
cayenne

PREPARATION

Sauté the bacon until it is crisp. Chop it.
Brown the pot roast in the bacon fat.
Deposit the roast and the bacon in a casserole, along with all other ingredients.
Cover the casserole. Shove it into a 350° oven and forget about it for 2 hours.
(The final sauce will be thin but delicious. If you prefer a thick meat sauce, thicken with a little flour mixed with cold water about 10 minutes before serving.)

P.S. *Mealy boiled potatoes are perfect with this.*

Casserole Stroganov

TIME: 1½ hours   SERVES: 4

COMPOSITION

2 pound beef tenderloin in 1-inch squares
salt
pepper
2-3 green onions (scallions)
butter
1 teaspoon powdered ginger
1½ cups beef stock
1 tablespoon tomato paste
1 pint sour cream

PREPARATION

Beat the meat until it is thin. Dust it with salt and pepper. Let it stand at room temperaure for a couple of hours.

Chop the onions.

Dry the meat. Brown it in butter. Add the chopped onions. Sprinkle with the ginger.

Cast it into a casserole. Add the stock. Bake, minus cover, for 1 hour at 350°. (There should be very little liquid remaining).

Blend the tomato paste into the sour cream. Stir the mixture into the casserole. Let it heat but not come to a boil.

CASING THE CASSEROLE CIRCUIT

Veal Birds en Casserole

TIME: 1 hour   SERVES: 6

COMPOSITION

6 bacon slices
2 tablespoons chopped parsley
¼ teaspoon tarragon
¼ teaspoon basil
½ teaspoon rosemary
2 garlic cloves
¼ teaspoon thyme
nutmeg
salt
pepper

6 slices of veal (preferably from the leg) about 5 by 3 inches
2 tablespoons olive oil
1 6-ounce can mushrooms
½ cup finely diced green pepper
¼ cup finely diced onion
7-8 peppercorns
1 cup dry white wine

PREPARATION

Broil the bacon until crisp. Dice.

Chop the parsley. Mash together the bacon, the parsley, the tarragon, the basil, the rosemary, and the crushed garlic.

Mix together the thyme, a man-sized pinch of nutmeg, and a liberal helping of salt and pepper.

Lay the veal slices on a sturdy work surface. Sprinkle them with the thyme mixture. Beat them until flat with a rolling pin, a cleaver, or the broad side of a knife.

Place a generous amount of the bacon mixture on each piece of beaten meat. Roll each into a tight cylinder, fastening with string or toothpicks.

Brown the "birds" in oil on all sides. Place them in a casserole. Slice the mushrooms, chop the green pepper and the onions, and crush the peppercorns.

Heat the wine in the pan used for browning the meat. Pour it over the birds. Toss in the vegetables and the pepper.

Bake in a 350° oven for 45 minutes or more without lifting the cover.

CHICKEN CASSEROLES

The Best Chicken Breasts in the World

TIME: Just over an hour   SERVES: You choose it

COMPOSITION

1 chicken breast per serving *garlic*
olive oil *curry powder*
butter *cayenne*
salt *Parmesan cheese*
pepper *bread crumbs*

PREPARATION

Brown the breast in oil and butter, using 1 tablespoon of oil and 1 tablespoon of butter per breast.
Cover the pan. Cook the breast slowly for 45 minutes.
Transfer the chicken to a casserole.
Over each breast sprinkle ½ teaspoon of salt, ¼ teaspoon of pepper, ½ pressed garlic clove, a generous pinch of curry and a dash of cayenne. Toss in at least 1 heaping tablespoon of grated cheese per breast. Top with bread crumbs and a light drizzle of oil.
Bake at 400° for 15 minutes.

P.S. *This recipe is divisible into two parts for those who get home from work a few minutes before guests are due. Prepared, precooked, and residing in the casserole with all the trimmings, it can be readied hours—even 24—in advance and popped into the oven for final baking—allow 20 minutes if the breasts are stone cold.*

Chicken with Oysters

TIME: 3½-4 hours   SERVES: 6-8

COMPOSITION

- 1 roasting (or stewing) chicken weighing about 5 pounds
- 1 garlic clove
- 1 celery stalk
- 3-4 parsley sprigs
- tarragon
- 1 bay leaf
- ¼ pound butter
- 1 cup raw rice
- ½ pound mushrooms
- ¼ cup flour
- 1½ pints heavy cream
- ¾ cup milk
- ¼ cup dry white wine
- salt
- pepper
- 1 teaspoon monosodium glutamate
- 1 package frozen peas
- 1 pint raw oysters
- 1 cup dry bread crumbs

PREPARATION

Stew the chicken (in well-salted water) with the garlic, the celery, the parsley, a pinch of tarragon, and the bay leaf. When the chicken is tender, skin and bone it, then chop the meat. Strain the broth; you need 4 cups.

Melt a generous tablespoon of butter. Add the rice and 2 cups of the broth. Cover and let the rice simmer over low heat until done.

Sauté the small whole mushrooms in a tablespoon of butter.

Melt 4 tablespoons of butter. Blend in the flour. Add 2 cups of the broth, stirring continuously until the sauce is smooth. Add the cream, the milk, and the wine.

Season to taste with salt and pepper and a teaspoon of monosodium glutamate.

Combine all ingredients in a large casserole. Top with the bread crumbs and a few lumps of butter.

Thirty minutes in a 350° oven just before dinner will thoroughly heat it.

Ham and Chicken Casserole

TIME: About 2 hours   SERVES: 2-4

COMPOSITION

1 stewing chicken
8 thin ham slices
1 large onion
1 pint mushrooms
½ cup grated Parmesan cheese

¼ pound butter
2 cups heavy cream
1 teaspoon salt
nutmeg
1 tablespoon paprika

PREPARATION

Stew the chicken as in the preceding recipe. Slice or chop the chicken meat.

Chop the onion.

Slice the mushrooms.

Grate the cheese.

Sauté the onion and the mushrooms in butter.

In a casserole, place layers of chicken meat, ham and the onion-mushroom mixture. Add cream to cover. Season with the salt and a pinch of nutmeg. Top with grated cheese and the paprika.

Bake for ½ hour at 350°. Brown the top under the broiler before serving.

Corn and Chicken Casserole

TIME: 2½ hours   SERVES: 4-6

COMPOSITION

1 stewing chicken (minimum weight, 5 pounds)	*1 cup raw rice*
	1 cup chicken broth
1 onion	*6 tablespoons butter*
1 carrot	*salt*
1 celery stalk	*pepper*
1 cup corn (fresh or whole-kernel canned variety)	*1 egg*

PREPARATION

Take a middle-aged hen and let it simmer for 1-1½ hours in plenty of salted water with the onion, the carrot, and the celery stalk. When the meat falls from the bones, toss them out.

Chop the meat. Strain the stock. Remove the fat.

Cook the corn on its cob (1-2 ears to obtain 1 cup of kernels). Scrape.

Cook the rice according to your favorite method or mine (p. 374). When done, stir in 2 tablespoons of butter.

Turn on the oven, set at 350°.

Combine the chicken meat and the corn.

Place a layer of drained rice in the casserole, using one-half of the total. Add the chicken mixture. Pour in a cup of chicken stock. Toss in the rest of the butter, in chunks.

Season to taste with salt and pepper.

Cover with a rice layer.

Beat the egg with a little water. Spread it over the rice.

Bake for 20-25 minutes until the top is well tanned.

Casserole Chicken Newburgh

TIME: 4 hours   SERVES: 8-10

Serve this with caution. You may be stampeded and never taste it yourself.

COMPOSITION

2 roasting chickens (total weight, 8-10 pounds)
1½ teaspoons salt
3-4 chicken bouillon cubes
2 garlic cloves
1 carrot
2 celery stalks
1½ pounds mushrooms
¼ pound butter
5 tablespoons flour
4 cups chicken broth
1 bay leaf
½ teaspoon pepper
cayenne
4 egg yolks
½ cup heavy cream
½ cup sherry

PREPARATION

Cut up the chickens. Cover them with about 7 cups of cold water. Bring to a boil. Throw in the salt, the bouillon cubes, the garlic, the carrot, and the celery.

Simmer gently for 3 hours, adding water to maintain the level. Remove the chicken meat and discard the skin and bones. Mince the meat. Strain the broth and skim off the fat.

While chickens are simmering, slice the mushrooms. Sauté them in half of the butter.

Place mushrooms and chicken meat in a large casserole.

Melt the rest of the butter, blend in the flour and let it brown briefly. Stir in 4 cups of chicken broth. Season with the pulverized bay leaf, pepper, and a pinch of cayenne.

Beat the egg yolks into the cream. Add this to the sauce, blending well. Add the sherry, stirring well.

Taste and adjust the seasonings.

Pour the sauce over the chicken, deposit the casserole in a 300° oven, and let it remain for at least 30 minutes.

Chicken en Cocotte

TIME: 1½ hours   SERVES: 4, possibly

COMPOSITION

8-10 *boiling onions*
3-4 *small carrots*
2-3 *parsley sprigs*
2 *bacon slices*
4 *tablespoons butter*
1 *4-pound chicken (or 2 2-pound chickens)*

¼ *cup dry white wine*
½ *cup chicken stock*
1 *teaspoon sugar*
salt
pepper
¼ *pound mushrooms*

PREPARATION

Peel the onions. Chop the carrots and the parsley.

Dice the bacon. Brown it in half of the butter. Remove and reserve the crisp bits.

In the same skillet brown the chicken on all sides for about 15 minutes. Place it in a casserole.

Cook and stir the onions, carrots, and parsley for 10 minutes in the remaining fat, adding more butter if necessary. Deposit them with the chicken.

Cleanse the skillet with the wine and pour the liquid over the chicken. Add the heated stock and the seasonings.

Bake for an hour at 350°, uncovered.

Clean, slice, then sauté the mushrooms in the rest of the butter. Add to the casserole about 15 minutes before serving.

Sprinkle the crisp bacon bits over the surface at the very last minute.

P.S. *This has that particular flavor of chicken which one finds usually only in France.*

Casserole Chicken for Four

TIME: About 2 hours   SERVES: 4, of course

COMPOSITION

2 2-pound broilers
3 pounds small boiling onions
½ pound butter
3½ cups chicken stock
1 cup rice

1 pint cream
salt
pepper
2 tablespoons chopped chives
1 jigger (plus) brandy

PREPARATION

Quarter the chickens.

Peel the onions.

Melt the butter in the top of a double boiler. Cook the onions in it, over boiling water, for almost an hour.

Simmer the chickens in the chicken stock for the same amount of time. When very tender, remove and skin them.

Remove much of the fat from the broth. Cook the rice in 3 cups of broth, over moderate heat, for 40-45 minutes. Keep the pot covered tightly.

Deposit the chickens in a casserole. Add the onions. Pour in the cream. Sprinkle with salt and pepper. Keep the casserole warm in a very slow oven until the rice is cooked to a turn.

Drain the rice, stir the chives into it and add it to the casserole. Sprinkle on the brandy just before serving.

FISH AND SHELLFISH CASSEROLES

Stuffed Flounder

TIME: An hour or so SERVES: 4-6

COMPOSITION

1 small onion
1 celery stalk
3 cups bread crumbs
2 tablespoons lemon juice
½ pound butter
salt
pepper
thyme
2 large skinned fillets of flounder (about 1 pound each)
3 bacon slices

PREPARATION

Mince onion and celery.

Prepare bread crumbs.

Squeeze lemons.

Sauté the onions and the celery until soft in 4 tablespoons of the butter. Combine them with the bread crumbs.

Melt 8 tablespoons of the butter and add it to the mixture. Season with 1 teaspoon salt, ⅛ teaspoon pepper, and 1 teaspoon thyme.

Rub the fish with ⅛ teaspoon pepper, 1 teaspoon salt, and the lemon juice. Compose layers of fish and stuffing in a casserole.

Top with the bacon. Melt the rest of the butter. Pour it over all.
Bake for 40 minutes in a 350° oven.

P.S. *Stuffing individual lemon sole or other small whitefish with the stuffing and cooking them the same way would work equally well.*

A Casserole of Sole or Halibut (or almost any other fish)

TIME: 1 hour plus 30 minutes   SERVES: 6

COMPOSITION

2 pounds fillet of sole (or any white fish)
½ cup lemon juice
½ cup water
2 tablespoons wine vinegar
½ teaspoon sugar
1 cup shrimp (canned or fresh, but cooked)
½ cup chopped mushrooms
4 tablespoons butter
¾ cup grated Parmesan cheese
½ cup chopped chives
¾ cup finely minced parsley
1 teaspoon pepper
Worcestershire sauce
1 can mushroom soup
½ cup sherry

PREPARATION

Wash and dry the fish fillets. Marinate them in lemon juice for an hour.
Mix the water, the vinegar, and the sugar in a saucepan. Simmer the shrimp for several minutes.
Sauté the mushrooms in butter.
Grate cheese.
Chop chives and parsley.
Place the fish in a wide shallow casserole. Sprinkle them with fresh pepper, Worcestershire, and most of the parsley.
Add the shrimp and then the mushrooms. Dust with the grated cheese, the chives, and the rest of the parsley.

Blend the soup with the sherry. Pour over the fish.
Cover the casserole and bake at 400° for 15-20 minutes.

P.S. *This tastes like an* haute cuisine *creation. Don't tell your guests how easy it is.*

Fish Pudding

TIME: 1½ hours   SERVES: 4-6

COMPOSITION

1 3-*pound whitefish (haddock, halibut, whitefish, or salmon)*
½ *cup raw rice*
1 *dozen large cooked shrimp*
pepper
curry powder
⅛ *pound butter*
3 *eggs*
2½ *cups milk*

PREPARATION

Poach the fish in salted water until tender. Drain, skin, and bone it. Flake the meat.

Cook the rice (p. 374).

Clean and cook the shrimp.

Butter a large casserole.

Melt ⅛ pound of butter.

Alternate layers of fish and rice in the casserole. Season each with salt, pepper, and curry. Sprinkle each with some of the melted butter.

Arrange the shrimp on top.

Beat the eggs into the milk. Pour over the fish.

Bake uncovered at 350° for an hour.

Fish Baked in Coconut Cream

TIME: Almost 2 hours SERVES: 4-6

COMPOSITION

½ pint heavy cream
½ pint coffee cream
1½ cups flaked or grated coconut
butter
1½ pounds mild fish or fish fillets (sole, halibut, or whitefish)
1 tablespoon salt

PREPARATION

Mix together the two creams. Soak the coconut in them for 30 minutes. Simmer mixture for 10 minutes. Cool. Strain, and squeeze the coconut to extract all the liquid. (The coconut has now been had; discard it.)

Butter a shallow casserole.

Rub the fish with salt. Place them in the casserole and add the coconut cream.

Bake at 350° for an hour.

Crab Casserole

TIME: 1½ hours (with canned crab meat) SERVES: 6

COMPOSITION

6 eggs
1 cup chopped walnuts
⅔ cup grated Parmesan cheese
2 cups crab meat
½ cup bread crumbs
½ pound mushrooms
6 tablespoons butter
1 cup milk
2 tablespoons flour
salt
pepper
¼ cup sherry

CASING THE CASSEROLE CIRCUIT

PREPARATION

Hard-cook, then slice the eggs.
Chop walnuts.
Grate cheese.
Obtain crabmeat from crabs or cans.
Make bread crumbs.
Butter a casserole.
Clean and sauté the mushrooms in 3 tablespoons of the butter.
Heat the milk to scalding. Add the rest of the butter. When it has melted, stir in the flour. Cook and stir for 4-5 minutes. Season with salt and pepper. Continue cooking and stirring until the sauce is thick. Add the cheese and the sherry.
Stack alternate layers of crab meat, sliced eggs, mushrooms, and walnuts in the casserole. Cover with the sauce. Top with bread crumbs and a final sprinkling of cheese.
Bake for 60 minutes in a 350° oven.

Crab Chevalier

TIME: 40 minutes, approximately   SERVES: 4

COMPOSITION

1 pound crab meat	2 tablespoons butter
½ lemon	1 egg
½ cup dry bread crumbs	12 capers
½ cup grated Parmesan cheese	salt
	pepper
2-3 parsley sprigs	good mayonnaise
1 small onion	

PREPARATION

Obtain the crab meat, either fresh or canned.
Squeeze the lemon. Crumble bread crumbs and grate cheese.

An Oyster Casserole

Chop the parsley. Grate the onion. Butter individual casseroles lavishly.

Beat the egg and stir in the crab meat, the lemon juice, the capers, the parsley, and the onion scrapings. Add salt and pepper to taste.

Bind the mixture with mayonnaise, using as little as possible.

Heap the mixture in the casserole, sprinkle with bread crumbs and cheese, topped with morsels of butter.

Place under the broiler (not too close) or in a very hot oven (450°) for 10 to 15 minutes.

An Oyster Casserole

TIME: 45 minutes   SERVES: 4

COMPOSITION

1 cup bread crumbs
1 cup sliced mushrooms
¼ pound butter

1 cup milk
½ cup heavy cream
2 pints shucked oysters

PREPARATION

Make crumbs.

Clean and slice mushrooms.

Butter your best casserole.

Melt a third of the butter in a skillet. Sauté the mushrooms for a couple of minutes.

Place a third of the crumbs in the casserole. Add half of the mushrooms.

Make alternate layers of crumbs, oysters, mushrooms, and crumbs.

Melt the rest of the butter. Mix with the milk and the cream.

Pour the mixture into the casserole.
Bake in a 350° oven for 30 minutes.

Baked Scallops

TIME: 1 hour   SERVES: 4-6

COMPOSITION

- 2 pounds scallops
- 2 cups dry white wine
- ½ pound mushrooms
- 1 medium onion
- 1 parsley sprig
- 6 tablespoons butter
- 1 teaspoon lemon juice
- 4 tablespoons flour
- 2 egg yolks
- ¼ cup cream

PREPARATION

Simmer the scallops in the wine for 10 minutes. Drain. Save the wine. Dice the scallops if you prefer smaller bites.

Chop the mushrooms, the onion, and the parsley.

Butter a shallow casserole.

Melt a third of the butter. Sauté the mushrooms, the parsley, and the onion. Add the lemon juice and 2 tablespoons of water. Cook for 10 minutes.

Heat the remaining butter. Stir in the flour. Cook and stir for 3 minutes. Add the wine. Let mixture thicken as you stir steadily.

Remove the pan from the fire and let the sauce cool.

Beat together the egg yolks and the cream. Stir the mixture gently into the sauce.

Add the scallops and the mushroom mixture.

Pour into the casserole.

Bake for 12-15 minutes in a very hot oven (450°) or under the broiler.

Quick Sea Food Casserole

TIME: 45 minutes   SERVES: 4

COMPOSITION

⅔ cup dry bread crumbs
⅔ cup grated sharp cheese
6 tablespoons butter
3 tablespoons flour
1½ cups milk
salt
pepper

1 teaspoon Worcestershire sauce
1 small can crab meat
1 small can shrimp
½ pint oysters (shucked)

PREPARATION

Make bread crumbs. Grate cheese.
Butter a casserole.
Melt the butter. Add the flour, the milk, and the seasonings. Mix, cook, and stir until thickened.
Add the sea food.
Pour into a casserole. Sprinkle with bread crumbs.
Bake for 15 minutes at 400°. Top with the cheese.
Continue baking for 5-10 minutes before serving.

Shrimp Mornay

TIME: 25-35 minutes   SERVES: 4

COMPOSITION

- 2 pounds fresh shrimp
- 1 pint water
- 1 pint vermouth or dry white wine
- 1 lemon slice
- few parsley sprigs
- 1 small onion
- 2 cloves
- 3-4 peppercorns
- 1 teaspoon salt
- 1 small bay leaf
- fish trimmings (if possible)
- ¾ cup grated Parmesan cheese
- ½ cup grated Gruyère cheese
- 2 cups cream
- 3 egg yolks
- salt
- pepper
- paprika
- cayenne

PREPARATION

Cook the shrimp by your method, or by mine, which follows:

Dump them into a deep pot. Add the water and the wine. (In case of severe drought, use water only.)

Add the lemon slice, the parsley, the onion, the cloves, the peppercorns, the salt, the bay leaf, and the fish trimmings.

Simmer the shrimp for 5-6 minutes only. Clean them now if necessary. Reserve the juice for another day.

In a double boiler, cook the cream and the cheeses until creamy, using only two-thirds of the Parmesan.

Beat the egg yolks slightly. Stir them into a small portion of the hot cheese. Add this slowly to the pot. Stir persistently. Season with salt, pepper, paprika, and cayenne.

Heap the shrimps in individual casseroles (or a single large one). Cover with the sauce. Top with a generous grating of Parmesan. Place under the broiler until lightly tanned.

P.S. *Shrimp marries well with cheese in a variety of casseroles. This is only one. Read on!*

Shrimp Casserole I

TIME: About an hour SERVES: 4-6

COMPOSITION

2 pounds shrimp
1 tablespoon butter
6 bay leaves
¼ cup grated sharp cheese
3 bacon slices
4 egg whites

salt
2 egg yolks
1 cup sour cream
pepper
Tabasco
¼ cup brandy

PREPARATION

Cook the shrimp. (I prefer the method given with Shrimp Mornay, p. 266. Use it, or your own.)
Butter a casserole liberally and thoroughly.
Pulverize the bay leaves.
Grate the cheese.
Sauté, drain, and crumble the bacon.
Beat the egg whites with ½ teaspoon of salt until very stiff.
Beat the yolks and stir in the sour cream.
Fold the whites into the yolks with a rubber dishscraper or wooden spoon. Ladle a third of the egg mixture into the casserole. Add about half of the shrimp.
Sprinkle with salt, pepper, and Tabasco.
Add half of the bay leaves, half of the brandy, half of the bacon and a third of the cheese.
Make another layer of egg, another of shrimp, and another of

CASING THE CASSEROLE CIRCUIT

seasonings. Top with the rest of the egg mixture and grated cheese.

Bake at 350° for 20-25 minutes.

Another Casserole of Shrimp

TIME: 30 minutes   SERVES: 4

COMPOSITION

½ dozen boiling onions
2 cups shrimp
¼ cup grated sharp cheese
2 bay leaves
2-3 whole cloves
1 garlic clove
1½ cups milk

2 tablespoons butter
2 tablespoons flour
⅛ teaspoon salt
⅛ teaspoon pepper
⅛ teaspoon celery salt
1 egg yolk

PREPARATION

Peel, then boil the onions in salted water until tender. Set the onions aside for the moment. Save the flavored water for soup, any soup.

Cook, drain, and clean the shrimp.

Grate cheese.

Butter a casserole.

Toss the bay leaves, the cloves, and garlic into the milk. Heat it. When it is scalding but not boiling, strain it.

Melt the butter. Stir in the flour until smooth. Season with the salt, the pepper, and the celery salt.

Add the hot seasoned milk slowly, stirring constantly until the sauce is thick. Cover and simmer for about 5 minutes.

Beat the egg yolk. Add it, slowly and gradually, to the sauce. Stir and cook for another 3 minutes.

Add the shrimp and the onions to the sauce. Pour into the casserole. Sprinkle with the cheese.

Place the casserole under the broiler (or in a 450° oven) until the top is tanned.—10-12 minutes should do it in either case.

Still Another Shrimp Casserole

TIME: 1½ hours   SERVES: 4-6

COMPOSITION

6 slices bread
butter
dry mustard
1½ pounds cooked shrimp
½ pound sharp cheese
salt

pepper
paprika
cayenne
5 eggs
2 cups milk

PREPARATION

Decrust bread. Butter it. Smear lightly with mustard. Cut into bite sizes.

Cook, clean, and chop shrimp.

Grate cheese.

Butter a casserole.

Create alternate layers of bread, shrimp, and cheese in the casserole. Season each layer with salt, pepper, paprika, and cayenne.

Beat the eggs. Combine them with the milk. Pour the blend into the casserole.

Bake in a shallow pan of water for 1¼ hours at 350°.

CHEESE AND EGG CASSEROLES

Egg and Cheese Casserole
(M-in-I)

TIME: 45 minutes   SERVES: 4-6

COMPOSITION

6 eggs
1 cup grated sharp cheese
2 tablespoons butter
2 tablespoons flour
1½ cups milk

salt
pepper
Worcestershire sauce
bread crumbs

PREPARATION

Hard-cook, cool, shell, and chop the eggs.
Grate cheese.
Butter a casserole.
Melt the butter and stir in the flour. Add the milk slowly. Blend until smooth. Season with salt, pepper, and Worcestershire. Cook until the sauce is thick.
Alternate layers of eggs, sauce, and cheese in the casserole.
Top with cheese and crown with crumbs.
Bake 30 minutes at 350°.

P.S. *No addenda is needed for breakfast. For lunch, serve a French Tomato Salad (p. 417) as a first course.*

Casserole Fondue
(M-in-I)

TIME: 1½ hours, including plenty of time off for drinks

SERVES: 6-8

COMPOSITION

10 slices white bread
butter
1 pound sharp cheese in 10 slices
¼ pound bacon
5 eggs

1 teaspoon prepared mustard
2 teaspoons salt
½ teaspoon pepper
1 teaspoon Worcestershire sauce
1 12-ounce can beer

PREPARATION

Decrust the bread. Butter each slice on both sides.

Lay alternate slices of bread and cheese in a casserole, topping with cheese.

Chop the raw bacon to a fare-thee-well.

Beat the eggs together with the mustard, the salt, the pepper, and the Worcestershire. Add the beer. Combine thoroughly.

Pour the egg-beer mixture into the casserole.

Throw in the chopped bacon.

Bake at 325° for about an hour.

P.S. *The component parts of this dish can be prepared hours in advance, combined in a matter of seconds and served on a variety of occasions. Served with a tartly dressed salad or a not-too-sweet fruit dessert, it makes a wonderful supper.*

CASING THE CASSEROLE CIRCUIT

Cheese and Wine Casserole (M-in-I)

TIME: 40 minutes   SERVES: 4-6

COMPOSITION

- 2 garlic cloves
- 6 tablespoons butter (preferably sweet)
- 6 slices dry bread
- 2 cups grated sharp cheese
- 3 eggs
- 1 cup dry white wine
- ½ cup rich chicken stock or bouillon made from cubes
- 1 teaspoon salt
- ½ teaspoon prepared mustard
- ½ teaspoon paprika
- cayenne
- 1 tablespoon Worcestershire sauce

PREPARATION

Press the garlic into the softened butter. Combine the two thoroughly.

Butter the bread liberally. Place it on the bottom and around the sides of a deep casserole.

Grate the cheese into a mixing bowl. Add all other ingredients. Stir well. Pour the mixture over the bread.

Bake at 325° for 30 minutes.

PRESENTATION

Try this with a Beet Salad (p. 410).

Cheese and No Wine Casserole (M-in-I)

TIME: 20 minutes to arrange
1-12 hours to saturate
45 minutes to bake

SERVES: 4

COMPOSITION

6 slices buttered bread (garlic butter or plain)
½ pound grated cheese, sharp variety

4 eggs
1 teaspoon dry mustard
1 teaspoon salt
2 cups milk

PREPARATION

Arrange the bread in a casserole.
Grate the cheese.
Beat the eggs. Add the seasonings, the milk, and the cheese.
Pour the liquid into the casserole. Let it stand for an hour or so, or overnight.
Bake for about 45 minutes in a 325° oven.

P.S. *For the timid host who likes to do his cooking in private, this recipe will be comforting. A preprepared dish of Chilled Stuffed Tomatoes (p. 416) will complete the picture.*

VEGETABLE CASSEROLES

Asparagus Casserole

TIME: About 45 minutes   SERVES: 4-6

COMPOSITION

6 eggs	4 tablespoons flour
3 pounds fresh or frozen asparagus	1 cup milk
	¾ cup chopped almonds
¾ cup asparagus juice	salt
¾ cup grated cheese	pepper
⅛ pound butter	

PREPARATION

Hard-cook, shell, and slice the eggs.

Cook the asparagus until tender yet crunchy. Chop coarsely. Drain, reserving ¾ cup of the juice.

Grate the cheese.

Melt the butter. Stir in the flour until smooth. Continue to stir and blend, adding the milk and the asparagus juice. Cook the sauce over low heat until it is thick.

Butter a casserole. In it, spread a thick layer of sauce, a thin layer of asparagus, and a layer of egg slices. Toss in a few of the nuts and sprinkle with cheese, salt, and pepper.

Repeat the layers until you run out of ingredients.

Deposit the casserole in a 350° oven. Let it remain there until the top is nicely browned, about 15-20 minutes.

MASTER MENU-MAKER

DIRECTIONS

Select a principal dish for your meal according to the amount of time at your disposal and the number of people you are serving. The time allotted represents the total cooking time, from start to finish, and obviously does not mean that every moment is spent tending that one dish.

Then choose other recipes which can be carried out in the same time or less and which will complement the main dish.

* *indicates additional time for marinating or freezing—before or after preparation*

SAUCES

Under 30 minutes	SERVES
Béchamel Sauce	1 cup
Mornay Sauce	2 cups
Hollandaise	1 cup
Hollandaise, Simplified	1 cup
Béarnaise Sauce	1 ½ cups

Sauces for Meat	
Cold Meat Sauce	1 ½ cups
Hot Meat Sauce	four to six
Mushroom Sauce for Ham	four to six
Mustard Sauce	1 ½ cups
Pine Nut Sauce	1 ½ cups
Sauce for Meat Loaf I	1 cup
Sauce for Meat Loaf II	¼ cup
Sauce for Meat Loaf III	4 cups

Sauces for Fish	
Anchovy Sauce	four
Almond Sauce	two to four

Sauces for Meat and Fish	
Shrimp Sauce	four to six
Sweet-Sour Sauce	1 cup

Vegetable Sauces	
Anchovy Sauce	¾ cup
Sauce for Baked Potatoes	2 cups
Mon Dieu Sauce for Rice	1 cup
Nut Butter	½ cup
Lemon Herb Butter	½ cup
Sour Cream Sauce, Hot	1 cup
Mayonnaise	½ pint
Aïoli	1 cup
Pseudo-*Aïoli*	1 cup
Vinaigrette	1 cup

SAUCES (*continued*)

Dessert Sauces

Fruit Sauce IV	four to six
Dessert Sauce, Donn's	six to eight
Hard Sauce	four to six

30 to 60 minutes

Brown Stock on the Double	1 ½ cups
Meat Glaze, Quick	1 cup
Sauce *Espagnole**	5–6 cups

Sauces for Meat

Almond Sauce	1 cup
Barbeque Sauce, A Good	2 ½ cups

Dessert Sauces

Fruit Sauce I	1 ½ cups
Fruit Sauce II	four to six
Fruit Sauce III	four to six

1 to 2 hours

Brown Stock*	2 quarts
Demi-Glace	2 cups
Glace de Viande	1 cup

APPETIZERS

Under 30 minutes   SERVES

Cheese Dabs	four
Cheese Puffballs	four
I'a Maka*	four to six
Mushrooms *à la Gage*	six to eight
Mushrooms for Cocktails (Cooked)	four to six
Mushrooms for Cocktails (Raw)	
Pâté Maison*	six to twelve
Shrimp, Cajun	two to four
Shrimp in Beer	four
Zucchini, Marinated*	six to eight

30 to 60 minutes

Cheese Rounds*	four to six
Chicken Liver *Pâté**	four to six
Fondue Bourguignonne	six
Shrimp Butter*	six to eight
Shrimp *Pâté**	four

1 to 2 hours

Eggplant Caviair *pour l'homme sans sous*	four to six
Liver *Pâté**	six to ten
Octopus in Wine	six

SOUPS

Under 30 minutes	SERVES
Beer Soup	four
Black Bean Soup	four
Buttermilk Soup, Cold*	six
Cheddar Soup	four to six
Coconut Soup	four
Corn Chowder, Canned	four
Crab Soup with Beer	four
Cucumber Soup*	six
Curry Soup, Iced*	four
Garlic Soup	six
Lobster Pea Bisque	six
Onion Soup for Two, Quick	two
Pumpkin Soup	four to five
Singhalese Soup, Simple*	four
Tomato Soup, Cold*	six

30 to 60 minutes	
Almond Chicken Soup	six
Corn Soup, Cream of	six
Onion Soup	four to six
Oysters Abstruse	two to four
Watercress Soup	six

1 to 2 hours	
Minestrone*	six
*Vichyssoise**	six to eight

2 to 3 hours	
Borscht	eight
Chicken Soup	six
Lentil Soup*	six

4 to 5 hours	
Pot au feu	six to eight

EGGS

Under 30 minutes	SERVES
Eggs Avocado	one to two
Eggs Diable	one
Eggs *Funghi*	one
Eggs in Ale	one to two
Eggs in Beer	one
Eggs in Cream	one
Eggs Mornay	one
Eggs *Obstaculos*	one
Eggs Orsini	two
Eggs, Quick Curried	one
Eggs Riviera	one
Eggs with Mushrooms	one
Ham and Eggs, Baked	one
Ham and Eggs *en Soufflé*	six
Ox-Eyes	one
Swiss Eggs	one to two
The Prairie Oyster	one

30 to 60 minutes	
Eggs *à la Russe**	one
Egg and Cheese Casserole	four to six

BREADS

	SERVES
Under 30 minutes	
Baking Powder Biscuits	14–16 biscuits
Biscuits, Cheese	14–16 biscuits
Biscuits, Herb	14–16 biscuits
Biscuits, Jam	14–16 biscuits
Butterscotch Rolls	14–16 rolls
Cinnamon Bread	four to six
Cinnamon Toast	four
Cornbread	four to six
French Toast, Coconut	four
French Toast, Delectable	six
Muffins	
Onion Cakes	14–16 cakes
Pancakes, Utopian	four to six
Pretzels	
Sausage Rolls	12 rolls
Shortcakes, Individual	six to ten
30 to 60 minutes	
Bread, Garlic	1–2 loaves
Bread, Sourdough*	1 loaf
Coffee Cake, Filled	four to six
Coffee Cake, Quick	four to six
Noodles, Homemade*	six
Popovers	four to six
1 to 2 hours	
Bread, Brown	1 loaf
Bread, Grapenut	2 loaves
Corn Pie, Mexican	six to eight
Pastel de Elote	six to eight
2 to 3 hours	
Frenchified Bread	1–2 loaves

BREADS (*continued*)

3 to 4 hours
Bread, White 2 loaves

7 to 8 hours
Croissant, Operation* 18 crescents

3 to 4 days
Sour-Dough Starter never ending

CHEESE

Under 30 minutes	SERVES
Cheese Dabs	four
Cheese Fondue I	four
Cheese Fondue II	four
Cheese Fondue III	four
Cheese Puffballs	four
Cheese Sandwiches, Toasted	three
Dessert Cheese I*	four to six
Dessert Sheese II*	four to six
Onion Cheese Soufflé*	two
Welsh Rabbit for Two	two

30 to 60 minutes	
Cheese and No Wine Casserole*	four
Cheese and Wine Casserole	four to six
Cheese Soufflé	four
*Croustade Jurasienne**	four to six
Macaroni and Cheese	four to six
Onion Cheese Soufflé*	two
Quiche Lorraine	four to six

1 to 2 hours	
Casserole Fondue	six to eight

DESSERTS

Under 30 minutes	SERVES
Applesauce, Alchemy for Canned	two to four
Apples, Stuffed	six
Avocodo, Sherbet	six to eight
Bananas, Candied	four
Bananas, *Flambé*	six
Bananas, à la West Indies	six
Cantaloupe *Escoffier**	six
Casaba *Rafraîchi*	six to eight
Cheese, Dessert I*	four to six
Cheese, Dessert II*	four to six
Cranberry Ambrosia*	six to eight
Crowns for Cakes	
Cream Cheese	
Chocolate Cheese	
Date Topping	
Lemon Butter	
Rum Butter	
Sour Cream	
Fabulous Frosting	
Dessert Sauce, Donn's	six to eight
Figs Eden	
Figs, Just	
Ice Cream, Inimitable*	four to eight
Chocolate	
Coffee	
Ginger	
Maple	
Mocha	
Peach	
Strawberry	
Vanilla	
Lime Pie*	six to eight
Pastry Mix, Donn's*	3–4 pies
Peaches, Packed *au Xérès*	six
Pears Poached in Sauterne	six
Pie Crust	1 pie
Pie Crust, Crumb	1 pie

DESSERTS (continued)

Pie Shell	1 pie
Pineapple *Kauai**	four to six
Prunes in Wine*	six to eight
Soufflé Flambé	two
Strawberry Shortcake, Wined*	four
Tortoni*	four to six
Waffles, Brandy Pecan	four to six

30 to 60 minutes

Applejack Crisp	four to six
Apples, Baked	six
Chocolate Bars, Brandied*	six to eight
Chocolate Soufflé	four to six
Crème Brûlée*	four to six
Lemon Pudding	four to six
My Fancy	six to eight
Pastry, Simple	1 two-crust pie
Peaches in Champagne*	six
Pears in Red Wine*	six
Pears, Stuffed	six
Pear Tarts	six
Prunes, Whipped*	four to six
Walnut Pudding	six to eight

1 to 2 hours

Almond Cheese	four to six
Almond Tarts*	six to twelve
Apple Crumb Tarts	six to eight
Apple Tart, Wined*	six to eight
Apple Thing	eight to ten
Apricot Soufflé	four to six
Babas au Rhum vite faits	six to eight
Black Walnut Cake	six to ten
Cheese Cake*	six to ten
Chocolate Cream Pie*	six to eight
Cranberries, Baked Brandied	six to eight
Cream Puffs	six to eight

DESSERTS (*continued*)

Cream Puff Pie*	eight to ten
Cointreau Soufflé	four
Date Delight	six to eight
Date Nut Cake	six to ten
Figs Adam*	
Figs Eve	
Genoise	six to eight
Hazelnut *Torte*	six to ten
Ice Cream Pie*	four to eight
Jelly Coffee*	four
Jelly, Wine*	four to six
Lemon Soufflé	four to six
Pecan Pie	six to eight
Pears in Red Wine and Applesauce	six
Meringue Pie Crust	2 pies
Rum Pie*	six to eight
Sponge Cake	six to eight
Upside-Down Cake, Preferably Pineapple	six to eight

2 to 3 hours

Orange Dessert Chiffon Cake	six to twelve
Pecan Cake	six to twelve

3 to 4 hours

Fig Pudding*	six to eight

FISH AND SHELLFISH

Under 30 minutes

	SERVES
Caviar Mousse*	six
Crab, Quick Luncheon	two to four
Fish, Barbecued Hawaii*	four
Fish Steaks, Curried	six
Fish Steaks with Olive Sauce, Broiled	six
I'a Maka*	four to six
Lobster Marsala	four
Shrimp, Another Casserole of	four
Shrimp, Balls of	four to six
Shrimp, Cajun	two to four
Shrimp in Beer	four
Shrimp Mornay	four
Shrimp Pâté*	four
Sole Véronique	six
Trout, Poached	four
Tuna Steaks, Broiled	four
Tuna Terrific	six

30 to 60 minutes

Crab Chevalier	four
Court Bouillon	
Eggplant aux palourdes	six to eight
Eggplant and Clam Casserole	six to eight
Eggplant and Shrimp	six
Fish Fillets Marguéry	four to six
Fish Steaks, Kazia's	four
Fish, Stuffed	six to eight
Oyster Casserole	four
Oysters Poulette	six
Salmon Soufflé	four to six
Scallops, Baked	four to six
Scallops, St. Jacques	four to six
Seafood Casserole, Quick	four
Shrimp Butter*	six to eight
Shrimp Casserole I	four to six
Shrimp with Wild Rice	six to eight
Tomatoes, Shrimp Stuffed	four

FISH AND SHELLFISH (*continued*)

1 to 2 hours

Cioppino	four
Crab Casserole	six
Fish Baked in Coconut Cream	four to six
Fish Pudding	four to six
Flounder, Stuffed	six
Octopus in Wine	six
Oysters Roffignac	four
Potatoes, Shrimp Stuffed	six
Salmon Aspic*	eight to ten
Salmon in Wine Sauce	six to eight
Shrimp Casserole, Still Another	four to six
Sole or Halibut, Casserole of	six

4 to 5 hours

Chicken with Oysters	six to eight

MEATS

Under 30 minutes

	SERVES
Beef in Cream	four
Beef *Vinaigrette**	four
Filet aux Champignons	four
Filet Flambé	four
Ham and Beans Steffy	four
Ham and Eggs *en Soufflé*	six
Ham *Nivernaise*	four
Ham with Bananas	six
Hamburgers, Stuffed	four
Lamb *Diable*	three to five
Lamb Hash	four to six
Liver and Onions	four
Liver, Chanfaïna of	four to six
Liver, Herbed	three to six
Liver in Sour Cream	three to four
*Pâté Maison**	six to twelve
Roast, Cold in Wine Sauce I	two to four
Roast, Cold in Wine Sauce II	four
Shashlik	
Steak, Chopped	two
Steak, Brandied Sirloin	two
Steak, Stuffed	four
Steak with Cheese	two
Veal Marsala	four
Veal Salad, Cold	four

30 to 60 minutes

Beef Filet in a Crust	two
Beef Hash	four to six
Beef Hash, Baked	six
Beef, *Salpicon* of	four to six
Corned Beef Hash	four
Cervelle Parisienne	four
Fondue Bourguignonne	six
Ground Beef Delight	six to ten
Ground Beef Pie	two to four

MEATS (continued)

Ham Casserole for Two, Quick	two
Ham Soufflé	four
Lamb Chops in Wine	three to six
Meat Loaf, Italian	four
Meat Loaf, Wined*	six to eight
Meat Loaf Sauces	
Sauce for Meat Loaf I	1 cup
Sauce for Meat Loaf II	¼ cup
Sauce for Meat Loaf III	4 cups
Sweetbreads, Braised	one
Veal Birds *en Casserole*	six
Veal, Cold with Tuna Sauce	six
Veal *Parmigiana*	six
Veal, *Salpicon* of	four to six
Veal, *St. Marcoux*	three to six

1 to 2 hours

Boeuf Stroganov	six
Boeuf Stroganov, Casserole	four
Boeuf Stroganov, Tamara's*	four to six
Brains, Empty	four
Flank Steak, I, II, III*	four
Ham and Chicken Casserole	two to four
Ham, Baked *en Casserole*	four to six
Ham Loaf	six to eight
Ham Sandwich in a Casserole*	four to six
Lamb and Eggplant Casserole	four
Lamb Shanks, Cora's	four
Liver, Baked Casserole Style	four
Meat Jambalaya	six
Meat Loaf, Jellied*	six to eight
Pain de Boeuf, Variation I	four to six
Pastetseo	four to six
Pork Chop Casserole	eight
Pork Chops, Marinated*	four
Pork Chops, Stuffed	six
Pork Chops Stuffings	
Mushroom Stuffing	six
Pork Stuffing	six

MEATS (*continued*)

Pork Chops, Wined	six
Pork Chops with Almonds	six
Short Ribs in Burgundy	six
Short Ribs, Marinated*	six
Spareribs in Wine	two
Steak, Swiss Style Garlic	four

2 to 3 hours

Boeuf à la Mode du Barry	four to six
Chateaubriand en Casserole	four
Ham, Fresh with Capers*	six
Meat Loaf, Plain	six to eight
See *Sauces* above	
Lamb, Anchovy Stuffed	four
Lamb, Roast Shoulder of*	four
Oiseaux sans Têtes	six
Pain de Boeuf (Cold)*	four to six
Pain de Boeuf (Hot)	four to six
Pot Roast in Beer*	six to eight
Pot Roast in Beer, Casserole	four to six
Spareribs, Glazed*	two
Veal, Roast	six
Veal Salad, Cold	four

3 to 4 hours

Ham Calvados	four to six
Lamb, Stuffed Leg of	eight
Osso Buco	four
Venison, Roast Haunch of*	ten to twelve
Vitello Tonnato	six

6½ hours

Beef, Smothered	six to eight

LEFT-OVERS

	SERVES
Under 30 minutes	
Beef in Cream	four
Beef *Vinaigrette**	four
Ham and Beans Steffy	four
Lamb Hash	four to six
Roast, Cold in Wine Sauce I	two to four
Roast, Cold in Wine Sauce II	four
Veal Salad, Cold*	four
30 to 60 minutes	
Beef Hash	four to six
Beef Hash, Baked	six
Corned Beef Hash	four
Chicken Hash Parmesan	four
Veal, Cold with Tuna Sauce	six
1 to 2 hours	
Fowl, Casserole of Left-over	four
2 to 3 hours	
Turkey Soufflé	six

STEWS AND RAGOUTS

	SERVES
Under 30 minutes	
Oyster Stew for Two	two
30 to 60 minutes	
Fish Stew	four to six
1 to 2 hours	
Rabbit Stew	six
Son-of-a-Bitch Stew	eight to ten
Veal Stew	four to six
Veal, Wine Stewed	four to six
Venison Stew	four
4 to 5 hours	
Boeuf Bourguignonne	six to eight
Lamb Ragout*	

POULTRY

30 to 60 minutes	SERVES
Chicken Breasts, The Best in the World	two
Chicken Breasts with Mushrooms	four
Chicken Hash Parmesan	four
Chicken Livers and Mushrooms	four
Chicken Liver *Pâté**	four to six
Chicken Liver *Risotto*	four
Chicken Marsala	two to four
Chicken Tarragon*	two
Stuffing For Turkey	18-20 lb. bird
Brandied Chestnut Turkey Stuffing	5 cups
Turkey Florentine	six

1 to 2 hours	
Almond Chicken	six
Casserole for Leftover Fowl	four
Chicken *Cacciatora*	six
Chicken and Corn Casserole	four to six
Chicken and Ham Casserole	two to four
Chicken, Casserole for Four	four
Chicken *Cocotte*	four
Chicken, Cold with Tuna*	four
Chicken, Oven Fried	two
Chicken with Lemon Sauce	four
Coq au vin*	four
Duck, Brandied*	four to six
Chestnut Turkey Stuffing	18-20 lb. bird
Turkey with Ham and Chestnuts	six

2 to 3 hours	
Arroz con Pollo	eight to ten
Chicken for Every Pot, The	six
Chicken, Charcoaled*	two to four
Duckling, Roast with Oranges	four to six
Poule au Pot, Henri IV	six

POULTRY (*continued*)

Rock Cornish Game Hen, San Francisco	six
Rock Cornish Game Hen, Vermouth	six
Turkey Soufflé	six

4 to 5 hours

Chicken Brazil*	eight to ten
Chicken Newburgh, Casserole	eight to ten
Chicken with Oysters	six to eight

CASSEROLES

Under 30 minutes	SERVES
Ham and Eggs *en Soufflé*	six
Shrimp, Another Casserole of	four
Shrimp Mornay	four
Vegetable Mishmash	six to eight
Zucchini Mousse	four

30 to 60 minutes	
Asparagus Casserole	four to six
Cheese and Wine Casserole	four to six
Cheese and No Wine Casserole*	four
Chicken Breasts, The Best in the World	two
Crab *Chevalier*	four
Egg and Cheese Casserole	four to six
Ground Beef Delight	six to eight to ten
Ham Casserole for Two, Quick	two
Ham Soufflé	four
Lamb Chops in Wine	three to six
Oyster Casserole	four
Onion Casserole	four to six
Pea Casserole	four to six
Peppers, Stuffed *à la Grecque*	six
Peppers, Stuffed Pierce Style	six
Rice Pilaff	six to eight
Seafood Casserole, Quick	four
Scallops, Baked	four to six
Shrimp Casserole I	four to six
Veal Birds *en Casserole*	six

1 to 2 hours	
Baked Beans, Authoritative	eight to ten
Casserole Fondue	six to eight
Chicken, Casserole for Four	four
Chicken *en Cocotte*	four
Corn and Chicken Casserole	four to six

CASEROLES (*continued*)

Crab Casserole	six
Eggplant Casserole, Rich	four
Fish Baked in Coconut Cream	four to six
Fish Pudding	four to six
Fowl, Casserole of Left-over	four
Ham and Chicken Casserole	two to four
Ham, Baked *en Casserole*	four to six
Ham Sandwiches in a Casserole*	four to six
Lamb and Eggplant Casserole	four
Liver, Baked Casserole Style	four
Meat Jambalaya	six
Pastetseo	four to six
Pork Chop Casserole	eight
Potatoes, Casserole	four to six
Shrimp, Still Another Casserole of	four to six
Sole or Halibut, Casserole of	six
Stroganov, Casserole	four
Wild Rice Casserole*	four to six

2 to 3 hours

Boeuf à la Mode du Barry	four to six
Chateaubriand *en Casserole*	four
Lasagna	six
Pot Roast in Beer, Casserole	four to six

3 to 4 hours

Chicken Newburgh, Casserole	eight to ten
Chicken with Oysters	six to eight

4 to 6 hours

Cassoulet, One Version of*	six to eight

A MEAL-IN-ITSELF

	SERVES
Under 30 minutes	
Croque Monsieur	four
30 to 60 minutes	
Chow Mein	six to eight
Croque Madame	four to six
Fondue Bourguignonne	six
Nasih Goreng	four to six
Onion Sludge	four
Ratatouille	four to six
Baked Spaghetti	four to six
Breakfast Sausage Pie	four
Wine Baked Veal	four
1 to 2 hours	
Cioppino	four
Curry	six to eight
Eggplant Caviar	four to six
Paella	ten to twelve
Sukiyaki for Six	six
Tomato Sauce for Spaghetti	four to six
2 to 3 hours	
Arroz con Pollo	eight to ten
3 to 4 hours	
Meat Sauce for Spaghetti	four to six
4 to 6 hours	
Choucroute a l'Alsacienne	six to eight

VEGETABLES

Under 30 minutes

	SERVES
Artichokes, Just Boiled	one to eight
Asparagus *Parmigiana*	four
Avocado, Baked	six
Green Beans *au Naturel*	six to eight
Lima Beans in Sour Cream	six
Beets Sauterne	six
Beets with Orange	six
Broccoli	four
Brussels Sprouts, Savory	six
Cabbage with Caraway	six
Cabbage, Sweet-Sour (Hot)	four to six
Carrots, Brandied	six
Carrots, Pierce Style	four to six
Cauliflower *à l'individu*	one, plus
Celery *Amandine*	four
Celery *Provençal*	six
Corn on the Cob	
Corn in the Husk	
Corn in Sour Cream	four
Corn Baked in Its Husk	one to eight
Eggplant *aux palourdes*	four
Hominy in Sour Cream	four
Leeks in Red Wine	four
Mushrooms *à la Gage*	six to eight
Mushrooms for Cocktails, Cooked*	four to six
Mushrooms, Just	two
Mushrooms in Brandy	four
Mushrooms for Cocktails (Raw)	
Onion Cheese Soufflé*	two
Peas *à la Bonne Femme*	four
Peas, Perfect Plain	four
Peas, Creamed	four
Green Peppers Sauté	four to six
Green Peppers with Corn	four
Snow Peas, Chinese	six
Potatoes, Parmesan	four to six
Spinach, Sesame	four

VEGETABLES (*continued*)

Spinach, Simply	four
Spinach, *Valenciennes*	four
Spinach with Savory Mushrooms	four
Tomates Fromagées	six
Tomatoes with Sour Cream	six
Turnips, Baked	four
Turnip *Purée*	four
Vegetable Mishmash	six to eight
Yams, Sherried	six
Sweet Potatoes, Sherried	six
Zucchini	six
Zucchini in Sour Cream	four
Zucchini, Marinated*	six to eight
Zucchini Mousse	four

---

30 to 60 minutes

Artichokes, Roast	six
Artichokes, Stuffed	four
Asparagus Casserole	four to six
Asparagus Pie	six to eight
Green Beans with Water Chestnuts	six
Beets, California	six
Cabbage, Red with Sour Cream	six
Corn with Mushrooms	four to six
Eggplant and Clam Casserole	six to eight
Eggplant and Shrimp	six
Leeks Mornay	four
Onion Sludge	four
Onion Casserole	four to six
Onion Soufflé	four to six
Parsnips, Baked	four to six
Pea Casserole	four to six
Peppers, Stuffed *à la Grecque*	six
Peppers, Stuffed, Pierce Style	six
Potatoes, Perfect Baked	one to ten
Potatoes, Perfect Mashed	two to eight
Potato Soufflé	four
Rice	two to twenty

VEGETABLES (continued)

Rice, Baked	six to eight
Rice, Orange	four to six
Rice Pilaff	six to eight
Snow Peas with Wild Rice	six
Spinach Soufflé	four to six
Tomato Eggplant Surprise	four to six
Tomatoes, Scalloped	six
Tomatoes, Shrimp Stuffed	four
Tomatoes, Stuffed*	six
Zucchini, Stuffed	six

1 to 2 hours

Baked Beans, Authoritative	eight to ten
Corn and Chicken Casserole	four to six
Corn and Eggplant Pudding	six to eight
Eggplant Casserole, Rich	four
Eggplant Caviar	four to six
Garbanzos with Herbs*	six to eight
Onions, Baked	six
Onions, Brandied Baked	six
Potatoes, Baked with Mushrooms	six
Potatoes, Casserole	four to six
Potatoes, Shrimp Stuffed	six
Potatoes, Stuffed	six
Squash, Summer, Stuffed	four
Wild Rice Casserole*	four to six
Wild Rice Soufflé	four to six
Yams and Brazil Nuts	six

4 to 5 hours

Cassoulet *	six to eight

SALADS

Under 30 minutes

	SERVES
Artichoke and Romaine Salad*	four
Artichokes, Cold*	
Beet Salad	four
Carrot Salad*	four to six
Cole Slaw, Savory*	four to six
Green Bean Salad*	six to eight
Kidney Bean Salad*	six
Leeks *Vinaigrette*	four
Potatoes, Cold	
Rice Salad*	four to six
Spinach, Salad	
Tomato *Babiche**	six
Tomato Salad, French*	six to eight
Turnip Salad*	four to six
Zucchini, Marinated	six to eight

Salad Dressings

Anchovy Caper Dressing*	1 ½ cups
Roquefort Dressing*	2 cups
Sour Cream Dressing	3 cups
Vinaigrette	1 cup

30 to 60 minutes

Bean Sprout Salad	six
Caesar Salad	six to eight
Salad *Nicoise*	four to six
Tomatoes, Chilled Stuffed*	six
Tomato Pepper Salad	six

2 to 3 hours

Potato Salad, Champagne*	six to eight

Authoritative Baked Beans

TIME: 2 hours   SERVES: 8-10

COMPOSITION

2 No. 2 cans red kidney beans
2 tablespoons bacon fat
1 garlic clove, pressed
2 whole cloves
thyme
rosemary
1 bay leaf
1 teaspoon salt
1 teaspoon dry mustard

¼ teaspoon cayenne
2 tablespoons cider vinegar
½ cup pickled peach juice
   (hoping you have some
   pickled peaches)
4 bacon slices
1 large onion
¼ cup very strong coffee
1 jigger brandy

PREPARATION

Combine all ingredients with the beans, except for the bacon, the coffee, the brandy, and the onion.

Bake at 275° for 1¼ hours.

Chop the bacon and slice the onion. Add them to the beans. Bake for 15 minutes.

Add the coffee and continue baking for 30 minutes.

Pour in the brandy 10 minutes before serving.

P.S. *This is a far cry from the Boston bean, but Bostonians will love it. So, too, will you.*

CASING THE CASSEROLE CIRCUIT

Eggplant and Clam Casserole

TIME: About an hour SERVES: 6-8

COMPOSITION

1 large eggplant
1 large onion
2 celery stalks
1 green pepper
2 7-ounce cans minced clams
1 cup bread crumbs
butter
clam juice (quantity unknown
—it depends upon your
casserole)

PREPARATION

Peel and chop the vegetables. Parboil them in salted water for about 8 minutes. Drain well.

Make bread crumbs and sauté them in a quantity of butter.

Butter a casserole. Place half of the vegetables in it and add a can of clams and half of the bread crumbs. Repeat the process.

Pour in enough clam juice to cover.

Cover the casserole and bake at 350° for 30-45 minutes.

P.S. *When you buy minced clams, buy a small bottle of clam juice. You'll need it.*

Eggplant Casserole

TIME: 1¼ hours (excluding SERVES: 4
time for amalgamation)

COMPOSITION

1 large eggplant
soda crackers
⅛ pound butter
½ cup cream
salt
pepper

PREPARATION

Peel and dice the eggplant. Simmer it in salted water until tender. Drain and mash the pieces.

Prepare 1 cup of crushed soda crackers.

Melt the butter.

Mix together all ingredients. Season with salt and pepper.

Let the mixture amalgamate (or just stand) as long as possible.

Place it in a casserole and bake at 350° for 1 hour.

P.S. *Make this in the morning. Serve it in the evening.*

An Onion Casserole

TIME: About 1 hour   SERVES: 4-6

COMPOSITION

2 pounds small boiling onions   *2 tablespoons butter*
½ cup chopped walnuts   *salt*
½ cup grated sharp cheese   *pepper*
1 can cream of mushroom soup

PREPARATION

Peel the onions. Boil until tender.

Chop the walnuts.

Grate the cheese.

Butter a casserole.

Mix together all ingredients, saving some of the cheese and all of the butter for topping.

Season with salt and pepper.

Bake in a 350° oven for ½ hour.

A Pea Casserole

TIME: About 40 minutes SERVES: 4-6

COMPOSITION

3 tablespoons oil
1 cup diced cooked pork
salt
pepper
½ teaspoon soy sauce
1 tablespoon sherry
1 teaspoon sugar
1 small onion

1 small celery stalk
½ cup sliced mushrooms
1 package frozen peas
1 cup beef or chicken stock
2½ teaspoons cornstarch
¼ teaspoon powdered ginger
1 teaspoon monosodium glutamate

PREPARATION

Heat 2 tablespoons of the oil. Add the pork, salt, pepper, the soy sauce, the sherry, and the sugar. Cook over high heat until the meat is golden. Place in a casserole.

Chop the onion and the celery. Sauté in the same pan for 2 minutes. Add to the casserole.

Sauté the mushrooms in a tablespoon of oil in the same pan. Dump them into the casserole.

Cook the peas in the stock for 4-5 minutes. Drain them (saving the juice) into the casserole.

Mix together the cornstarch and the ginger. Stir into the pea juice, adding the monosodium glutamate. Cook and stir until the sauce is smooth and shiny. Add it to the casserole and stir everything together well. Taste and re-season.

Place the casserole in a 350° oven for no less than 20 minutes.

Stuffed Peppers à la Grecque

TIME: 45 minutes   SERVES: 6

COMPOSITION

1 cup raw rice
4 medium tomatoes
1 small onion
1 garlic clove
6 large green (bell) peppers
1 cup left-over meat tidbits (optional)
½ cup currants
salt
pepper
olive oil
½ cup nuts (unsalted)

PREPARATION

Cook the rice according to your favorite recipe, or mine (p. 374).

Peel, drain, and quarter the tomatoes.

Chop the onion.

Parboil the peppers for 3-4 minutes.

Meat is not absolutely necessary. If you have it, chop it.

Combine the tomatoes, the onion, the currants, the meat, and the pressed garlic with half of the cooked rice. Add salt and pepper to taste and then enough oil to make a smooth paste-like (yet grainy) substance.

Stuff the peppers loosely.

Place them in a baking dish or casserole. Pour a little oil over each. Bake at 350° for 25-30 minutes.

About 5 minutes before serving time, sprinkle the top of each pepper with nutmeats.

PRESENTATION

Mix the left-over rice with left-over nuts and left-over stuffing. Heat well. Make a bed of rice on a serving platter. Imbed the peppers and serve.

CASING THE CASSEROLE CIRCUIT

Stuffed Peppers Pierce Style

TIME: Not quite an hour   SERVES: 6

COMPOSITION

- 6 large green peppers
- 1 small green pepper
- 1 garlic clove
- 1 medium onion
- ½ cup grated Parmesan cheese
- 2 cups bread crumbs
- ¼ cup chopped parsley
- 2 cups mixed nuts (excluding peanuts)
- ½ pound ground pork
- ½ pound ground (or chopped) ham
- ⅛ pound butter oregano
- ½ cup currants
- ½ pint sour cream
- 2 eggs
- salt
- pepper

PREPARATION

Deseed, parboil (in salted water for 5 minutes), and drain the 6 large peppers.

Chop the small pepper, the garlic, and the onion.

Grate cheese. Make bread crumbs. Mince parsley. Chop nuts. Grind or chop pork and ham, then mix together.

Sauté the onions, the garlic, and the chopped pepper in the butter. Add the oregano, the parsley, the meats, the currants, and the nuts. Cook and stir for 10 minutes.

Blend in the sour cream. Simmer the mixture without boiling for about 10 minutes. Remove the pan from the fire. Stir in the eggs and the bread crumbs. Season with salt and pepper.

Stuff the peppers. Top with grated cheese. Place in a casserole or baking dish. Bake at 350° for 25-30 minutes.

Casserole Potatoes

TIME: 1¼ hours SERVES: 4-6

COMPOSITION

4 cups potatoes in thin slices
½ cup choped onion
¼ cup chopped celery (including some leaves)
¼ cup chopped parsley
¼ cup melted butter

1 cup grated cheese
1½ teaspoons salt
plenty of freshly ground black pepper
paprika
1½ cups milk

PREPARATION

Chop, grate, slice, hack, grind, melt (and cuss, if necessary). Mix all ingredients together. Season, adding the salt cautiously but to taste.

Slip the mixture into a well-buttered casserole. Slide it into a 350° oven.

Forget it for an hour.

P.S. *This is an excellent companion to cold roast beef or lamb or to baked ham, hot or cold.*

Rice Pilaff

TIME: About 45 minutes, excluding chopping SERVES: 6-8

COMPOSITION

¾ cup chopped celery
¾ cup chopped parsley
¾ cup chopped onion (preferably green)
1 cup (preferably more) chopped nuts

4 cups rich meat or fish stock
½ pound butter
2 cups raw rice
1 cup currants

CASING THE CASSEROLE CIRCUIT

PREPARATION

Chop, chop, chop.

Let the stock be heating.

Melt the butter. Add the rice. Agitate it with a fork or spoon until all grains are well tanned, about 8 minutes.

Pour the hot stock into a casserole. Add everything on the list. Stir once or twice.

Cover the casserole tightly. Bake at 375° for about 30 minutes. Kindly restrain the temptation to lift the lid until ready to serve.

Vegetable Mishmash

TIME: 20-25 minutes   SERVES: 6-8

COMPOSITION

1 package frozen green beans (French style preferred)	½ pint mayonnaise
1 package frozen baby lima beans	½ cup grated Parmesan cheese
1 package frozen peas	butter
½ pint whipping cream	salt
	pepper

PREPARATION

Cook the vegetables separately until tender but crunchy.

Whip the cream.

Make mayonnaise (p. 21).

Grate cheese.

Combine the whipped cream, the mayonnaise, and the cheese.

In a well-buttered casserole, make separate vegetable layers. Sprinkle each with salt and pepper.

Pour the sauce over all and brown quickly in a hot oven (450°) for about 8 minutes.

Zucchini Mousse

TIME: 20-25 minutes   SERVES: 4

COMPOSITION

1 *medium onion*
4 *tablespoons butter*
2 *pounds zucchini*
½ *cup dry bread crumbs*

PREPARATION

Mince the onion. Brown it in half of the butter.

Cook the zucchini in salted water until tender. Drain, then mash them.

Combine the vegetables. Deposit them in a buttered casserole. Top with bread crumbs and butter lumps.

Bake at 300° for 15-20 minutes.

A MEAL-IN-ITSELF

EVEN the most accomplished cook with an inexhaustible repertory of recipes has his own favorites. I believe he should use them as often as he likes without apology. Among them will be several that best fill the bill when one or another of the occasions inevitable to all genial (or bewildered) hosts arise —times when cocktail guests linger too long, when the budget has hit a new low, or when spur-of-the-alcohol invitations are given without thought to the larder.

Under such circumstances, a few stand-bys on the shelf pay off nicely. So do a few stand-by recipes which can be expanded to feed a small multitude, even during periods of financial drouth.

I'm not claiming to be the most knowledgeable cook, but I do claim that the following recipes serve me well. They could fit into other chapters but have the quality of being so rich and

A MEAL-IN-ITSELF

satisfying that little or nothing else is needed in the way of solid food (except possibly bread and salad or dessert). Liquid nourishment is not excluded. In fact, it is urged.

Try these, if you will, first. You will find others throughout the book, marked M-in-I. Suggestions are made for rounding out each meal. Don't be afraid to mix and match to your own desires.

Sausage Pie

TIME: 40-60 minutes   SERVES: 4 or more

COMPOSITION

3 *apples*
1 *pound link sausages*
2-3 *tablespoons sugar*
6 *tablespoons butter*

1 *cup flour*
1 *teaspoon salt*
1 *egg*
milk

PREPARATION

Peel, core, and slice apples.

Grease a large pie tin.

Preheat the oven to 400°

Toss the sausages into a skillet. Jab each with a fork. Cover with water. Cook for 5 minutes. Drain off the water. Brown the meat.

Place the meat in the pie tin.

Spread apple slices over the meat.

Sprinkle the sugar over the apples.

Mix together the butter and the flour. Add the salt. Stir in the egg and enough milk to make a stiff dough. Spread the dough over the apples with your hands. Brush it with butter (or some of the egg).

Poke a hole in the center for steam to escape.

Bake for 25-30 minutes.

PRESENTATION

Serve as is, or with tomato sauce. Fruit juice and coffee complete the breakfast picture.

P.S. *Try serving for breakfast or brunch with fruit juice and coffee.*

PASTA

To have spaghetti, you must get good spaghetti. Some of the packaged, processed tubes available on your grocery shelf have little resemblance to the real thing. Go to the Italians. They understand spaghetti. Find a *pasta* that suits you. Find several. Build a stockpile in your cupboard. Or, better still, make your own pasta (see Homemade Noodles, p. 293). And while you are in the Italian neighborhood, get a supply of cheese—Romano and Parmesan. Avoid the sawdust sold in prefab sprinkle cartons. Grate your own cheese as you need it.

Get out the largest pot you own. Fill it with salted water. Bring it to a brisk boil. Select the *pasta* of the evening from your stockpile. Don't break it up. Souse one end of a bunch in the water. As it softens, push in the rest, coiling it around the inside of the pan. Let the water come to a boil again, then reduce to a simmer. In five to six minutes you should have *al dente* spaghetti. If it must be soft to satisfy, cook it longer.

Spaghetti cannot be served elegantly without being unfit to eat. Serve it from pot to plate. Grab a gob with a fork (or with two forks). Hold it high to drain. Drop it on the plate. Let each diner then help himself to the sauce of his choice. If there is only one sauce, his choice is limited, but he will undoubtedly love it.

One need not have a rich sauce. Butter and grated cheese is delicious. Butter, minced parsley, and grated cheese is better. Butter in which garlic, parsley, and basil have been quickly sautéed is best. If your tastes differ from mine, here are other sauces to please.

P.S. *Chopped anchovy fillets or minced clams added to the "best" are superlative.*

Meat Sauce for Spaghetti

TIME: 3 hours, more or less   SERVES: 4-6

COMPOSITION

1 medium onion
1 medium carrot
1 medium green pepper
1 celery stalk
2-3 garlic cloves
¼ cup olive oil
⅛ pound butter
1 pound ground chuck
½ pound ground pork
½ pound chopped veal
2 bay leaves

2-3 whole cloves
1 teaspoon thyme
1 large can tomatoes or 4-5 fresh tomatoes
salt
pepper
sugar
1 cup beef stock
1 cup red wine
1 can tomato paste

PREPARATION

Peel and chop the vegetables.

Heat the oil and the butter. Sauté the pressed garlic and the onion.

Brown the meats. Add the chopped carrot, the celery, the green pepper, the crushed bay leaves, the cloves, the thyme, and the tomatoes. (If fresh tomatoes are used, please peel them first.)

Season to taste with salt, pepper, and sugar.

Add the stock, the wine, and the tomato paste. Cover.

Simmer the sauce for 2-2½ hours. Stir it from time to time and taste it frequently. Adjust the flavors as you see fit.

Let it cook uncovered for the final ½ hour or so to reduce and thicken the sauce.

A MEAL-IN-ITSELF

Baked Spaghetti

TIME: 50-60 minutes   SERVES: 4-6

COMPOSITION

1 medium onion
2 garlic cloves
1 medium green pepper
grated Parmesan cheese
½ cup olive oil
1 can condensed tomato soup
1½ teaspoons salt
cayenne
paprika
Worcestershire sauce

1 12-ounce can of whole-kernel corn
3 ¼-ounce can of pitted ripe olives
3-ounce can of button mushrooms
1 pound ground beef
1½ pounds cooked spaghetti (al dente)

PREPARATION

Chop the onion, the garlic, and the green pepper.
Grate cheese (½ cup).
Sauté the onion and the garlic in oil until golden. Add the soup, the seasonings, and the green pepper. Stir in the cheese. Cook and stir until it melts.
Add the corn, the olives, and the mushrooms.
Break the ground beef into small lumps. Throw them into the pot. Cook for about 8 minutes.
Cook the spaghetti.
Turn the mixture into a large casserole.
Add the cooked spaghetti.
Sprinkle heavily with additional grated cheese.
Bake for 30 minutes at 350°.

Tomato Sauce for Spaghetti

TIME: About 1½ hours   SERVES: 4-6

COMPOSITION

1 small celery stalk
1 small onion
2 parsley sprigs
1 garlic clove
¼ cup olive oil
1 large can Italian style tomatoes or 4-5 large fresh tomatoes
1 medium size can (8 oz.) tomato purée
½ teaspoon salt
½ teaspoon pepper
1 tablespoon (or more) sugar
½ teaspoon basil
½ teaspoon oregano
1 bay leaf

PREPARATION

Chop the vegetables, the parsley, and the garlic.
Heat the oil. Brown the vegetables.
Add the tomatoes and the purée. Blend well.
Season. The amount of sugar depends on the acidity of the tomatoes.
Simmer for about 45 minutes.
Add the herbs. Taste and reseason.
Cook for another 15 minutes.

Homemade Noodles

TIME: 20 minutes to prepare
Up to 1 hour to dry
5-8 minutes to cook

YIELD: About 1 pound
SERVES: 6

COMPOSITION

3 cups sifted flour
3 eggs
1 teaspoon salt
2 tablespoons water

A MEAL-IN-ITSELF

PREPARATION

Sift the flour into a large bowl. Fashion a well in the center with fingertips.

Break the unbeaten eggs into the well. Add the salt and the water.

Mix with the hands until the dough can be gathered into a ball.

Dust a wood or marble work surface with flour.

Knead the dough by pressing with fingers and heels of your hands, pushing down and away. Fold the dough and press again. Repeat the process for a good 5 minutes.

Divide the resulting stiff dough into thirds.

Roll out each portion on a lightly floured surface until it is paper thin. Roll up each sheet like a jelly roll and cut into strips ½ inch wide.

Spread the noodles out on a floured surface, toss them lightly to separate, cover with a towel and let stand for 30-60 minutes.

Cook in a large kettle of boiling salted water for 5-8 minutes. Drain thoroughly.

P.S. *The new pasta machines are a great joy to noodle lovers. The dough is the same; it's the cutting that's different. Follow the directions that come with the machine. Dry the noodles thoroughly if they are not to be used immediately.*

Fondue Bourguignonne

TIME: Up to 1 hour, depending upon the variety of dips

SERVES: 4

COMPOSITION

THE MEAT:

1½ *pounds tender fillet of beef in ¾-inch cubes*
½ *pound butter*
⅔ *cup olive oil*

THE DIPS:

mayonnaise (plain or seasoned with garlic, mustard, curry powder, or tarragon)
chili sauce or catsup
Vinaigrette Sauce (p. 22)
Hollandaise Sauce (p. 19)
Béarnaise Sauce (p. 18)
Pine Nut Sauce (p. 12)
sour cream
horse-radish
capers
minced parsley and chives, mixed
ground almonds or peanuts
chopped hard-cooked egg

PREPARATION

Prepare a selection of sauces and dips. Place them in small dishes, one of each for each place setting.

Heat the butter in a fondue pan or in the blazer of a chafing dish. (Lacking these, an electric popcorn popper works beautifully.) Add the oil and bring the mixture to a boil.

A MEAL-IN-ITSELF

Adjust the heat to keep it bubbling throughout the meal. Supply each guest with a long-handled fondue fork. Let each spear his own cube of raw meat and cook it to his own taste, before dipping into the dips.

PRESENTATION

Crusty French bread and red wine are essential.

Veal Ragout

TIME: About an hour   SERVES: 4

COMPOSITION

1½ *pounds tender veal*	1½ *cups milk*
1 *small onion or 1-2 scallions*	½ *teaspoon salt*
1 *small green pepper*	*coarse pepper*
1 *garlic clove*	⅓ *cup dry white wine or dry vermouth*
¼ *pound butter*	
1 *tablespoon flour*	1 *3-ounce can chow mein noodles*

PREPARATION

Cut the veal into small cubes.
Peel and mince the onion. Mince the green pepper.
Melt the butter in a heavy pan. Add the onion and the garlic. Sauté them quickly.
Add the meat. Push it around the pan for a few minutes.
Cover. Let the meat steam for about 20 minutes.
Uncover the pan. Let the meat get well browned.
Blend in the flour. Add the milk by degrees. Stir.
Continue cooking and stirring until a smooth sauce forms.
Add the green pepper, the salt, and a generous grind of black pepper.

Cook for another 45 minutes.
Stir in the wine. Let it heat.
Serve the stew.

PRESENTATION

Distribute the noodles over all just before serving. White wine must be served with this dish.

Paella

TIME: 1½ hours   SERVES: 10-12

There are many ways of making *paella*. This one was taught me by my cook in Spain. I have made a few minor adjustments to make it simpler.

COMPOSITION

- 1 *large frying chicken*
- ½ *pound pork* or *beef*
- ½ *pound chorizo (Spanish sausage)*
- 2 *large onions*
- 3 *garlic cloves*
- 3-4 *tomatoes*
- 1½ *cups peas*
- 1 *pound small raw shrimp*
- 1½ *pounds lobster, cooked*
- 12 *clams (or mussels, or both)*
- 4 *cups (minimum) chicken stock*
- ½ *cup (plus) olive oil*
- 2 *cups raw rice*
- 1 *teaspoon Spanish saffron*
- 1 *7-ounce can pimientos*
- 6-8 *artichoke hearts*
- 1½ *teaspoons salt*
- ½ *teaspoon pepper*
- 1 *teaspoon capers*
- ½ *teaspoon coriander*
- 1 *teaspoon oregano*

PREPARATION

Cut up the chicken in small serving pieces, cube the pork, and slice the *chorizo*.

A MEAL-IN-ITSELF

Chop the onions and mince the garlic.
Peel, seed, and chop the tomatoes.
Shell the peas and the shrimp.
Cut up the lobster, shell and all.
Clean and steam the clams (or mussels).
Heat the chicken stock.
Heat the oil in a large skillet. Sauté the chicken, the pork, and the sausage, turning frequently until the chicken is golden. Remove the pieces to a *large*, well-oiled baking dish or casserole.
Add more oil to the skillet, if needed. Sauté the onion and the garlic until both are transparent.
Add the rice. Sauté, stirring constantly, until golden.
Add the saffron and the hot stock. Cook over a very low flame until all liquid is absorbed.
Deposit the rice in the casserole. Add the tomatoes, the peas, the pimientos, the artichoke hearts, and the sea food—including clam or mussel shells.
Season. Stir once or twice to distribute everything equally through the casserole.
Bake the *paella*, uncovered, in a 350° oven for 50-60 minutes.

PRESENTATION

Serve with a salad, nothing more.

Arroz con Pollo

TIME: 2½-3 hours SERVES: 8-10

COMPOSITION

2 fine chickens
1 onion
3-4 celery stalks, including leaves
several parsley sprigs
salt
¼ cup chopped onions
6 shallots
6 medium tomatoes
2 green peppers
2 tablespoons finely chopped parsley

½ pound chorizo (Spanish sausage)
¼ cup olive oil
1 garlic clove
¾ teaspoon saffron
2 bay leaves
4 whole cloves
1¼ cups raw rice
1 teaspoon monosodium glutamate
1 jigger sherry

PRELIMINARY PREPARATION

Skin the chickens. Remove the meat. Chop it. Dredge it in flour. Set aside.

Cleave an onion into chunks.

Place the onion chunks, the celery stalks, the parsley sprigs, a teaspoon of salt, and the chicken carcass (including skin) into a large pot. Add 3½ cups of water.

Simmer the pot for 2 hours, adding more water as necessary to end up with 3 cups of rich chicken broth.

Strain the broth, skim off the fat, and save it. (Broth, not fat.)

PREPARATION

Chop ¼ cup of onions, the shallots, the green peppers, and more parsley. Peel the tomatoes. Break up the sausage.

Sauté the shallots and onions in oil until transparent.

Add the chicken meat. Cook until it is well tanned. Add the tomatoes and the pressed garlic. Stir.

A MEAL-IN-ITSELF

Add the broth, the chopped parsley, the saffron, the crushed bay leaves, and the cloves.
Simmer for 25 minutes, covered.
Stir in the rice and the green pepper.
Simmer for another 25 minutes, still covered.
Add 1 teaspoon of salt, the monsodium glutamate, the sausage chunks, and the sherry.
Cover and simmer for 10 minutes.

PRESENTATION
Red wine and good bread are all that is necessary.

Cioppino

TIME: Slightly over 1 hour   SERVES: 4 very hungry people

COMPOSITION

THE SAUCE:

- 1 cup chopped onions
- 1 cup chopped green onions
- 2-3 garlic cloves
- ½ cup chopped green pepper
- ¾ cup minced parsley
- ½ cup olive oil
- 1 8-ounce can tomato sauce
- 1 No. 2½ can tomatoes
- 2 cups red wine or sherry
- 1 teaspoon salt
- ¼ teaspoon pepper
- ¼ teaspoon oregano or marjoram
- ¼ teaspoon basil
- 1 teaspoon monosodium glutamate

THE FILLER:

- 1½-¾ pound raw shrimps
- 1½-2 pound assorted fish (sea bass, rock cod, red snapper)
- 1½-2 pounds cooked, cracked crabs (Western or Maryland)
- 1 dozen clams in their shells

PREPARATION

Chop the vegetables.

Heat the oil. Sauté the green vegetables, the onion, and the pressed garlic.

Add the tomato sauce, the tomatoes, the wine, and the seasonings. Cook, in a large pot, for 10-15 minutes.

Shell and clean the shrimp.

Chop the fish. Clean and crack the crab. (Let your guests extract the meat when they are eating.)

Add the sea food (except clams) to the pot. Cook over a low flame until the fish is done. (No more than 25 minutes at the most.)

Add the clams. As soon as they open up, serve the stew.

PRESENTATION

Let each help himself from the community bowl. Sour-dough bread and red wine are essential.

Croque Monsieur

TIME: None at all, all things being relative   SERVES: 4

COMPOSITION

1 cup grated Swiss cheese
2 cups Béchamel Sauce
8 slices bread (thin)
4 slices cooked ham (thick)
¼ cup heavy cream
1-2 eggs
butter

PREPARATION

Grate cheese.

Prepare Béchamel Sauce (p. 8), adding ¼ cup of the grated cheese.

Slice bread and ham.

A MEAL-IN-ITSELF

Mix the remainder of the cheese to a paste with the cream.

Spread the paste on the bread. Add a ham slice. Make a sandwich.

Dip the sandwiches in beaten egg.

Sauté them in butter until golden.

PRESENTATION

Serve them topped with the sauce.

Croque Madame

TIME: Less than 45 minutes   SERVES: 4-6

COMPOSITION

¼-½ cup diced ham
¾ cup grated Swiss cheese
¼ pound mushrooms
1 loaf bread
2 tablespoons wine vinegar
1 teaspoon grated onion
¼ teaspoon pepper
2 egg yolks

¾ cup butter
1½ tablespoons flour
¾ cup milk
1 tablespoon dry white wine
3 tablespoons cream
salt
pepper

PREPARATION

Shred or chop the ham. Grate cheese.

Slice mushrooms and bread.

Make the sauce: heat the vinegar with the onion and the pepper. Boil down by half.

Beat the egg yolks. Stir in the onion-vinegar. Blend in 6 tablespoons of butter.

Melt 4 tablespoons of butter. Stir in the flour. Add the milk, the wine, and the cream. Combine with the other mixture.

Season with salt and pepper.
Simmer and stir until it is thick.
Sauté the bread on both sides in butter.
Sauté the mushrooms in butter. Mix together mushrooms, ham, and sauce. Spread it on the bread.
Make sandwiches. Place them on an oven-proof platter. Sprinkle with cheese.
Broil until the cheese melts.

P.S. Mesdames *are always more complicated than* Messieurs.

Curry

Face it: curry is a stew—an exotic and practical stew. It is not a thing that grows on trees. Curries can be made from any combination or selection of left-overs or started from scratch. The main essential is a good curry powder. Mixing and blending your own combination of spices into the perfect powder is more than a day's work. Unless you are a specialist or want to impress, buy it. Buy the best, in small quantities. It loses its potency with age.

Curry takes time: anywhere from 1 to 6 hours. The end results can be worth while. Preparation of the basic sauce is mess-making and time consuming. Start early—even the day before. Get the job behind you and permit the sauce to mellow. It does improve with age. No need to spend the day chained to the stove. Add the meat, fish, or whatever during the final heating.

Curry requires good rice: boiled rice, in large quantities. Learn how to make this by reading p. 374.

It also requires side dishes, called sambals. The more sambals, the merrier. Six seems to be the absolute minimum.

A MEAL-IN-ITSELF

The selection should include things that are sweet, crisp, hot, tart, soft, and bland. Both texture and taste are important. Serve them on the side, in small bowls (with demitasse spoons) from which each guest helps himself to the quantity he desires.

The following recipe may not be strictly authentic from an East Indian point of view, but it has all the marks. Try it and have fun. Assemble the ingredients. The list *is* longer than your arm. Surprisingly, it is not expensive. You are now about to turn out a perfect curry sauce.

TIME: 1-2 hours to 5-6 hours   SERVES: 6-8

COMPOSITION
THE BASICS

2 pounds chopped cooked lamb
or
2 pounds chopped cooked beef
or
2 pounds chopped cooked chicken
or
2 pounds chopped cooked shrimp

or
2 pounds raw scallops
or
2 pounds flaked crab meat
or
2 pounds lobster meat
or
1 dozen hard-cooked eggs

Curry

CURRY SAUCE

1 cup flaked coconut and ½ cup milk; or ½ cup frozen coconut milk
2 large onions
1-2 tart apples
1-2 tomatoes
½ cup olive oil (or ¼ pound butter or a half-and-half combination of the two)
2-3 garlic cloves
1 cup seedless raisins or currants
juice and grated rind of ½ lemon
1 cup rich stock (to match the main ingredient being curried)
½ cup brandy or dry white wine
2-3 tablespoons curry powder
salt
pepper
cayenne
1 teaspoon powered ginger
1 teaspoon powdered turmeric
cardamom
thyme
2 bay leaves, crushed
1 chili pepper, crushed or ½ teaspoon chili powder
ground cloves
2-3 teaspoons sugar
arrowroot or cornstarch

SAMBALS

chutney
chopped salted nuts
toasted coconut
toasted flaked coconut
chopped hard-cooked egg
crumbled crisp bacon
chopped parsley
chopped chives
chopped green onions
French fried onions
sliced bananas sprinkled with oil and vinegar
chopped green pepper
diced celery
raisins or currants soaked in brandy
toasted flaked codfish
chopped dried herring
minced green or ripe olives
watermelon pickles
orange marmalade
crumbled potato chips
chopped sweet pickles
shredded pineapple
finely chopped lime, lemon, or orange peel
sliced cucumbers
chopped candied ginger
toasted sesame seeds
hot cucumber relish
melon balls
shredded Bombay duck
pickled walnuts

A MEAL-IN-ITSELF

ADDITIONS WHICH ADD A LOT

3 medium bananas
2-3 carrots
cucumber, diced
chopped peel of 1 orange
chopped peel of 1 lime
chutney
candied citron

PRELIMINARY PREPARATION

Make coconut milk: soak a package of grated coconut in milk as long as possible. Squeeze out the coconut and discard it. Save the milk.

PREPARATION

Cut the onions into chunks. Peel and dice the apples. Peel and quarter the tomatoes.

Heat the oil. Sauté the peeled and minced garlic.

Add the fruit, the vegetables, the stock, the liquor, and the coconut milk. Cook and stir constantly for about 8 minutes. Add water to make a thin sauce.

Mix the dry spices into a paste with a little water. Go easy. You can always add more later on.

Blend the paste into the sauce.

Continue cooking at a simmer. Stir occasionally to prevent sticking. The final sludge should be nasty in appearance and it *should* be sludge. Cook it for at least 45 minutes to an hour. (If you are the lazy type, turn it into a casserole and let it repose in a slow oven.)

Meanwhile, prepare the sambals and rice (p. 374).

About 10-15 minutes before serving, add the cooked meat or sea food or fowl to the curry sauce.

PRESENTATION

Serve over rice. Accompany it with beer. Follow with a light salad and fresh fruit, and be replete.

P.S. *Once you've made this curry, all other home-made varieties will suffer abysmally in comparison.*

Ratatouille

TIME: 45 minutes   SERVES: 4-6

COMPOSITION

1 fat eggplant, unpeeled
3-4 firm tomatoes
2 large onions
1 green pepper
1 garlic clove
1 chili pepper or *pimiento*
½ pound mushrooms

¾ cup olive oil
½ teaspoon Spice Islands Beau Monde seasoning
salt
pepper
basil
1 cup grated Parmesan cheese

PREPARATION

Cut all the vegetable into a heap of bite-size cubes.

Heat the oil. Add the vegetables. Let them simmer for about 20 minutes.

Season.

Simmer for another 10 minutes. The final result should be neither juicy nor dry. If moistening is necessary, use stock.

Just before serving, stir in the grated cheese.

PRESENTATION

Serve hot or chilled with stacks of sour-dough bread.

A MEAL-IN-ITSELF

Nasih Goreng

TIME: 25 minutes for rice (during which chopping may be accomplished) 25 minutes for the final brew

SERVES: 4-6

Everyone who has lived in the Far East thinks he has the only authentic recipe (and spelling) for *Nasih Goreng*. Here is one—mine. Spell it as you will. Vary it as you like. You can never do it much harm. You can feed a few or a multitude—well.

COMPOSITION

2 cups (minimum) cooked chopped meat, fowl, sea food or *a combination of any or all*
2-3 garlic cloves
4 medium onions
½ pound fresh mushrooms
4-5 chili peppers without seeds or *chili powder to taste*
soy sauce
ground coriander
cumin
mace
1 tablespoon monosodium glutamate
1 7-ounce can salted peanuts
½ cup minced chives and parsley mixed
3 cups beer (about 2 12-ounce cans)
1½ cups raw rice
8 tablespoons butter or *bacon fat*
chutney

PREPARATION

Chop the principal element of the dish, whether it be pork, ham, beef, chicken, shrimp, or what-have-you.

Chop the vegetables.

Assemble the seasonings.

Heat the beer to a boil. Add the rice. Cover and simmer about 25 minutes. When cooked, keep it hot.

Melt the butter. Add the garlic and the onions. Sauté them

briefly. Add the cooked rice. Stir seriously until it is richly tanned.

Toss in the principal element. Let it cook for 2-3 minutes.

Season. Start modestly. If you like what happens, add more.

Add the peanuts and the mushrooms. Mix well. Remain at your post for about 10 minutes, stirring and sampling. Adjust the seasonings as you like. The final conglomeration should be very hot and fairly dry.

PRESENTATION

Transfer to a large warm serving dish. Toss chives and parsley over all and serve forth—with chutney and plenty of beer.

Choucroute à l'Alsacienne

TIME: 4½ hours   SERVES: 6-8

COMPOSITION

2 pounds sauerkraut
1 large onion
2 carrots
1 large sweet apple
8-10 bacon slices
2 garlic cloves
2 teaspoons coarse pepper
6 juniper berries (optional)
6 whole cloves
salt

6 pork loin cutlets
6 pig's feet or knuckles
1 cup consommé
dry white wine
1 garlic sausage
6 knockwurst
6 frankfurters (optional)
6 thin slices cooked ham (optional)
8-10 potatoes

PREPARATION

Wash, drain, and press the water from the sauerkraut.

Chop the onion and the carrots.

Pare, core, and slice the apple.

A MEAL-IN-ITSELF

Cover the bottom of a large casserole with half of the bacon. Add a layer of sauerkraut, using about a half. Cover with half of the fruit and vegetables. Using a garlic press, press 1 garlic clove over all. Sprinkle with half of the pepper. Toss in the juniper berries and the cloves. Salt lightly.

Add the loin chops.

Cover with a layer of the sauerkraut. Top with the remaining onion, carrot, and apple. Press another garlic clove over all.

Add the pig's feet. Cover with the remaining sauerkraut. Sprinkle with the rest of the pepper and salt again, lightly.

Top with the remaining bacon slices.

Pour in the consommé and enough dry white wine to cover.

Cover the casserole. Simmer gently (or bake at 325°) for 4 hours. Add more wine if the combination seems too dry.

Add the sausage for the last 25 minutes.

Add the knockwurst for the last 15 minutes.

If frankfurters or ham are used, add them for the last 5 minutes.

Meanwhile, boil the potatoes in their jackets for about ½ hour.

PRESENTATION

Place the sauerkraut in the center of a large platter. Surround it with the meats and the potatoes. Serve with beer, please.

P.S. *Be kind to yourself; prepare this the day or night before and reheat it well just before serving.*

Chow Mein

TIME: About an hour, including chopping
SERVES: 6-8

COMPOSITION

2 cups onions, cut in strips
3 cups celery, cut in strips
1 can bamboo shoots
1 pound pork, beef, shrimp, or chicken
1 1-pound can bean sprouts
1 tablespoon fresh ginger

¾ cup rich stock (meat, chicken, or fish)
1 teaspoon sugar
5 tablespoons soy sauce
1 pound rice or noodles
4 tablespoons oil
1 3-ounce can chow mein noodles

PREPARATION

Cut the onions, the celery, the bamboo shoots, and the raw meat into matchstick strips. Keep them separated.

Drain the bean sprouts.

Dice the ginger.

Put the stock to heat over a low fire. Add the sugar, the ginger, and the soy sauce.

Start cooking the rice or the noodles (see pp. 374 and 293).

Sauté the meat in a tablespoon of oil.

In another pan, sauté the onions in a tablespoon of oil. Add them to the meat.

Sauté the celery in a tablespoon of oil. Add to the meat-onion mixture.

Sauté the bean sprouts in the rest of the oil. Add to the meat-onion-celery mixture.

Add the hot stock. Stir gently.

Thicken the sauce with cornstarch if desired.

PRESENTATION

Preferably in bowls, over rice or noodles. Sprinkle each generously with the chow mein noodles.

VARIOUS VEGETABLE VIGNETTES

IN THIS ERA of instant everything, some poor ignorants are convinced that processed, frozen, dehydrated, and revitaminized vegetables are better than the fresh variety. In this illusion they are not thinking of taste, texture, or appearance; they are only concerned with speed and convenience, and with this we cannot argue. There are times when a frozen vegetable is the frenzied cook's best friend. At best they cannot compete with fresh young things that the best shops (and gardens) afford.

Once the fresh vegetable is found, there are fabulous things to do with it. If you don't believe me, peruse the following pages. One word of caution: you may turn vegetarian even if you've been avoiding vegetables for years.

* * *

VARIOUS VEGETABLE VIGNETTES

P.S. *Read this chapter with particular care because Donn Pierce's vegetable vernacular is very special and includes points that make you understand what "a great great love his vegetable love can be."*

P.P.S. *When you finish reading this chapter, take a glance at the vegetables in the casserole chapter.*

ARTICHOKES

Certain parts of the country are fortunate enough to have real live artichokes. The rest of the United States is out of luck because artichokes to be at their best are always firm well packed, and with bright green leaves, and they invariably lose their vigor traveling. The poor sick shrouded variety found in many supermarkets are a far cry from the fresh thing. (Given no choice, however, I personally would choose withered artichokes rather than none at all.)

In any event, choose the best available: large ones for stuffing and roasting; small ones (edible throughout) for just boiling. Trim off a few of the very coarse outer leaves. If they are very large (and the spines especially sharp) cut the leaf-tips back slightly. (Kitchen shears are the perfect tool.) Cut the stem back to the base. Don't discard the stems. Peeled, then cooked until tender, they are wonderful for salads.

Don't serve cooked bugs: soak the 'chokes in salt water to force them out, either before or after trimming. Cooking time for an artichoke depends entirely upon the artichoke. Stand it upright in a deep pot of salted, boiling water. Boil. Test for tenderness from time to time by pulling at a leaf. If it slips off with a minimum of resistance, the 'choke is done. Its color should remain green, not battleship gray.

If you are not already an artichoke fan, try one of the following.

VARIOUS VEGETABLE VIGNETTES

Artichokes, Just Boiled

TIME: 15-20 minutes, depending upon artichoke size SERVES: 1-8

COMPOSITION

artichokes (1 large or 2 small per serving)
salt
lemon juice
water
a dunking sauce

PREPARATION

Bathe the artichokes in salt water to bring out lurking insects.
Bring a large pot of salted and lemon-juiced water to a boil.
Drop the artichokes into the pot, right side up.
Cook until they are done. Test with a fork or by pulling at a leaf. Some (but not total) resistance should be met in either case.
At the same time prepare the dunking sauce. Melted butter, Lemon Butter (p. 14), Mayonnaise (p. 21), Hollandaise (p. 19) and *Aïoli* (p. 20) are typical. Allow at least ¼ cup per serving.

PRESENTATION

Serve on individual plates as separate course. Provide a large bowl for discarded leaves.

Roast Artichokes

TIME: less than 1 hour SERVES: 6

COMPOSITION

6 artichokes, medium to large
¾ cup chopped parsley
2 garlic cloves
salt
pepper
about ½ cup oil
water

Stuffed Artichokes

PREPARATION

Remove a layer of tough outer leaves from each artichoke. (If the spines annoy you, cut about ½ inch from the top of each remaining leaf.) Bang each artichoke a blow on the counter to spread the foliage. Soak them in salted and lemon-juiced water to dislodge the animals.

Chop parsley and garlic. Mix them together with a liberal seasoning of salt and pepper.

Stuff the mixture between the artichoke leaves. Press the leaves back together as closely as possible.

Place the artichokes upright in a pan. They should be snug, but not squeezed. Pour the oil over them and into the pan. Cook over a hot flame for about 10 minutes. Watch closely to avoid burning.

Add ½ cup of water. Lower the heat. Cook (*without* lid) for another 8-10 minutes or until all water evaporates.

Add another ½ cup of water. Cover the pan. Continue cooking for 15-20 minutes.

PRESENTATION

On individual plates, as is or with one of the dunks mentioned in the previous recipe.

Stuffed Artichokes

TIME: 30-40 minutes   SERVES: 4

COMPOSITION

1 2-ounce can anchovies   4 fat artichokes
1 garlic clove   olive oil
1 cup bread crumbs

PREPARATION

Chop and combine anchovies, garlic, and bread crumbs. Clean, bang, soak, and boil the artichokes. (See preceding

recipes.) Drain them when they barely pass the leaf test.
Trim off the spines and open out the leaves. Stuff them, reshape them, and place, tight and upright, in a baking dish.

Dribble liberally with oil.

Bake, covered, for about 15 minutes at 325°.

Cold Artichokes
—A Reminder

Don't overlook them. Soak the artichokes (after cooking) in Vinaigrette Sauce (p. 22). Or serve them with mayonnaise or Aïoli (p. 20). They are just as good one way as the other.

If you can obtain only the canned or frozen variety, my advice is to serve them in a salad. See p. 409.

ASPARAGUS

No matter what your source of supply, choose fresh, young, tender asparagus of uniform size.

Bathe the stalks. Remove the tough section. (Given half a chance it will separate, when you bend the stalk, of its own accord at the point between delicacy and pith.) Snap it; don't operate with a knife.

For cooking, choose a deep narrow pot in which the stalks can stand upright. Use very little water; more than ½ to ¾ cup per bunch is too much. Bring the water to a boil; salt it lightly. Add the asparagus, closely packed. Cover the pot. 10-12 minutes should be sufficient cooking time for asparagus of an edible age. Test with a fork for doneness, drain, and serve.

Asparagus is finger food. Serve it with grated cheese and fresh pepper, or dunks of melted butter, or sour cream or Hollandaise. (If you do belong to the knife and fork school, serve the dunks as sauces.) In any event, enjoy it.

Asparagus Parmigiana

TIME: 15-20 minutes   SERVES: 4

COMPOSITION

asparagus for 4 (which means about 3 pounds, if you all love it)
⅛ pound (or more) butter
salt
pepper
1 cup (plus) grated Parmesan cheese

PREPARATION

Cook the asparagus, properly bathed and trimmed, until almost tender.

Drain it immediately.

Lay the spears in a buttered oven-proof platter.

Cover with melted butter. Sprinkle with salt and pepper. Top with a heaping cup of grated Parmesan cheese.

PRESENTATION

Place the platter in a very hot (450°) oven until the cheese becomes swarthy and partially melted.

VARIOUS VEGETABLE VIGNETTES

Asparagus Pie

TIME: 45-60 minutes   SERVES: 6-8

COMPOSITION

1 prebaked 9-inch pie shell	4 tablespoons flour
2 pounds fresh asparagus (or 1 large can)	2 cups milk
⅛ pound butter	salt
	pepper

PREPARATION

Clear the counter, get out your own pastry mix (pp. 516–518), and prepare a pie shell. Line a 9-inch pie tin with the pastry. Fill it with beans, rice, or anything heavy to weight it down. Bake in a 425° oven until delicately tanned.

Melt the butter, stir in the flour, and gradually add the milk, stirring until thickened.

Cook the asparagus in the usual way. Dry it well. Lay it in the shell if you feel fancy, or just toss it in.

Pour sauce over it.

Return to the hot oven for 10 minutes.

P.S. *This is one asparagus recipe that can be mostly prepared in advance. The shell, asparagus, and sauce can be cooked before and combined just before the last 10 minutes of oven treatment.*

Baked Avocado

TIME: 25 minutes   SERVES: 6

COMPOSITION

3 large *avocados*
lemon juice
1-2 *tomatoes*
1 *small onion*
¾ *cup grated sharp cheese*
1 *small garlic clove*

2 *tablespoons butter*
2 *tablespoons flour*
1 *teaspoon best chili powder*
salt
1 *cup whole-kernel corn* *(drained)*

PREPARATION

Set the oven at 200°. Turn it on.

Cut in half and deseed the avocados. Sprinkle them with lemon juice. Place in a shallow buttered baking dish. Bake for 5-8 minutes. Keep warm.

Peel the tomatoes. Chop the onion. Grate cheese.

Sauté the pressed garlic clove and the onion in the butter. Blend in the flour, the chili powder and salt to taste. Add the corn and the tomatoes. Continue cooking for about 10 minutes. Add the cheese.

Stuff the avocado halves when the cheese has melted and spread throughout the mixture.

Serve immediately.

VARIOUS VEGETABLE VIGNETTES

GREEN BEANS

Beans blossom with tender care. They seldom receive it. The usual store-bought limp and lifeless strings bear little similarity to the succulent vegetable. Look for crisp young beans. Snap a sample. If it refuses to snap, discard it (as well as the idea of serving fresh beans). Continue your search in the frozen-food department.

Fresh beans need little preparation. Wash them. Remove any stems. "French" slice them if you prefer or if they are ungainly.

In cooking, please use restraint. Do it quickly. The very best beans always retain some of their original crispness.

Green Beans au Naturel

TIME: 10 minutes   SERVES: 6-8

COMPOSITION

2 pounds green beans or 2 boxes frozen beans
butter (4 to 6 tablespoons)
½ teaspoon sugar
1 teaspoon monsodium glutamate
2-3 chopped green onions (scallions)

PREPARATION

Place the ingredients in a shallow pan or skillet.
If the beans are fresh, add ½ cup of water. If frozen, skip the water completely and increase the quantity of butter.
Cover the pan tightly and simmer for 7-8 minutes, no more.

Green Beans with Water Chestnuts and Bean Sprouts

PRESENTATION

As is. There is no better way, in my book.

For variations, cook with garlic or tarragon or rosemary. Or serve with freshly ground pepper, butter, nutmeg, or capers.

Green Beans with Water Chestnuts and Bean Sprouts

TIME: 40-50 minutes   SERVES: 6

COMPOSITION

1½ pounds green beans or
2 boxes frozen beans
1 cup sliced water chestnuts
1 cup bean sprouts
1 medium onion
1 pint cream
2 tablespoons butter

PREPARATION

Slice the beans into French-style strips. (Slap a frozen box against the counter before opening to separate the beans.)

Slice the water chesnuts.

Drain a can of bean sprouts.

Chop the onion.

Butter a deep baking dish. In it place a layer of water chestnuts, a layer of bean sprouts, a layer of green beans and a layer of onion. Add the cream and several lumps of butter.

Bake at 400° for no more than 30 minutes.

VARIOUS VEGETABLE VIGNETTES

LIMA BEANS

Buy lima beans in the pod: they are far better. With very little moral encouragement, shelling them is really no problem.

Feel the pods. Tiny beans make tiny lumps. If the lumps are large, resort to the frozen variety. (If you really prefer, buy frozen limas at the outset: they go through the freezing process with flying colors.)

Cook the beans in just enough water to cover, using about ¼ teaspoon of salt per cup of water. The best test for edibility is to sample. If a large bean be tender but not mushy, serve his fellows as soon as possible.

For baby limas, a simple dressing of melted butter and freshly ground black pepper is great. For variety, use the Béchamel Sauce on page 8. Or use sour cream, as in the following recipe.

Lima Beans in Sour Cream

TIME: 25 minutes   SERVES: 6

COMPOSITION

2 pounds shelled lima beans (4 cups)
1½ cups sliced mushrooms
3 tablespoons butter
½ pint sour cream

½ teaspoon salt
¼ teaspoon pepper
¾ teaspoon basil
paprika

PREPARATION

Cook the beans in salt water for about 6 minutes.
Butter an oven-proof vegetable dish.
Clean and slice mushrooms. Sauté them in butter just until tender.
Add the sour cream and the seasonings.
Place the drained beans in the vegetable dish. Add the mushroom sauce. Sprinkle generously with paprika. Bake at 300° for 15-20 minutes.

BEETS

Beets are best when small, smooth, and solid. Give a wide berth to the wizened oldsters. They will invariably taste like wood pulp.

Beets bleed. Don't be too vigorous when cleaning them. Cook them unskinned, with roots and an inch or so of leaf-stem intact. Drop the nuggets into boiling salted water. (A dash of lemon juice or vinegar will help preserve their color.) Cook them covered until they are just tender. Test with a fork after 15-20 minutes: it should pierce them easily, yet meet some resistance. The actual cooking time will depend on the size and age of the beets. When they are cooked to your idea of firmness (or pulpiness), remove the stems and slip off the skins. Slice, dice, or sliver as desired and serve as you see fit.

VARIOUS VEGETABLE VIGNETTES

California Beets

TIME: 30-40 minutes   SERVES: 6

COMPOSITION

10 medium beets
4-5 green onions (scallions)
⅛ pound butter
1 teaspoon sugar
1 teaspoon salt
1 small head of lettuce (iceberg variety)

PREPARATION

Scrub the beets gently. Slice them very thin without peeling.
Chop the onions.
Melt the butter. Add the beets and onions. Stir well. Sprinkle with sugar and salt.
Break apart the head of lettuce (or use several large leaves). Hold them under the faucet, then add them, dripping, to the pan.
Cover very tightly.
Simmer over low heat for 25-30 minutes.

Beets Sauterne

TIME: 25 minutes   SERVES: 6

COMPOSITION

½ cup sugar
4 tablespoons lemon juice
½ teaspoon cornstarch
2 tablespoons butter
⅓ cup sauterne
3 cups cooked beets

PREPARATION

Combine everything (except beets) in a saucepan.
Cook for 5 minutes.

Add the beets.

Cover and continue cooking at reduced heat for about 15 minutes.

Beets with Orange

TIME: About 20 minutes   SERVES: 6

COMPOSITION

2 *oranges*
3 *cups tiny beets (fresh or canned)*
1½ *tablespoons butter*
2 *tablespoons flour*
1 *tablespoon honey*
2 *tablespoons brown sugar*
1-2 *tablespoons lemon juice*

PREPARATION

Squeeze the oranges to give 1 cup of juice. Chop the orange peel very fine.

Boil the choppings in salted water for a minute or two. Drain.

Cook the beets (or open the can).

Melt the butter. Blend in the flour, the honey, the brown sugar, and the juices. Cook and stir until the sauce is thick.

Add the orange peel and the beets. Mix carefully to coat each beet with sauce.

Heat thoroughly.

Serve hot or cold.

P.S. *These are almost too good-looking to eat, but one can overcome that easily.*

VARIOUS VEGETABLE VIGNETTES

BROCCOLI

In full bloom, broccoli makes a delightful flower arrangement. For normal dinner table use, the heads should be firm, with tight, bright-green buds. When yellow flower color begins to show, it is past its prime.

Select stalks of uniform size. Clean them. Soak briefly in salt water to coax out any skulking animals. The tender flower buds cook very quickly. Leave the heads as is but split the coarse stems vertically to speed up the cooking process. Keep the cooking time short to have crisp and attractive broccoli rather than a gray and sodden mess.

Broccoli needs little companionship other than freshly ground pepper and butter. For a change in pace, serve it with Nut Butter for vegetables (p. 18) or Hollandaise (p. 19). Or chill and serve with a Sauce Vinaigrette (p. 22).

Broccoli à la Grecque

TIME: 15 minutes   SERVES: 4

COMPOSITION

8-10 broccoli stalks
2-3 green onions (scallions)
2-3 tablespoons butter
½ cup water

1 garlic clove
½ teaspoon sugar
pepper
1 lemon, quartered

PREPARATION

Clean the broccoli. Slit the stems.
Chop the onions.

Melt the butter with the water. Press the garlic into the pan, add the onions, the sugar, and a good grinding of black pepper.

Place the broccoli in the pan with flower heads up. Cover tightly. Cook for about 12 minutes. The time will vary with the broccoli. Test it with a fork after a few minutes.

PRESENTATION

Arrange on a warm platter together with the lemon quarters.

BRUSSELS SPROUTS

These can be cabbage at its best, but only if selected wisely and cooked properly. Nothing could be worse than the gray flavorless lumps which are too often served.

Pick out the smallest of the small. Large ones with loose and yellow leaves are too old to bother with. The color should be fresh and bright. The size should be uniform. They should feel firm and fully packed. The quantity (for 4) should total 1 pound.

To prepare these miniatures, first discard any withered outer leaves. Make a slit in the base of each to hasten cooking time. Soak them (to dislodge bugs) in salt water for at least 10 minutes.

Don't torture them. Cook gently in just enough salted water to cover until they are tender when jabbed with a fork; 8-10 minutes should do the trick.

VARIOUS VEGETABLE VIGNETTES

Simple and effective companions are butter, nutmeg, or grated cheese.

Savory Brussels Sprouts

TIME: 20-25 minutes SERVES: 6

COMPOSITION

1½ pounds fresh sprouts or 2 boxes frozen sprouts	3 tablespoons butter pepper
½ teaspoon sugar	1 onion slice
1 teaspoon monosodium glutamate	lemon juice nutmeg

PREPARATION

Make ready the Brussels sprouts. If fresh, remove the coarse outer leaves and let them soak. If frozen, whack the box against the counter to separate the mass.

Into a deep pan with a cover, put ½ cup of water, the sugar, the monosodium glutamate, the butter, and a generous helping of freshly ground pepper. When the liquid boils, add the sprouts.

Cover the pot. Cook for 8-10 minutes (longer will make them mushy, gray, and tasteless).

Place the sprouts in a hot serving dish. Keep them warm.

Add the onion slice and a dash of lemon juice to the pan juice. Cook rapidly to reduce the sauce somewhat.

Drain it over the Brussels sprouts, sprinkle them lightly with nutmeg, and serve.

CABBAGE

These old warhorses should receive more (and more careful) kitchen cultivation. Overlong cooking can kill them. In the dying process the odors of decay can kill the cook and remain to greet the guests.

Cook cabbage quickly in very little water. Keep it crisp. You can change the course of your personal gastronomic history if you treat it with due regard.

Cabbage with Caraway

TIME: 20 minutes or so   SERVES: 6

COMPOSITION

1½-pound cabbage
3-4 parsley sprigs
⅛ pound butter

1 teaspoon sugar
freshly ground pepper
caraway seeds

PREPARATION

Slice the cabbage into wedges about 1½ inches thick.
Chop the parsley.
Melt the butter in a large skillet. Add the cabbage, the parsley, and the sugar. Pour in about ½ cup of water. Cover the pan and cook for almost 15 minutes.
Sprinkle heavily with caraway and pepper at the last minute.

P.S. *Try this with a roast of pork.*

VARIOUS VEGETABLE VIGNETTES

Red Cabbage with Sour Cream

TIME: Depends upon the cabbage   SERVES: 6 or more

COMPOSITION

1½- to 3-pounds red cabbage   2 tablespoons sugar
½ cup vinegar   salt
½ teaspoon caraway seeds   1 pint sour cream

PREPARATION

Choose a deep covered pot into which the cabbage will fit with little or no room to spare. Push the cabbage into the pot.

Add enough water to come midway. Add the vinegar, the caraway, the sugar, and a dash of salt.

Cover tightly and cook until the cabbage is tender. Judge by jabbing into the cabbage core.

Meanwhile, warm but do not boil, the sour cream.

PRESENTATION

Drain the cabbage. Place it on a handsome platter. Cover with the sour cream.

Slice vertical sections and serve forth.

Sweet-Sour Cabbage (Hot)

TIME: 20-30 minutes   SERVES: 4-6

COMPOSITION

1 cabbage, 1½-3 pounds   2 tart apples
1 tablespoon lemon juice   ⅛ pound butter
2 tablespoons sugar   ⅓ cup brown sugar
3 tablespoons cider vinegar   ¼ teaspoon allspice
1 small onion   1 jigger brandy

PREPARATION

Clean the cabbage. Shred it with a sharp knife as for coleslaw. Cover with boiling water, the lemon juice, and the white sugar. Cover and cook for about 10 minutes. Drain it well.
Chop the onion and the peeled apples.
Melt the butter. Sauté the onion until tan. Add the cooked cabbage and the apple chunks. Stir in the vinegar, the brown sugar, the allspice, and the brandy.
Cook for 5 minutes before serving.

CARROTS

With peas, they are an abomination. Each is a fine vegetable which should shine in its own light.

Scrawny carrots should be avoided. Great overgrown plump ones should be evaded. Young, tender, pencil-slim carrots are the best choice. If properly treated, these can charm the most avid carrot-hater.

Cook the sylphs unpeeled and whole. The fat ones should be scrubbed, then slivered; the coarse core discarded. Cook carrots in just enough water to cover, in a flat, shallow covered pan. Make taste-tests after a few minutes. If you enjoy mushy carrots, let them cook indefinitely. If you prefer them somewhat crisp, limit the cooking time to 10-12 minutes.

Butter, chopped fresh mint, nutmeg, parsley, or freshly ground black pepper are fine accompaniments for this delicate root.

VARIOUS VEGETABLE VIGNETTES

Carrots, Pierce Style

TIME: 15-20 minutes   SERVES: 4

COMPOSITION

2 bunches (about 16) small carrots
6 tablespoons butter
½ tablespoon sugar
monosodium glutamate
salt
pepper

3 to 6 lettuce leaves
2 tablespoons sour cream
1 tablespoon chopped parsley
1 tablespoon chopped fresh mint
¼ teaspoon tarragon

PREPARATION

Purchase 4 small carrots per person. Scrub and cut into vertical strips.

Melt the butter in a skillet. Add the sugar, the monosodium glutamate, a small pinch of salt, and a generous twist of pepper.

Spread the carrot strips on the bottom of the pan. Cover them with the dripping-wet lettuce leaves.

Cover the pan tightly. Cook for 12-15 minutes. Start sampling after the first 10 minutes. Stop cooking when you obtain crisp tidbits and before you get mushy sticks.

PRESENTATION

Drain the carrots. Discard the lettuce. Stir in the sour cream. Sprinkle with the parsley, the mint, and the tarragon.

Brandied Carrots

TIME: 15 minutes   SERVES: 6

COMPOSITION

4 cups sliced (or chopped or matchsticked) carrots
⅛ pound butter
¼ cup water
juice of ½ lemon
2-3 parsley sprigs
salt
brandy

PREPARATION

Scrape or scour the carrots. Cut them into shapes of your own choice. Drop them into a pan.

Add the butter and the water. Cover and cook slowly until the carrots are tender and the water absorbed.

Add the lemon juice, the minced parsley, some salt and a jigger or so of brandy.

Heat, stir, taste, and then serve.

CAULIFLOWER

Each to his own taste in vegetables. Cauliflower is one of the best, and one of the best ways to serve it is raw.

The heads should be clean and white and firm. Yellowed foliage indicates old age, as does a head neatly trimmed by the grocer. Do your own cleaning and trimming.

Remove the leaves and any excess stem. Soak the head

VARIOUS VEGETABLE VIGNETTES

in salted water to dislodge hiding insects. Jab into the core with a fork to help it cook quickly.

Treated sympathetically, cauliflower should be crispy when cooked. A flaccid mess is a bore and a culinary crime. Twenty to twenty-five minutes in boiling salted water should transform any head to an edible morsel.

Cauliflower à l'individu

TIME: 20-25 minutes   SERVES: Any number

COMPOSITION

cauliflower (1 small head per serving)
lemon juice
sugar
monosodium glutamate

PREPARATION

Remove extraneous leaves and bugs from the cauliflower heads. Jab into each stem with a sharp knife.

Pack the cauliflowers in a a deep pan, upright and with little room to spare. Add boiling water to about ½ the heads' height.

For each head, add the juice of ½ lemon, ½ teaspoon of sugar, and a dash of monosodium glutamate.

Cover the pan tightly. Cook for 20 minutes or more. Test with a probing fork. It should slip in easily but with some resistance.

PRESENTATION

Remove the heads to individual platters. Cover with melted butter or the sauce of your choice.

P.S. *If only large cauliflowers reach your market, divide into halves or quarters and trim each to make replicas of the parent.*

CELERY

Celery is most often designated as rabbit food. If lifted out of that category and cooked, it is a delightful new addition to the vegetable line.

Celery comes either green or bleached. If you prefer the anemic variety, use it. The fresh green variety has far more flavor to the eyes and the palates of discriminating vegetable lovers.

Read farther for delicious ways and means to cook it.

Celery Amandine

TIME: 10-12 minutes   SERVES: 4

COMPOSITION

4 cups chopped celery
¾ cup mixed chopped chives and green onions (scallions)
1 garlic clove
¼ pound butter
1 cup almonds, blanched and slivered
1 jigger dry vermouth

PREPARATION

Roll up your sleeves. Chop celery, medium fine and chives and onions very fine.

Cook the celery slowly in ½ of the butter. Stir constantly to prevent scorching. After a few minutes add the chives, the onions, and the pressed garlic.

VARIOUS VEGETABLE VIGNETTES

Sample. By all means let the vegetables remain crisp although cooked.

In another pan, melt the rest of the butter. Brown the nuts.

Add the vermouth to the celery just before serving.

PRESENTATION

Arrange the celery on a warm serving platter.
Top with the nuts.

Celery Provençal

TIME: 12-15 minutes   SERVES: 6

COMPOSITION

6 *celery hearts*
2-3 *medium tomatoes*
1 *cup rich beef stock* or *consommé*

2 *garlic cloves*
1 *tablespoon olive oil*

PREPARATION

Split the celery hearts lengthwise.

Peel, chop, and deseed the tomatoes.

Cook the celery in the stock until tender yet crisp. Remove when done to your taste. Keep it warm.

Reduce the stock by half over a hot fire.

Sauté the pressed garlic in the oil. Add the tomatoes.

Stir the tomatoes into the stock. Cook for 3-4 minutes.

Spoon the final sauce over the celery.

CORN

Despite its appearance, corn is a delicate thing. It seldom receives the devotion it deserves.

Lucky people harvest their own just before cooking. Those of us who rely on the grocer should let the suckers be taken in by the partially stripped (and therefore dehydrated) ears. The few worms which may be hiding under the husks cost little. Sweeter and fresher kernels will be hiding there also—especially if the husks are fresh and green. Strip an ear and see: firm fat kernels which resist a fingernail jab are the best. With this corn under your arm, rush home. Toss it into a pail of cold water or wrap it in a wet towel and store it in the refrigerator. Forget it for a while.

When the time is ripe, choose your largest kettle and consider the following recipes.

Corn on the Cob

TIME: 15 minutes at most SERVES: Any number

COMPOSITION

fresh corn, preferably unhusked
salt
sugar (optional)
freshly ground pepper
butter

PREPARATION

Consider the foregoing remarks.

Choose your largest pot. Judge its size by the quantity of corn.

VARIOUS VEGETABLE VIGNETTES

Let there be plenty of room for each ear to bounce around in. Fill the pot with fresh water. Add salt.
(If you think the corn is over age, add sugar, too.)
Let the water come to a healthy rolling boil.
Dehusk the corn. Throw it into the pot, for 3-4 minutes only. Unless you know the age and pedigree of your corn, the exact time is hard to judge. Far better to have it slightly undercooked and crisp than tough.
Rush the final results to the table and provide plenty of salt, fresh pepper, and melted butter for companionship.

Corn in the Husk

TIME: 10-15 minutes   SERVES: You count them

COMPOSITION

corn, unhusked   *pepper*
salt   *butter*
sugar

PREPARATION

Again, choose a large pot, fill with water. Add salt and sugar and bring to a boil.
Toss the corn into the pot unhusked. Tackle husks and silks after it has cooked, using mitts or towels. (This is actually an easier process than removing them beforehand.)
With salt, fresh pepper, and butter this is the end.

P.S. *When corn is eaten on the cob it requires the consumer's entire concern, so serve it as a separate course. For real enthusiasts it need be the only course.*

Corn Baked in its Husk

TIME: 20-25 minutes SERVES: Any number

COMPOSITION

fresh corn, unhusked
salt
pepper
butter

PREPARATION

Hold each ear of corn under the cold faucet. Let water run inside the husk.

Bake in a 350° oven for 15-20 minutes.

Strip the ears and serve with the usual accompaniments.

Corn in Sour Cream

TIME: 30 minutes, including corn-scraping SERVES: 4

COMPOSITION

2 cups corn (preferably pulp scraped from the cob)
1 pimiento
6 bacon slices
3 tablespoons grated onion
1 teaspoon sugar
salt
pepper
1½ cups sour cream

PREPARATION

Scrape the corn. Cook it in its own juice for 2-3 minutes only, stirring constantly.

Chop the pimiento.

Dice the bacon.

Grate the onion.

VARIOUS VEGETABLE VIGNETTES

Sauté the bacon bits until they are crisp. Remove them from the pan.

Sauté the grated onion in the bacon fat. Add the sugar, the corn pulp, and the pimiento. Add salt and pepper to taste.

Cook for about 10 minutes.

Stir in the bacon. Fold the sour cream into the mixture.

Heat but do not boil.

Serve right now.

Corn and Eggplant Pudding

TIME: 1¼ hours   SERVES: 6-8

COMPOSITION

2 tomatoes
1 onion
1 eggplant
2 eggs
1 garlic clove
6 tablespoons butter
salt
pepper

paprika
cayenne
2 tablespoons olive oil
flour
2 cups cream-style corn (or 2 cups fresh corn plus ¼ cup cream)

PREPARATION

Turn on the oven at 325°.

Peel and seed the tomatoes.

Slice the onion.

Peel the eggplant. Cleave it into 1-inch cubes.

Separate the eggs.

Grease a baking dish.

Sauté the onion and the pressed garlic in 4 tablespoons of the butter. Add the tomatoes. Season to taste.

Heat the oil in another pan.

Dredge the eggplant chunks in flour. Sauté them in oil until just tender. Place them in the baking dish. Top with the tomato mixture and bake, covered, for about 15 minutes.

Mix the corn with the egg yolks. (If the corn is fresh, scrape the kernels from the cob, boil for 2-3 minutes only, and combine with the cream.) Melt the rest of the butter. Add it.

Beat the egg whites until very stiff. Fold them into the batter. Pour it over the eggplant.

Bake until an inserted knife comes out clean as a whistle.

Corn with Mushrooms

TIME: About 1 hour   SERVES: 4-6

COMPOSITION

2 cups cooked corn pulp	*2 tablespoons flour*
1 cup chopped mushrooms	*1 cup milk*
6 tablespoons butter	*3 egg yolks*

PREPARATION

Scrape, grate, cut, or obtain the corn pulp by any means possible. (If this means opening a can, use whole-kernel style.)

Clean and chop the mushrooms.

Set the oven to 375°.

Butter a baking dish.

Melt 4 tablespoons of the butter. Sauté the mushrooms briefly. Add the corn pulp. Cook and stir until there is no more juice.

Let the milk be heating in a second pan.

In another pan, melt the rest of the butter. Stir in the flour.

Blend in the hot milk. Cook and stir until the sauce is thick (about 15 minutes).

Add the egg yolks, one by one, beating well after each.

Add the corn-mushroom mixture.

Pour the combination into the baking dish. Bake it for 20-25 minutes.

EGGPLANT

Eggplants *can* be used for sheer decoration, and often are. They can also be cooked in a number of ways. If you like the taste and flavor at all, they combine well with many other foods. (Check other recipes in the index for ideas not included in this section.)

Good eggplants are heavy and solid and have a rich, shiny color. Bad eggplants are soft and flabby and shriveled. In either case, they are most often egg shaped. When shopping, look for small ones. Weigh them. It takes 1½-2 pounds for 4 good servings.

If you have never experienced anything other than "fried" eggplant, attempt one of the following recipes. You'll soon learn how delicious and delicate the fruit can be.

Eggplant and Shrimp

TIME: About 1 hour   SERVES: 6

COMPOSITION

3 medium eggplants
1 garlic clove
1 small onion
1 large celery stalk
½ pound cooked shrimp (or 2 small cans)

¾ cup fine bread crumbs
6 tablespoons butter
sage
¼ teaspoon thyme
salt
pepper

PREPARATION

Cut the eggplants in half lengthwise. Place them in a flat baking dish, cut side exposed. Cover with about ½ inch of water. Bake at 400° for about 30 minutes. Drain well.

Scoop out the meat and save it. Save the shells also. (If you puncture them, toss them out. Butter a casserole instead.)

Chop the garlic, the onion, and the celery as fine as possible.

Produce the cooked shrimp, shelled and cleaned.

Make bread crumbs. Sauté them quickly in 2 tablespoons of butter.

Melt 4 tablespoons of butter. Sauté the garlic, the onion, and the celery. Add the herbs and the shrimp. Season to taste with salt and pepper. Cook for a minute or two. Combine with the eggplant pulp.

Stuff the shells (or the casserole). Spread the buttered crumbs on top. Bake at 350° for 10-15 minutes.

VARIOUS VEGETABLE VIGNETTES

Eggplant Caviar pour l'Homme sans Sous

TIME: An hour or so   SERVES: 4-6

COMPOSITION

1 eggplant	*salt*
3-4 large fresh tomatoes	*pepper*
1 large onion	*olive oil*
1 garlic clove	*wine vinegar*

PREPARATION

Bake the eggplant in a 350° oven for about 15 minutes until tender. Let it cool; then peel, and chop very fine.

For each cup of eggplant, chop a small ripe tomato and a small onion. Add ½ clove of pressed garlic (more or less) for each cupful.

Combine all ingredients. Add salt and pepper to taste.

For each cup of stuff, stir in a tablespoon of olive oil. When the oil is absorbed, stir in a tablespoon or so of wine vinegar.

Before serving, let the "caviar" mellow.

PRESENTATION

To be smeared on thick slabs of sour French bread.

For hors d'oeuvres, for a vegetable course, for an entire lunch (what I call a Meal-in-Itself).

Eggplant aux Palourdes

TIME: 25 minutes   SERVES: 4

COMPOSITION

1 eggplant
¼ cup chopped parsley
¼ cup chopped chives

1 small (8-ounce) can minced clams
2 garlic cloves
⅛ pound butter

PREPARATION

Peel the eggplant. Cleave it into 1-inch-square chunks.

Mince the parsley and the chives.

Separate clam juice from clams.

Press the garlic into the butter. Sauté it quickly. Add the clam juice. After 2-3 minutes add the eggplant. Cook for 10 minutes. Turn the chunks often.

Throw in the herbs. Cook for another minute or so.

Add the clams, stir once or twice, then serve.

Garbanzos (Chick Peas) with Herbs

TIME: 24 plus 1½-2½ hours,   SERVES: 6-8
and worth every hour

COMPOSITION

1 pound dried garbanzo beans
1 No. 2½ can Italian style tomatoes
1 garlic clove, pressed
1 onion, sliced
⅛ cup olive oil
salt

pepper
a good pinch each of
basil
oregano
savory
thyme

VARIOUS VEGETABLE VIGNETTES

~~~~~~

PRELIMINARY

Soak the beans for 24 hours in salted lukewarm water to cover.

PREPARATION

Add more water if necessary and bring the beans to a boil. Simmer. Skim the top until the water is clear.

Add everything except the herbs. Continue cooking until the beans are tender.

Remove the pot from the stove. Add the herbs. Stir well. After a minimum 30-minute rest (maximum 1 hour), return the pot to the stove. Cook until hot. Serve.

Hominy in Sour Cream

TIME: 15 minutes   SERVES: 4

COMPOSITION

2 tablespoons chives
1 2-pound can of hominy
⅛ pound butter

1 heaping tablespoon curry powder
½ pint sour cream

PREPARATION

Chop the chives.

Stew the hominy in its own juice until it is thoroughly heated. Drain off any remaining liquid.

Melt the butter. Stir in curry powder. Blend well. Pour over the hominy. Blend again.

Swathe the hominy in the sour cream. Let it reheat but not boil. Serve with chopped chives.

Leeks Mornay

TIME: 30-40 minutes   SERVES: 4

COMPOSITION

2 pounds leeks
1½ cups Béchamel Sauce
3 tablespoons grated Gruyère cheese

3 tablespoons heavy cream
2 tablespoons butter
¼ cup grated Parmesan cheese

PREPARATION

Wash the leeks thoroughly. Chop them into 2-inch lengths. Simmer in salted water until barely tender.

Meanwhile, prepare the sauce (p. 8), adding the Gruyère and the cream.

Drain the leeks. Sauté them in butter for about 10 minutes. Place them in a shallow buttered baking dish. Cover with sauce. Top with grated Parmesan cheese.

Bake 5-8 minutes in a 350° oven.

Leeks in Red Wine

TIME: 20 minutes   SERVES: 4

COMPOSITION

2 pounds leeks
¼ cup olive oil
1 teaspoon (more or less) salt
cayenne

¼ cup beef or chicken stock
¾ cup dry red wine
nutmeg

PREPARATION

Buy the smallest leeks available. Clean them, removing only an inch or so of the green top. Stand them upside down in a small deep pot or pitcher of water. After a long soak of at least ½ hour, excess grit should have disappeared.

Heat the oil in a skillet. Sauté the leeks on each side. Sprinkle them with salt and a dash of cayenne. Add the stock and the wine. Cook, uncovered, for 8-10 minutes. Remove the leeks to a hot serving platter.

Boil down the sauce to half its quantity. Pour it over the leeks. Dust with nutmeg.

PRESENTATION

Serve as a separate course or to accompany pork or lamb.

Leeks Vinaigrette

See p. 414 in the salad chapter.

MUSHROOMS

Dark and wrinkled mushrooms (unless completely dehydrated) can never compare with chubby youngsters. Freshness counts. Size is unimportant in most cases.

Mushrooms and water don't mix. They lose much of their flavor in a bath. Clean them with a brush or a moist sponge. If you insist on removing the peel, do it immediately before cooking.

Don't overlook the stems: they may be tough, but they are still all mushroom. Chop them finer and cook them longer.

Mushroom cooking-time should be extremely brief. A quick pass through hot oil or butter is more than enough, even for the canned variety.

Mushrooms in Brandy

TIME: 30 minutes SERVES: 4

COMPOSITION

10-12 green onions (scallions) *¼ cup sherry*
2 pounds mushrooms *1 jigger brandy*
¼ pound butter *½ pint heavy cream*

PREPARATION

Chop the onions.
Clean and trim the mushrooms, leaving them whole.
Sauté the onions in butter. Add the mushrooms. Simmer for 5-6 minutes. Add the sherry, the brandy and the cream. Continue cooking for about 20 minutes.

PRESENTATION

Serve with boiled rice (p. 374) or on toast or just as is.

VARIOUS VEGETABLE VIGNETTES

Les Champignons de Mon Ami—Baked and Stuffed

TIME: 25-30 minutes   SERVES: 6-8

COMPOSITION

24 large *mushrooms*
lemon juice
⅛ *cup minced parsley*
⅛ *cup minced chives*
2 *tablespoons minced onions*
1 *minced garlic clove*
½ *cup bread crumbs*

¼ *cup grated Parmesan cheese*
salt
pepper
6 *tablespoons butter*
¼ *cup sherry*

PREPARATION

Clean the mushrooms, remove the stems, and sprinkle lemon juice (lightly) in each cap. Set them aside.

Mince the mushroom stems, the parsley, the chives, the onions, and the garlic.

Crumble bread crumbs and grate cheese.

Combine everything except bread crumbs, cheese, and sherry. Season lightly with salt and pepper. Sauté briefly in 3 tablespoons of the butter.

Add the bread crumbs and the sherry. Continue cooking and stirring for 2 minutes.

Pile the filling high in the mushroom caps. Sprinkle them with cheese. Dot them with butter. Bake them for 15 minutes in a 350° oven.

PRESENTATION

Serve at once with cocktails or as a vegetable course.

Cocktail Mushrooms (Raw)

TIME: 10-15 minutes   SERVES: ???

COMPOSITION

Vinaigrette Sauce   large fresh mushrooms

PREPARATION

Make the sauce (p. 22).

Clean the mushrooms. Sample a stem. If they seem coarse and woody, discard them or save them for later use.

PRESENTATION

Dip a mushroom in sauce. Eat it.

Cocktail Mushrooms (Cooked)

TIME: About 10 minutes to make   SERVES: 4-6
At least 60 minutes to chill

COMPOSITION

1 pound mushrooms   1 jigger brandy
¼ cup grated onion   1 tablespoon lemon juice
2 tablespoons butter   1 pint sour cream
salt   ¼ cup chopped chives

PREPARATION

Clean the mushrooms. Remove the stems. Cut the caps into quarters.

Grate the onion.

Sauté mushrooms and onion in butter for 4-5 minutes. Remove the pan from the fire. Dust its contents with salt. Pour in the brandy and the lemon juice.

VARIOUS VEGETABLE VIGNETTES

Chill for several hours, or at least one.

Just before serving, mix lightly with the sour cream. Throw the chives over all.

Just Mushrooms

TIME: 4-5 minutes   SERVES: 2

COMPOSITION

1 garlic clove
½ cup chives and parsley (chopped and mixed)
1 pound mushrooms
⅛ pound butter
½ teaspoon powdered ginger (or an equal amount of grated fresh variety)
salt
pepper

PREPARATION

Chop the garlic, the chives, the parsley, and the cleaned mushrooms.

Melt the butter. Sauté the garlic. Stir in the chives and the parsley. Add the mushrooms, leaving them whole.

Sprinkle lightly with ginger, salt, and freshly ground pepper.

Serve.

P.S. *Lightly sautéed rounds of French bread makes a good base for this delicacy.*

ONIONS

If onions are provoking, cut down on your personal contact with them. Mitigate tears to a degree by eliminating the peeling process. Slice them, then pick out the rims of skin. Or halve and quarter them, pick out the peel, and chop as needed.

If the onions are strong willed, soak the slices or chunks in milk before using: the onions become milder and the milk becomes the basis for a terrific sauce. Or remove some of the sting by permitting them to rest under a sprinkling of sugar before further use.

It is lamentable that onions are wooed with such lack of imagination. They should be more than just a seasoning agent. They can stand alone—as onions.

Use the yellow ones for stewing, the white for boiling, Bermudas and Italians for broiling and in the raw, and green onions (scallions) however you like.

Baked Onions

TIME: 75 minutes   SERVES: 6

COMPOSITION

36 small white onions
1 cup nutmeats (no peanuts and no salt)
¾ cup butter
1-2 tablespoons brown sugar

1 teaspoon salt
cayenne
nutmeg
ground cloves

VARIOUS VEGETABLE VIGNETTES

PREPARATION

Peel the onions.
Chop the nuts.
Melt the butter in a casserole. Add all other ingredients. Combine thoroughly. Stir to coat the onions completely.
Cover the casserole and shove it into the oven.
Bake at 350° for about an hour. Shake the pot occasionally to keep the onions from sticking.

Brandied Baked Onions

TIME: 75 minutes   SERVES: 6

COMPOSITION

3 dozen small white onions
1 cup blanched, shredded almonds
¼ pound sweet butter
1 garlic clove
1 tablespoon brown sugar
1 teaspoon salt and pepper, mixed
1 jigger brandy or white wine

PREPARATION

Peel the onions.
Chop the nuts.
Melt the butter in a baking dish.
Sauté the garlic. Add the other ingredients.
Bake, covered, at 350° for one hour.

Onion Soufflé

TIME: 45-50 minutes   SERVES: 4-6

COMPOSITION

6 medium onions
½ teaspoon salt
¼ teaspoon pepper
nutmeg
cayenne

3 eggs
⅛ pound butter
4 tablespoons flour
⅓ cup heavy cream
⅓ cup onion water

PREPARATION

Peel and chop the onions. Boil them in lightly salted water until very soft. Fish them out. Season with salt, pepper, nutmeg, and cayenne. Set aside for the moment. Reserve the onion water.

Separate the eggs. Beat the yolks until lemon colored. Whip the whites until stiff and foamy.

Butter a soufflé mold.

Melt the butter. Add the flour, blending it in thoroughly. Stir continuously while adding the cream and ⅓ cup of the onion water. Keep stirring until the sauce is thick and smooth.

Combine the egg yolks and the cooked onions. Add these to the sauce.

Fold in the egg whites. Turn into the soufflé dish. Bake at 350° for 25-30 minutes.

VARIOUS VEGETABLE VIGNETTES

Onion Sludge
(M-in-I)

TIME: About 45 minutes   SERVES: 4

COMPOSITION

8 large onions
1 cup grated Swiss cheese
about ½ loaf stale sour dough bread
⅛ pound butter
4 tablespoons flour

2 cups rich stock
2 cups milk
1 jigger brandy (if available)
salt
pepper
nutmeg

PREPARATION

Cut the onions into thick peeled slices.
Grate the cheese.
Tear the bread into chunks.
Sauté the onion slices in some of the butter. Place them in groups of 2 or 3 in a large shallow baking dish. Make a checkerboard pattern, alternating onions and bread chunks. A single layer is preferable.
Melt the rest of the butter in a skillet. Blend in the flour. Stir. Add the stock and the milk. Continue stirring until smooth. Add the brandy. Pour the sauce into the baking dish. Sprinkle lightly with salt, pepper, and nutmeg. Sprinkle heavily with grated cheese.
Bake at 350° until hot and crusty (about 20-25 minutes). The liquid should be almost completely absorbed.

PRESENTATION

With a salad.

P.S. *Mr. Pierce "discovered" this dish in a peasant farmhouse near Vence, France. It has all that's necessary for a hearty lunch or supper—and it's wonderfully delicious.*

Onion Cheese Soufflé
(M-in-I)

TIME: 20 minutes to concoct
   60 minutes to bake

SERVES: 2, possibly 3

COMPOSITION

*4 cups white onions
 in thin slices*
½ cup finely minced parsley
1½ cups grated sharp cheese
*1½ cups coarse dry bread
 crumbs*
¼ pound butter

3 cups milk
1 teaspoon salt
½ teaspoon celery salt
¼ teaspoon paprika
¼ teaspoon dry mustard
generous dash cayenne
4 eggs

PREPARATION

Slice the onions. (Avoid a few tears by eliminating the peeling process. Cut completely through each slice and pick out the circles of skin as they fall away.)

Chop the parsley, grate the cheese, and prepare the bread crumbs.

Let the butter be melting in one pan and the milk be heating in another.

Butter a baking dish.

Place onion slices, cheese, parsley, bread crumbs, and seasonings in a large bowl. Mix. Pour in the melted butter. Mix again.

Beat the eggs lightly. Stir them into the scalded milk. Add to the onion mélange. Combine thoroughly.

Pour it into the baking dish and bake in a 325° oven for an hour.

PRESENTATION

Serve on the dot, hot and steamy. Accompany with a green bean salad (p. 409), and there's your whole meal.

PEAS

The very best peas come encased in pods. They require work, which is never really work if one loves peas. It all starts with the picking, whether from vine or vegetable market.

Look for shiny bright green pods with small lumps. Help yourself to one. Why not? Who can honestly say he has never swiped a grape or a berry? Chew on a single pea. If it is tender and sweet and juicy, continue gathering. Two pounds of unshelled peas should serve 4 people more or less adequately. Refrigerate them until just before cooking time. Shell them at the very last minute (Of course this is often impossible. In any event wait as long as possible and avoid soaking them in water after they are shelled. They do lose flavor this way.)

Cook peas quickly in very little water until tender but still crunchy. Drain and serve them as you see fit. As I see it, melted butter and freshly ground black pepper are very fit.

Perfect Plain Peas

TIME: 15 minutes to shell   SERVES: 4
5-7 minutes to cook

COMPOSITION

2 pounds unshelled peas
⅛ pound butter
1 teaspoon sugar
1 teaspoon monosodium glutamate
1 teaspoon Spice Islands Beau Monde seasoning

PREPARATION

Shell the peas.

Melt the butter in a skillet having a tight-fitting cover. Add 4-5 tablespoons of water, the peas, and the seasonings. Cover the pan.

Steam the peas for 5-7 minutes, depending on their age, their size, and the total quantity.

Peas à la Bonne Femme

TIME: 25-30 minutes, including pea-shelling   SERVES: 4

COMPOSITION

- 2 pounds unshelled peas (or 1½ packs frozen peas)
- 4-5 chives
- 4-5 parsley sprigs
- 1 bay leaf
- 1 teaspoon sugar
- 1 teaspoon monosodium glutamate
- ¼ pound butter
- 1 small head iceberg lettuce (or 4-5 large leaves of any lettuce)
- pepper

PREPARATION

Shell the peas (or thump the frozen packages against the counter to separate the mass).

Chop chives and parsley.

Crush the bay leaf.

Place the peas in a wide shallow and covered pan. Sprinkle them with the sugar, the monosodium glutamate, and the herbs. Toss in half of the butter, in chips.

Break the lettuce into chunks. Immerse it (or the leaves) in cold water and spread it over the peas.

VARIOUS VEGETABLE VIGNETTES

Cover the pan. Cook the peas. In 4-7 minutes they will be crisp and firm, with the flavor of summer.

PRESENTATION

Remove them (and the bedraggled lettuce) to a hot serving dish. Drench them with the rest of the butter, melted. Sprinkle generously with freshly ground black pepper.

These deserve to be served as a separate course in themselves.

Creamed Peas

TIME: 20-25 minutes   SERVES: 4

COMPOSITION

2 pounds peas (or 1 10-ounce package frozen peas)
1 cup cream sauce
5-6 water chestnuts (optional)
1 tablespoon butter
pepper

PREPARATION

Shell the peas. Cook them. The recipe is on (p. 362).
Make a cream, or Béchamel, sauce. The recipe for it is on p. 8.
Drain and slice the water chestnuts. Sauté them very briefly in the butter.
Combine the ingredients. Dust with pepper. Serve.

GREEN PEPPERS

Rotund peppers with a bright, clean green complexion are choice peppers. Once middle age sets in, they are seldom fit companions for man.

Sad to state, just because they are hollow, peppers are almost exclusively served stuffed. They bulge with cheap hamburger, ooze tomato sauce, and swim in grease. Consequently they are repulsive, but they needn't be. Read Green Peppers Callas and see. As a seasoning they have a delicate sweet tang which not only compliments other food but can sing alone. If you haven't had a pepper lately, look at these recipes and rejoice.

Green Pepper Sauté

TIME: 10-15 minutes   SERVES: 4-6

COMPOSITION

8 green peppers
1 medium onion
¼ pound butter
⅛ cup olive oil
1 tablespoon sugar

1 teaspoon monosodium glutamate
salt
pepper

PREPARATION

Clean the peppers. Cut them into thin strips. Chop the onion.

VARIOUS VEGETABLE VIGNETTES

Melt the butter together with the oil. Add the onion, the sugar, the monosodium glutamate, and the pepper strips. Cook gently until the peppers are tender. Avoid overcooking. They should remain a fresh green and not become nasty.

PRESENTATION

Just before serving, sprinkle with salt and freshly ground coarse pepper.

Stuffed Peppers Espagnole

TIME: 45 minutes   SERVES: 6

COMPOSITION

1 cup lean chopped veal
1 cup chopped ham
2-3 parsley sprigs
juice of ½ lemon
¼ cup Parmesan cheese
2-3 tomatoes
1 cup chopped mushrooms
¼ pound butter

2 garlic cloves
6 green peppers
1 tablespoon basil
2 egg yolks
salt
pepper
1 cup chicken stock

PREPARATION

Chop the meats.
Mince the parsley.
Squeeze the lemon.
Grate cheese.
Peel, quarter, and drain the tomatoes.
Chop the mushrooms very fine. Sauté them quickly in 2 tablespoons of the butter, together with the pressed garlic.
Cut the peppers in half, lengthwise. Deseed them. Toss them into boiling salt water for 2-3 minutes. Drain.

Combine the meats, the parsley, the lemon juice, the cheese, the mushrooms, and the seasonings. Add the egg yolks.
Stuff the peppers. Place them in a baking dish.
Melt the rest of the butter. Pour it over them.
Heat the stock. Pour it around them. Place the tomatoes around them also.
Cover the baking dish. Bake for 20 minutes at 350°.

PRESENTATION

Place the peppers on a serving platter. Strain the juice, boil it down by half, and pour it over the peppers.

Green Peppers with Corn

TIME: 30 minutes   SERVES: 4

COMPOSITION

½ medium green pepper
½ medium red pepper
1 tablespoon parsley
1 tablespoon chives
1 package frozen corn or 1½ cups canned whole kernel corn

6 tablespoons butter
tarragon
¼ cup white wine
1 tablespoon brandy

PREPARATION

Chop the peppers coarsely.
Mince the parsley and the chives.
Defrost the corn or open a can.
Heat 2 tablespoons of the butter. Add the corn. Cook and stir for a minute or two. Add the rest of the butter, the herbs, and the peppers, After another minute, add the wine.
Cover the pot. Simmer it for 20 minutes.
Uncover, add the brandy, stir and serve.

VARIOUS VEGETABLE VIGNETTES

POTATOES

Potatoes occupy a preferred place on many menus. They are served more often (and are more often ruined) than any other vegetable. Blame the cook and not the potato. If it is carefully chosen to suit its eventual end, it can be a great delicacy.

Besides baking and mashing, which I will spell out for you, there are countless ways of serving the spud. You have your favorites. I have mine. Here they are.

Perfect Baked Potatoes

TIME: 30 minutes to 1 hour   SERVES: Any number

No greater love can be given a potato than to bake it. Thoughtful attention before and after the oven sojourn is required. For baking, use baking potatoes—nothing else.

For potato accompaniments you are on your own. Here are a few reminders from a long list: butter, sour cream, chopped crisp bacon, chives, softened Roquefort cheese, grated sharp cheese, lemon-butter, parsley, thyme, marjoram, chervil, curry powder, or nutmeg.

COMPOSITION

1 baking potato per person   *salt*
butter or oil   *pepper*

Perfect Mashed Potatoes

PREPARATION

Scrub the potatoes. Dry them. Coat them with oil or butter. Send them to a preheated 425° oven. Let them remain until done to a turn. (Check with the potatoes for this: 45 minutes is an average time for an average potato.)

Remove, split, dust with salt, pepper, butter or anything else which I have suggested above, or turn to page 17 for a special sauce.

Perfect Mashed Potatoes

TIME: 30-45 minutes   SERVES: You name it

These need special attention from beginning to end. Select regular Irish potatoes of a uniform size. Allow 1 large or 2 medium potatoes per serving. Never cook them to a state of sogginess, and be more than liberal with the butter and the cream.

This, man, is eating!

COMPOSITION

4-8 potatoes   *butter*
salt   *cream*
pepper   *baking powder (optional)*

PREPARATION

Peel the potatoes or not as you desire. (If peeled, toss them into cold water immediately to avoid browning.) If unpeeled, slip off the skins as soon as they are done.

Put them through a ricer.

Add the seasonings to taste and at least ¼ pound of butter (melted) and ½ cup of cream (scalded) per pound of

VARIOUS VEGETABLE VIGNETTES

potatoes. (They respond well to a pinch of baking powder in addition.)
Beat them, fast and hard.
Serve them quickly before the froth gets cool.

Potatoes Baked with Mushrooms

TIME: Almost 1¼ hours   SERVES: 6

COMPOSITION

6 baking potatoes   *1 egg*
½ pound mushrooms   *salt*
6 chives   *pepper*
⅔ cup bread crumbs   *1 jigger dry white wine*
2 tablespoons butter

PREPARATION

Peel, then cut a lid from the side of each potato. Hollow out the core in the easiest way.
Clean and chop the mushrooms.
Chop chives.
Make fine bread crumbs.
Preheat the oven to 450°.
Sauté the mushrooms in the butter. Leave any remaining butter in the pan.
Combine the mushrooms, the chives, the breadcrumbs, and the egg. Season with salt and pepper.
Fill the hollowed potatoes with the mixture. Top with an additional lump of butter. Replace the lids and fasten them with toothpicks.
Fit the potatoes in a butter-laden baking dish.
Pour the wine into the pan, heat, and spoon over the potatoes.
Cover the dish and bake for 45 minutes.

Shrimp Stuffed Potatoes

TIME: 1¼ hours   SERVES: 6

COMPOSITION

6 baking potatoes
¼ pound mushrooms
¼ pound cooked, cleaned
    shrimp
5-6 chives
⅔ cup bread crumbs

2 tablespoons butter
1 egg
salt
pepper
1 jigger dry white wine

PREPARATION

Follow the recipe for Potatoes Baked with Mushrooms. The end result is the same: good eating.

Parmesan Potatoes

TIME: 20-25 minutes   SERVES: 4-6

COMPOSITION

2 pounds small new potatoes
grated Parmesan cheese
2 eggs
flour

salt
pepper
butter

PREPARATION

Boil the potatoes in their skins.

Grate cheese. Beat eggs.

When done, remove the potato skins. Make a small hollow in the side of each potato. Fill it with grated cheese. Dip each in beaten egg. Roll each in flour seasoned with salt and pepper.

Sauté the potatoes in lots of butter until beautifully tanned.

VARIOUS VEGETABLE VIGNETTES

Stuffed Potatoes

TIME: 1½ hours   SERVES: 6

COMPOSITION

6 large baking potatoes
2 eggs
¼ pound cooked ham
½ pound mushrooms
1 small onion
2-3 green onions (scallions)

2-3 parsley sprigs
3-4 tablespoons butter
salt
pepper
1 cup rich stock

PREPARATION

Peel the potatoes. Cut a thick slice from the side of each. Scoop out the centers, leaving a ½-inch shell.

Hard-cook the eggs.

Chop separately the ham, the mushrooms, the onions, the parsley, and the eggs.

Melt the butter. Mix into it the chopped ingredients, excluding the green onions. Season with salt and pepper.

Fill the potato shells. Replace and fasten the lids with toothpicks.

Place the potatoes in a buttered baking dish. Toss in the green onions. Add the stock.

Bake. This will take an hour in a 350° oven.

Potato Soufflé

TIME: 40-45 minutes, using left-over potatoes   SERVES: 4

COMPOSITION

2 cups mashed potatoes	*½ cup cream*
¼ cup grated sharp cheese	*1 teaspoon salt*
4 eggs	*nutmeg*

PREPARATION

Serve mashed potatoes a day or two in advance. Restrain yourself. Let there be 2 cups left over. If this is impossible, start from scratch.

Reheat the potatoes in the top of a double boiler over simmering water. It may take slightly longer but it frees you for other work.

Grate the cheese.

Separate the eggs.

Add the cream, the salt, and a dash of nutmeg to the potatoes. Whip them. Add the cheese. Whip again.

Remove from the heat and beat in the egg yolks, singly. Keep the mixture warm over the same simmering water.

Beat the egg whites to a stiff froth and fold them into the potatoes.

Place in a well-buttered soufflé dish (only ¾ full, please) and bake.

Thirty minutes in a 375° oven will be ample.

PRESENTATION

Serve immediately before it flops.

VARIOUS VEGETABLE VIGNETTES

RICE

There is as much palaver about how to cook rice properly as there is rice in China, but most people make a gray and gummy mess of it. It's not that difficult. In fact, it's very easy.

Boiled Rice

Bring a kettle of water to a full rolling boil. Salt it generously. Pour white rice in a stream into the water. Give it a quick stir. Put on a cover, leaving about an inch for the steam to escape. Boil the rice *just* 17 minutes. Turn it into a collander and run cold water through it, fluffing the rice with your hands or, if you prefer, a fork. Now or later, reheat the rice in a very slow oven in a covered buttered vegetable dish for 25-35 minutes, or until very hot. The result of this simple process is the kind the Orientals boast of (but don't always produce)—each kernel completely separate. One cup of raw rice will yield four cups of the cooked variety.

Rice can be an accompaniment to hundreds of meat and poultry dishes. It is delicious just boiled and served with melted butter, salt, and pepper, or with other additives such as toasted chopped almonds or sautéed mushrooms, provided you use plenty of either. I like to stir in one or two beaten eggs with several lumps of butter, chopped chives and quantities of grated Parmesan cheese, or cover it with Sauce Mon Dieu (see page 17). Adding a generous pinch of saffron while boiling the rice gives a distinctive color and flavor. Here are a few more specific suggestions. You'll think of others.

Wild rice is a different story, and I've included a couple of recipes for that.

Baked Rice

TIME: 48½ minutes   SERVES: 6-8

COMPOSITION

1 cup raw rice
1 can consommé or beer
1 can water

¼ pound butter
2 teaspoons salt
½ cup chopped parsley

PREPARATION

Empty all the ingredients into a baking dish. Stir once or twice. Cover.
Bake for 45 minutes at 350°.

Orange Rice

TIME: 35 minutes   SERVES: 4-6

COMPOSITION

2 tablespoons grated orange peel
¾ cup orange juice
¼ cup diced celery
1 small onion

salt
⅛ pound butter
2 cups raw rice
2 cups water

PREPARATION

Grate and squeeze the oranges.
Dice the celery.
Mince the onion.
Combine all ingredients and cook in a tightly covered pan for about 25 minutes.

375

VARIOUS VEGETABLE VIGNETTES

~~~~~~

PRESENTATION

Serve with pork. This will delight guests to the point of delirium.

Wild Rice with Mushrooms

TIME: Overnight, plus 1 hour   SERVES: 4-6

COMPOSITION

1 cup raw wild rice	1 cup milk
⅛ pound butter	½ teaspoon salt
1 cup chopped mushrooms	pepper
2 tablespoons flour	

PREPARATION

Wash the rice. Soak it overnight in water to cover. Drain, cover with boiling salt water, and let it stand for 25 minutes.

Melt the butter. Sauté the chopped mushrooms very quickly and briefly. Stir in the flour. Add the milk. Cook and stir until the sauce thickens. Season with salt and pepper.

Drain the rice. Combine it with the sauce.

Bake in a buttered baking dish at 350° for 45 minutes.

Wild Rice Soufflé

TIME: 1¼ hours   SERVES: 4-6

COMPOSITION

1½ cups cooked wild rice	2 eggs
1 cup grated sharp cheese	⅔ cup olive oil
1 medium onion	1 cup milk
1 cup chopped parsley	salt
½ cup (or more) chopped blanched almonds	pepper

PREPARATION

Wash and cook the wild rice. Use the directions on the box.
Grate cheese.
Chop and mince onions and parsley.
Shell, blanch, and chop almonds.
Butter a soufflé dish.
Separate eggs. Beat the yolks well. Add the oil, the onion, the parsley and ¾ cup of the cheese. Stir in the rice, the milk, and the seasonings.
Whip the egg whites until stiff. Fold them into the rice mixture. Pour the batter into the soufflé dish. Top with almonds and the remainder of the cheese.
Set the dish in a shallow pan of hot water. Place both in a 325°-350° oven for 30-45 minutes.

SNOW PEAS

These tender, edible pods come under a variety of names: snow peas, pod peas, sugar peas, Chinese pea pods and *Mange-tout*. No matter the name, everyone should discover them, the sooner the better.

They are best cooked quickly and gently in very little water and very much butter. They must be crisp and not wilted. 8-10 minutes will do them very well.

Serve them simply, if you please. Drain them and provide a sauce of melted butter flavored very slightly with lemon juice. Or try them with Hollandaise Sauce. For variety, cover them with Vinaigrette Sauce, let them chill well, and serve as a crisp salad.

VARIOUS VEGETABLE VIGNETTES

For further variety, try either of the following; they are equally delicious.

Snow Peas with Wild Rice

TIME: 45 minutes   SERVES: 6

COMPOSITION

1 cup raw wild rice
2 green onions (scallions)
1 tablespoon butter
1½ teaspoons salt
2 cups chicken consommé
1 pound snow peas
¼ pound mushrooms
1 4-ounce can water chestnuts
1 tablespoon minced parsley
2 tablespoons oil
¼ teaspoon pepper
¼ cup whole toasted almonds

PREPARATION

Wash the rice thoroughly.
Mince the green onions.
Melt the butter. Sauté the onions. Add the rice, 1 teaspoon of salt, and the consommé. Bring to a boil, reduce the heat, cover the pot, and let it simmer for about 35 minutes. The juice should be completely absorbed.
Wash the snow peas.
Slice the mushrooms and the water chestnuts.
Mince the parsley.
Heat the oil in a skillet. Sauté the mushrooms and the water chestnuts quickly.
Add the peas and water to barely cover. Season with ½ teaspoon of salt and ¼ teaspoon of pepper. Cover and simmer for 8 minutes.
Combine the rice, the vegetables, the parsley, and the almonds. Mix lightly and serve.

Chinese Snow Peas

TIME: 20 minutes   SERVES: 6

COMPOSITION

1 pound snow peas (fresh or frozen)
1 small onion
1 teaspoon salt
1 teaspoon sugar
¼ cup melted butter
1 teaspoon soy sauce
1 teaspoon cornstarch

PREPARATION

Wash the pea pods.
Grate the onion. Toss the gratings and the snow peas into a skillet with water to barely cover.
Season with salt and sugar.
Cover and cook for 10 minutes.
Drain them well. Add the butter. Simmer for 2 minutes.
Add the soy sauce. Mix the cornstarch with very little water.
Simmer and stir until the cornstarch becomes transparent.

SPINACH

If you don't like it, don't bother. Far be it from me to proselytize. However, if you haven't eaten it for years, it might be interesting to try once again. Our recipes are for eating it raw or cooked. Some like plain and simple spinach; others go in for the sophisticated variety. We like it every way.

Buy spinach crisp, fresh, and, if possible, unpackaged.

VARIOUS VEGETABLE VIGNETTES

Bathe it well in several waters and remove the tough stems, if they are tough. After the final rinsing, toss it dripping into a pan and cook it just until it is wilted. If fresh spinach isn't available, there's always the frozen variety, which can be awfully good if treated with proper respect—still it's not the same as garden fresh.

Simply Spinach

TIME: 10-12 minutes   SERVES: 4

COMPOSITION

2 pounds fresh spinach　　*pepper*
6 tablespoons butter　　*lemon juice*
salt

PREPARATION

Buy the freshest youngest spinach possible. Wash it well. Cook it just until tender *without* extra water. Drain thoroughly.

PRESENTATION

Dress it with melted butter, salt, pepper, and lemon juice.

Spinach Valenciennes

TIME: 12-15 minutes   SERVES: 4

COMPOSITION

½ cup seedless raisins　　*2 pounds spinach*
¾ cup brandy　　*⅛ pound butter*
½ cup pistachio nuts

PREPARATION

Put the raisins to soak in warm brandy.
Shell the nuts.

Spinach with Savory Mushrooms

Clean the spinach. Cook it as usual.

Melt the butter in a skillet. Toss in the nuts. Move them about until they are tanned.

Add the raisins, the brandy, and the spinach. Mix, heat thoroughly without cooking, and serve quickly.

P.S. *If fresh spinach seems like too much effort, try this with the frozen variety.*

Spinach with Savory Mushrooms

TIME: 10-12 minutes   SERVES: 4

COMPOSITION

2 pounds spinach
¼ pound fresh mushrooms
⅛ pound butter
¼ cup soy sauce

1 tablespoon sugar
½ cup sherry
½ teaspoon salt
1 tablespoon cornstarch

PREPARATION

Work over the spinach and the mushrooms to make sure they are free from all grit. Sauté the mushrooms in the butter. Add the soy sauce, the sugar, the sherry, and the salt. Cook and stir until the sauce begins to bubble.

Blend the cornstarch into ½ cup of water. Add to the juice in the pan. Stir until the sauce thickens.

Hold the spinach under the faucet. Drop it, dripping with water, into a pan of its own. Cook it for a few minutes, stirring briskly. Drain it, if necessary, and place it on a hot serving platter.

Cover with sauce and serve quickly.

VARIOUS VEGETABLE VIGNETTES

~~~~~~

Sesame Spinach

TIME: About 10 minutes   SERVES: 4

COMPOSITION

2 pounds fresh spinach
2 tablespoons butter
1 garlic clove
1 tablespoon Spice Islands Beau Monde seasoning
sugar
pepper
1-2 tablespoons brandy
sesame seeds

PREPARATION

Clean the spinach.

Melt the butter. Press the garlic into it. Sauté briefly. Add the Beau Monde seasoning, about ½ teaspoon of sugar, and a generous twist of pepper.

Add the spinach.

Cover the pan. Simmer for 2-3 minutes.

Uncover the pan. Add the brandy.

Recover the pan. Cook for another minute.

Uncover the pan for the last time. Sprinkle the spinach with sesame seeds (toasted or not) and serve immediately.

Spinach Soufflé

TIME: 45-60 minutes   SERVES: 4-6

COMPOSITION

1 cup cooked chopped ham
½ cup grated Parmesan cheese
2 pounds spinach
½ cup milk
⅛ pound butter
1 tablespoon flour
1 teaspoon salt
¼ teaspoon pepper
⅛ teaspoon nutmeg
3 egg yolks
4 egg whites

PREPARATION

Chop (or grind) ham.

Grate cheese.

Butter a soufflé dish.

Clean, wash, and cook the spinach in little or no water. Drain it well. Chop it fine.

Heat the milk to scalding.

Melt a third of the butter in a skillet. Add the flour and the seasonings. Mix well. Stir in the hot milk. Add the spinach. Mix again. Cover and cook over low heat for 10-15 minutes.

Beat the egg yolks briefly. Beat the whites until stiff.

Melt the rest of the butter.

Remove the spinach from the fire. Stir in the cheese, the ham, the egg yolks, and half of the melted butter. Combine thoroughly.

Fold in the egg whites carefully.

Pour into the soufflé dish. Drizzle the remaining butter over the top.

Bake at 350° for 20-25 minutes.

TOMATOES

These are love apples. There are several varieties to choose from: fresh garden tomatoes and hothouse tomatoes, canned tomatoes and tomatoes picked green and shipped to the ends of the country.

VARIOUS VEGETABLE VIGNETTES

The first choice is the best. The second can be used if one is absolutely starved for a tomato. The same goes (except for cooking and seasoning) for the third class. Green-shipped tomatoes should be avoided at all costs.

Good edible tomatoes should be firm, not overripe and not puffy.

Tomato skin is edible, but why eat it? Blister the tomatoes over fire or plunge them into boiling water: the skins slip off easily. Tomato seeds are also edible. They are often bitter. Cut the tomatoes and squeeze out the seeds or let them drain upside down. The best part of a tomato is its shell, minus seeds, core, skin, and watery pulp. Use this and enjoy a love apple at its best.

Stuffed Tomatoes

TIME: 45-50 minutes after rice is cooked

SERVES: 6

COMPOSITION

6 ripe fat tomatoes
salt
sugar
2 medium onions
3-4 fresh mint leaves
3-4 parsley sprigs

¾ cup bread crumbs
1 cup cooked rice
1 tablespoon currants
1 tablespoon pine nuts
1 cup (plus) oil
tomato juice (optional)

PREPARATION

Wash the tomatoes. Cut a hole in the top of each. Remove some of the pulp and save it. Sprinkle the hollow cores with a little salt and sugar. Turn the tomatoes upside down to drain.

Chop the onions, the mint, and the parsley.

Make bread crumbs.

Heat 1 cup of the oil. Sauté the onions. Add the tomato pulp. Cook for 2-3 minutes. Stir in the rice, the currants, the nuts, the mint, and the parsley. Moisten with tomato juice if you have some. Cook for another 2-3 minutes.

Stuff the tomatoes. Place them in a baking dish. Dribble on some additional oil and sprinkle with the bread crumbs.

Bake at 350° for 15-20 minutes.

Cool for a few minutes before serving.

Tomato-Eggplant Surprise (M-in-I)

TIME: 50 minutes   SERVES: 4-6

COMPOSITION

1 small eggplant
1 medium onion
2-3 medium tomatoes
¼ cup grated sharp cheese
1 cup bread crumbs
¼ pound butter
1 garlic clove

1 egg
¼ cup milk
½ teaspoon salt
½ cup sifted flour
½ teaspoon baking powder
½ cup chopped parsley
paprika

PREPARATION

Peel and slice the eggplant into ½-inch slices. Soak them for 15 minutes in salted water.

Chop the onion and the parsley.

Peel and slice tomatoes.

Grate cheese.

Prepare bread crumbs. Sauté them in 3 tablespoons of butter.

Sauté the onions and pressed garlic in 2 tablespoons of butter.

VARIOUS VEGETABLE VIGNETTES

Prepare a batter by combining the egg, the milk, the salt, the flour, and the baking powder.

Melt 3 tablespoons of butter. Dip the drained eggplant slices in batter and sauté each for about 3 minutes on each side.

Lay half of the slices in a 9-inch pie tin. Cover with tomato slices. Sprinkle with the onion-garlic mixture. Cover with the remaining eggplant. Top with cheese, bread crumbs, parsley, and paprika.

Bake at 350° for 20 minutes.

PRESENTATION

Serve as a main luncheon dish or as a side dish with meat.

Tomatoes Fromagées

TIME: Less than 30 minutes   SERVES: 6

COMPOSITION

6 large tomatoes
1 cup grated Gruyère cheese
freshly ground pepper
cayenne

1 teaspoon French mustard
¼ cup dry white wine
1 garlic clove
paprika

PREPARATION

Cut off the tomato tops, scoop out the center, sprinkle with salt, and invert to drain.

Grate the cheese.

In a double boiler combine the cheese, pepper, and cayenne to taste, the mustard, the wine, and the pressed garlic clove. Cook and stir until it becomes the consistency of Welsh rabbit.

Place the tomatoes tightly in a shallow baking dish. Stuff them. Sprinkle with paprika.

Bake for 10 minutes in a 350° oven. Finish under the broiler for 3-4 minutes.

Scalloped Tomatoes

TIME: 45-60 minutes   SERVES: 6

COMPOSITION

1½ cups croutons (about 3 slices bread)
2 tablespoons grated onion
1 can tomatoes (1 pound minimum)
1 chicken bouillon cube
1 tablespoon brown sugar
¼ teaspoon pepper
¼ teaspoon basil
salt
1 tablespoon butter

PREPARATION

Prepare croutons. Toast them lightly.
Grate onion.
Drain the tomatoes. Combine and heat the tomato juice, the onion, the bouillon cube, and the brown sugar.
Place 1 cup of croutons in a buttered casserole.
Add the tomatoes. Sprinkle them with pepper, basil, and salt to taste.
Add the juice.
Melt the butter. Toss in the remaining croutons. Stir briefly. Spread over the tomatoes.
Bake at 350° for about 30 minutes.

VARIOUS VEGETABLE VIGNETTES

Shrimp Stuffed Tomatoes

TIME: About 45 minutes   SERVES: 4

COMPOSITION

1 cup cooked shrimp
4 large tomatoes
1 small onion
2 tablespoons minced parsley
¼ cup soft bread crumbs
2 tablespoons grated Parmesan cheese
1 tablespoon butter
⅛ teaspoon basil
salt
pepper

PREPARATION

Clean and cook the shrimp (or use the canned variety).
Cut the stem end from the tomatoes. Remove the centers. Invert them to drain.
Grate the onion. Mince the parsley.
Prepare bread crumbs. Grate cheese.
Melt the butter. Add the onion and sauté until tender. Add the shrimp, the crumbs, the parsley, the basil, and salt and pepper to taste. Cook and stir briefly.
Place the tomatoes in a buttered shallow baking dish. Stuff them. Top with cheese.
Bake 15-20 minutes in a 350° oven.

Tomatoes with Sour Cream

TIME: 15 minutes   SERVES: 6

COMPOSITION

6 fine tomatoes
1 small green pepper
1 medium onion
2 tablespoons butter
½ pint sour cream
salt
pepper
basil

PREPARATION

Peel and halve (lengthwise) the tomatoes. Set them aside to drain upside down on a rack.

Chop the green pepper and the onion.

Melt the butter in a large skillet. Sauté the pepper and onion bits. Pile them on one side of the pan. Sauté the tomatoes, first on the cut side and then on the other. Add more butter if necessary.

Remove the tomatoes to a warm serving platter.

Stir the sour cream into the onion-pepper mixture. Season. Warm thoroughly without boiling.

Pour the sauce over the tomatoes.

TURNIPS AND PARSNIPS

These are available for men and for cattle. Those meant for human consumption, to my way of thinking, should be white, smooth, firm, and heavy for their size. The tops should be young, fresh, and green. Leave the rutabagas for cattle.

The approach to turnips is simple. Peel them. Chop or slice them. Toss them into a full pot of rapidly boiling salted water. Let them remain there for 20-30 minutes. By that time they should be tender and edible. Little is *needed* other than salt, pepper, and butter. Other things *can* be added, as the following recipes indicate.

An illegitimate cousin to turnips, often equally maligned, is the parsnip. He certainly deserves mention.

VARIOUS VEGETABLE VIGNETTES

Baked Turnips

TIME: 30 minutes   SERVES: 4

COMPOSITION

6 turnips *basil*
butter *caraway seeds*
½ cup milk *½ pint sour cream*

PREPARATION

Peel and slice (or quarter) the turnips. Dump them into a generous quantity of salted water. Boil for about 10 minutes. Discard the water. Put the turnips in a well-buttered oven-proof vegetable dish.

Add the milk. Sprinkle liberally with basil.

Bake, covered, at 350° for some 20 minutes. Stop cooking before you obtain mush.

Drain off the juice, toss in a teaspoon or so of caraway seeds, and wrap the turnips in sour cream.

PRESENTATION

Serve immediately before the cream cools.

Turnip Purée

TIME: 20-25 minutes   SERVES: 4

COMPOSITION

6 medium turnips *paprika*
butter *pepper*
sour cream

PREPARATION

Peel, then cook the turnips in boiling salt water until they are very soft.

Mash them, adding plenty of butter and sour cream.

Cover lavishly with paprika and freshly ground pepper just before serving.

Baked Parsnip Purée

TIME: 45 minutes   SERVES: 4-6

COMPOSITION

- 1 pound parsnips
- 2 tablespoons finely chopped parsley
- 2 tablespoons (or more) butter
- 1 teaspoon salt
- ¼ teaspoon pepper
- 2 eggs

PREPARATION

Peel and boil the parsnips until they are soft. Mash them thoroughly.

Add the seasonings.

Beat in the eggs, one at a time.

Place the purée in a buttered baking dish. Set the dish in a shallow pan of hot water. Deposit both in a 350° oven.

Bake for 30 minutes.

VARIOUS VEGETABLE VIGNETTES

YAMS

Yams are not true yams, which may be beside the point. They are actually a type of sweet potato having white or red skin and deep orange flesh which is oily, moist, and sweet. Sweet potatoes, so-called, have fawn-colored skin and dry, mealy, pale-yellow flesh. In cooking they are interchangeable, so take your choice. I personally prefer yams.

Buy either variety well shaped and firm. Skip over those with cracks, bruises and odd shapes. Unless you want vines, store them in a dry place. Dampness will bring on quick decay or growth.

Whenever possible, cook them in their jackets. This not only saves peeling time, the yams taste better. The sweetness remains in the potato rather than dissipating into the water. Scrub them. Toss them into boiling salted water, cover, and cook until tender. Cool, slip off the skin, and use as you wish.

One very fit way is to mash them, using copious amounts of butter, milk, salt, and pepper. An even better way is to replace the milk with orange juice, adding a tablespoon or so of chopped orange peel. The best way is to forget the milk or juice and use brandy or sherry. For textural changes, chopped nuts (pecans, walnuts, almonds, or peanuts) or crisp bacon bits may be added. Some people even use marshmallows. If none of these ideas appeal, try one of the following recipes. They are good.

Yams and Brazil Nuts

TIME: About 1½ hours using real nuts
About 1 hour using shelled nuts

SERVES: 6

COMPOSITION

1½ cups chopped Brazil nuts
6 yams or sweet potatoes
1 cup crushed pineapple
2 tablespoons butter

1 teaspoon salt
1 jigger sherry
1 egg
sour cream

PREPARATION

Chop the shelled Brazil nuts coarsely.
Boil the yams until they are soft. Peel and mash them.
Drain a small can of pineapple. (Drink the juice with a dash of vodka).
Add the butter, the salt, the pineapple, the sherry, and the egg (slightly beaten) to the yams. Whip them into a soft, light mass. Add the nuts.
Deposit the mass in a buttered baking dish.
Bake at 400° for 30 minutes.

PRESENTATION

Spread the sour cream on top.

Sherried Yams (or Sweet Potatoes)

TIME: 25 minutes
SERVES: 6

COMPOSITION

6 yams or sweet potatoes
peel of ½ orange
¼ pound butter
½ cup sherry

¼ teaspoon nutmeg
¼ teaspoon cinnamon
salt
pepper

PREPARATION

Boil the yams until soft. Peel and mash them.

Dice the orange peeling very fine.

Stir all ingredients into the mashed yams. Place in a buttered heat-proof vegetable dish.

Bake about 15 minutes in a 350° oven.

ZUCCHINI

Zucchini are tender, delicate members of the squash family. The best ones are small, under six inches, with tender skins. Mature zucchini will often be tasteless and seedy, especially if their skin is sere and wrinkled. Two pounds of any size will provide four more than adequate servings.

Zucchini cook quickly. No need to peel them; merely wash, then slice into thin rounds or strips. Steam quickly in very little salted water or sauté gently in hot oil or butter, turning once to brown both sides. For variations, add a garlic clove or a grated onion or a peeled, seeded tomato. Use only one of each to avoid overpowering the delicate squash flavor. Or sprinkle them liberally with Parmesan cheese just before serving. Dress them with salt, freshly ground pepper, and butter and enjoy a treat, summer or winter.

Zucchini Semplici

TIME: 10 minutes   SERVES: 6

COMPOSITION

3-6 zucchini (quantity depends upon size)
1-2 onions
⅛ pound butter
1 tablespoon sugar

1 teaspoon monosodium glutamate
chopped chives
pepper
oregano

PREPARATION

Slice small zucchini lengthwise.
Slice the onions horizontally.
Place the butter, the sugar, the monosodium glutamate and ½ cup of water in a skillet.
Add the zucchini and the onions.
Cover the pan tightly. Cook for 5-8 minutes.
Sprinkle with chopped chives, pepper, and oregano just before serving.

Stuffed Zucchini

TIME: 45 minutes   SERVES: 6

COMPOSITION

6 large zucchini
2 cups finely chopped cooked meat (pork or beef or both)
½ cup bread crumbs
1 medium onion

1 garlic clove
½ cup chopped parsley
2 eggs
½ cup grated Swiss cheese
2 medium tomatoes

VARIOUS VEGETABLE VIGNETTES

PREPARATION

Hollow the zucchini. Chop the onion and parsley. Press the garlic. Beat the eggs lightly.

Combine all ingredients except tomatoes and cheese. Stuff the zucchini. Sprinkle with cheese. Place in a well-buttered baking dish.

Bake at 350° for about 30 minutes.

Lay tomato slices over the zucchini and bake 10 minutes before serving.

Zucchini in Sour Cream

TIME: 10-12 minutes   SERVES: 4

COMPOSITION

4 medium zucchini
2 tablespoons butter
1-2 tablespoons sour cream
¼ cup grated Parmesan cheese

1 tablespoon paprika
salt
pepper

PREPARATION

Wash the zucchini. Grate it into slivers.

Melt the butter. Sauté the slivers for a very few minutes. It *must* be crunchy.

Add the sour cream, the cheese, and the seasonings. Serve quickly.

TOSS AND SERVE

🝆🝆🝆🝆🝆🝆🝆🝆🝆🝆🝆🝆🝆🝆🝆🝆🝆🝆🝆🝆🝆🝆🝆🝆🝆

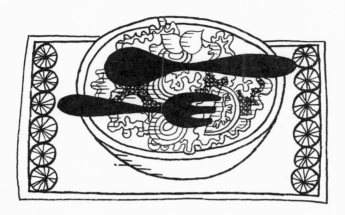

THERE ARE two salad schools. You may belong to both or either. Purists insist upon lettuce dressed with oil and vinegar. Others agree that anything goes. Whether the salad is offered as a side dish, a main course (after the entrée, of course) or as a taste-teaser, we take no sides. Our selections should keep everyone happy.

A green salad is no better than its greens. No matter how many are used—one or a combination—they should be selected with a view toward the other courses as well as each other. Lettuces (and other greens) are available sweet or bitter, sharp or delicate, tender or crunchy.

To be good, the green (or greens) should be fresh, clean and unwilted. Each leaf should be washed carefully. Each should be dried thoroughly. They should be handled gently. And they must be crisp. Wrap them in a moist towel (or plastic bag) and refrigerate until ready to use. Let them be chilled but never icy.

TOSS AND SERVE

It's the dressing that can make or break a salad. Choose one that combines (or contrasts) with the other courses of the meal. Make it fresh. Add it at the last minute (in most cases). Toss gently. Serve quickly. Savor completely and enjoy thoroughly.

DRESSINGS

French Dressing

TIME: 10 minutes   YIELD: ½ cup

COMPOSITION

2 tablespoons red wine vinegar
6 tablespoons good olive oil

¾ teaspoon salt
freshly ground black pepper
1 finely minced garlic clove

PREPARATION

Combine all ingredients.
Shake or stir to blend thoroughly.
Chill briefly before using.

Roquefort Dressing

TIME: 15 minutes plus 4-5 hours   YIELD: 2 cups

COMPOSITION

1 tablespoon minced parsley
5 ounces Roquefort cheese
1 tablespoon wine vinegar
2 teaspoons lemon juice
1 garlic clove

4-5 drops Tabasco
2 tablespoons sour cream
½ pint heavy cream
salt
pepper

PREPARATION

Chop parsley. Crush the garlic.
Crumble 2 ounces of the cheese. Set aside.
Mix the remaining cheese together with all other ingredients

TOSS AND SERVE

until well blended. Add the crumbled cheese. Mellow under refrigeration for half a day before using.

Anchovy-Caper Dressing

TIME: 1 hour preliminary
15 minutes preparation
2-3 hours chilling

YIELD: 1½ cups

COMPOSITION

½ teaspoon tarragon
¼ cup red wine
1 tablespoon chopped capers
1 tablespoon mashed anchovies
2 tablespoons minced parsley

1 tablespoon minced onion
½ garlic clove, pressed
1 cup mayonnaise
2 tablespoons cream
salt
coarse pepper

PRELIMINARY PREPARATION

Soak the tarragon in wine for 1 hour.

PREPARATION

Chop, mash, mince, and press as necessary.
Combine all ingredients.
Chill well before using.

PRESENTATION

Serve over crisp lettuce or use as a dunk.

Sour Cream Dressing

TIME: 15 minutes   YIELD: 3 cups

COMPOSITION

1½ cups sour cream
½ cup vinegar
¾ cup olive oil
2 tablespoons grated onion
2 tablespoons horse-radish

2 tablespoons chopped capers
1 teaspoon paprika
1 teaspoon salt
pepper

PREPARATION

Combine all ingredients. Mix well. Chill.

SALADS

Tomato-Pepper Salad

TIME: 45 minutes   SERVES: 6

COMPOSITION

3 *ripe tomatoes*
2 *green peppers*
1-2 *heads lettuce*
¾ *teaspoon salt*
2 *tablespoons sugar*

1 *tablespoon chopped parsley*
½ *cup minced onion*
¼ *cup olive oil*
¼ *cup red wine vinegar*

PREPARATION

Peel the tomatoes. Cut them in wedges.
Seed the peppers. Grind them or mince them very fine.
Wash the lettuce, mixing and matching the varieties you prefer. Tear it into bite-size pieces.
Prepare the dressing by combining the remaining ingredients.
Pile the lettuce in a bowl.
Arrange the tomato wedges in a circle on top of the lettuce.
Sprinkle the green peppers over the tomatoes.
Add the dressing.

PRESENTATION

This is attractive. Display it before tossing and serving.

Kidney Bean Salad

TIME: 3½ hours   SERVES: 6

COMPOSITION

2 No. 303 cans red kidney beans
1 cup chopped celery
3 green onions (scallions)
½ cup minced green pepper
¾ cup chopped sweet pickles
¼ cup olive oil
¼ cup red wine vinegar

1 garlic clove
3 drops Tabasco
½ teaspoon tarragon
½ teaspoon cardamon
½ teaspoon curry powder
½ teaspoon salt
lettuce

PREPARATION

Drain the beans. Rinse them in cold water. Drain again.

Chop and mince the celery, the onions, the green pepper and the pickles. Combine with the beans.

Prepare the dressing by combining the oil, the wine, vinegar, the crushed garlic, and the seasonings.

Marinate the bean mixture in the dressing for at least 3 hours before serving.

PRESENTATION

Serve ice cold on individual lettuce beds.

TOSS AND SERVE

Salade Nicoise (M-in-I)

TIME: 1 hour   SERVES: 4-6

COMPOSITION

1 8-ounce can tuna
1 2-ounce can anchovies
1 green pepper
¾ cup sweet red onions, sliced thin
1 cucumber
2 tomatoes
1 head romaine lettuce
2 tablespoons capers

1 teaspoon salt
½ teaspoon coarse pepper
½ cup olive oil
3 tablespoons red wine vinegar
½ teaspoon dry mustard
1 garlic clove
3 hard-cooked eggs
½ cup sliced ripe olives
basil

PREPARATION

Drain the tuna and the anchovies.

Sliver the pepper. Cut the onions and the cucumber into thin slices and the tomatoes into wedges.

Tear the lettuce into a bowl. Add the fish, the vegetables, the capers, and the salt and pepper.

Combine the oil, the vinegar, the dry mustard and the crushed garlic into a dressing. Pour over the salad and toss well. Chill briefly.

PRESENTATION

Garnish with egg slices and ripe olives. Sprinkle literally with basil.

P.S. *For a summer evening, this makes a meal that refreshes the palate as well as the eye. It calls for a luscious dessert to make a perfect supper.*

Caesar Salad

TIME: 45-60 minutes, including chilling   SERVES: 6-8

COMPOSITION

3 small heads romaine
1 2-ounce can anchovies
1 teaspoon salt
½ teaspoon dry mustard
½ teaspoon coarse black pepper
⅓ cup red wine vinegar
1 cup olive oil
2-3 garlic cloves
2 cups bread cubes
1 egg
¾ cup grated Parmesan cheese

PREPARATION

Wash, dry and chill the lettuce. Tear it into a bowl.
Add the drained and chopped anchovies, the salt, the dry mustard, the pepper, the vinegar, and ½ cup of the oil.
Toss until well coated. Chill.
Heat the rest of the oil. Sauté the minced garlic and the bread cubes until browned.
Coddle the egg for 1 minute in simmering water.
Break the egg into the salad. Toss until well distributed.
Add the cheese. Toss again.
Throw in the croutons just before serving.

TOSS AND SERVE

Champagne Potato-Shrimp Salad (M-in-I)

TIME: For preliminaries: 1¼ hours
For chilling: 12 hours
Final: 10 minutes

SERVES: 6-8

COMPOSITION

6 large potatoes
chicken stock
2 cups water
½ cup dry white wine
2 bay leaves
2 parsley sprigs
¼ teaspoon thyme
1½ teaspoons salt
½ teaspoon pepper
1 teaspoon whole cloves
1 pound small shrimp

4 eggs
2 cups ripe olives (pitted and halved)
⅔ bottle champagne
1 jigger brandy
⅓ cup olive oil
juice of 1 lemon
¼ teaspoon dry mustard
salt
pepper

PREPARATION

Cook the peeled potatoes in chicken stock to cover for 20-25 minutes. Cool and slice them paper thin.

Bring the water and the wine to a boil. Add the seasonings. Simmer for ½ hour.

Add the shrimp. Cook for 5 minutes. Shell and devein them.

Hard-cook the eggs. Slice them.

Pit and slice the olives.

Fill a large serving bowl with alternate layers of potato slices, shrimp, egg slices and olives.

Cover with champagne and give the rest to yourself. Chill overnight. Remove from the refrigerator for 1 hour before serving time. The salad should be cold but not chilled.

About 15 minutes before serving, sprinkle the salad with brandy.

Prepare the dressing by combining the remaining ingredients. Toss at the table.

PRESENTATION

Serve this with hot biscuits and cold champagne.

Artichoke and Romaine Salad

TIME: 8 hours plus 10 minutes   SERVE: 4

COMPOSITION

1 large can artichoke hearts
French dressing (1 cup)
hearts of romaine
salt
pepper

PREPARATION

Drain the artichoke hearts.

Prepare the dressing (p. 401). Let the artichokes marinate in the dressing (at room temperature) during the day.

Strip the romaine. Use only the small, beautiful inner leaves.

About ½ hour before serving time, combine the ingredients and chill.

Green Bean Salad

TIME: 4-5 hours   SERVES: 6-8

COMPOSITION

3 pounds tiny green beans
  (if not tiny, then
  "Frenched")
2 large onions
2 cups milk
1 7-ounce can pimientos
French dressing (p. 401)

TOSS AND SERVE

PREPARATION

Cook the beans in salted water until tender yet crisp. Drain. and cool.

Slice the onions as thin as paper. Marinate them in the milk for an hour. Drain. Save the milk for a sauce later.

Chop the pimientos.

Combine the ingredients gently.

Cover with French dressing.

Let stand for an hour.

Chill and serve.

Beet Salad

TIME: 15 minutes to prepare
      30 minutes to chill
SERVES: 4

COMPOSITION

4-5 beets (or 1 large can)   *pepper*
½ pint sour cream   *horse-radish*
salt   *3-4 green onions (scallions)*

PREPARATION

Cook, cool, skin and slice the beets paper thin. (Or drain the can well.)

Mince the onions.

Mix all other ingredients to taste into the sour cream.

Swathe the beets in the mixture.

Chill before serving.

Bean Sprout Salad

TIME: 45 minutes to 1 hour   SERVES: 6

COMPOSITION

1 pound fresh green bean sprouts (or 2 cans)
1 heaping tablespoon sesame seeds
1 tablespoon butter
3 green onions (scallions)
½ teaspoon sugar
1-2 tablespoons olive oil
3-4 teaspoons soy sauce
1 garlic clove
cayenne

PREPARATION

Wash the bean sprouts. Cook them in 2 cups of salted water for 2-3 minutes. Drain. (If you must use the canned variety, drain them into a sieve and wash under running cold water for a few minutes.)
Brown the sesame seeds in the butter.
Chop the onions fine. Press the garlic.
Combine all ingredients.
Mix. Chill. Serve.

Savory Cole Slaw

TIME: 1 hour to soak   SERVES: 4-6
20 minutes to prepare

COMPOSITION

2-pound cabbage
2 Bermuda onions
1 cup mayonnaise
½ cup sour cream
juice of 1 lemon
1 tablespoon sugar
1 teaspoon dry mustard
1 tablespoon horse-radish
salt
pepper

TOSS AND SERVE

PREPARATION

Shred the cabbage. Slice the onions.

Place them in layers in a large bowl. Cover with salted water and let stand for 1 hour.

Combine the remaining ingredients into a dressing, adding salt and pepper to taste.

Drain the cabbage thoroughly.

Add the dressing.

Mix and serve.

Carrot Salad

TIME: 20 minutes plus 2 days   SERVES: 4-6

COMPOSITION

1 pound tender young carrots
⅔ cup white wine vinegar
⅔ cup white wine
1 teaspoon salt
1 teaspoon sugar
½ cup olive oil

1 garlic clove
1 bay leaf
few parsley sprigs
thyme
cayenne
1 tablespoon French mustard

PREPARATION

Clean and quarter the carrots.

Toss everything except carrots and the mustard into a pot. Add ⅔ cup of water. Bring to a boil.

Add the carrots. Continue boiling rapidly until they are cooked but not overcooked, crisp but not soggy.

Blend in the mustard, working carefully and thoroughly.

Put carrots in a cool place.

Forget them for 2-3 days, until the flavors are interlaced.

Serve chilled.

Gazpacho

TIME: 3½ hours   SERVES: 6-8

Who does not know this liquid salad by now? If that man remains, he must try it. Why? First, and if for no other reason, it is good. It is also inexpensive. It is adaptable to the vagaries of the wallet and to the whims of the herb garden or the produce counter. It can, and should, vary with each man who makes it. And it *is* simple to make. Try it on one of those dehydrated mornings-after or as a complete meal-in-itself on a sagging summer day. You'll find it's here to stay.

COMPOSITION

- ¼ cup chopped chives
- ¼ cup chopped parsley
- 3 *(more or less, to taste)* garlic cloves
- 1 cup chopped green pepper
- 4 cups diced tomatoes
- ¾ cup minced onion
- ¾ cup olive oil
- 2 cups meat stock
- ½ cup lemon juice
- ½ cup fresh basil (or 1½ teaspoons dry)
- ½ teaspoon cumin
- salt
- freshly ground black pepper
- paprika
- Tabasco
- 1 cup *(plus or minus)* bread crumbs (optional)
- ½ cup chopped cucumber
- 1 cup (or more) croutons
- ice cubes

PREPARATION

Chop and mince the chives, parsley, garlic, green pepper, and tomatoes. Toss them into a blender. Blend.
Add the oil and the stock. Blend again.
Season to taste.
Let stand at room temperature for an hour.
Thicken with bread crumbs if desired.

TOSS AND SERVE

Garnish with the chopped cucumber, croutons, and several ice cubes just before serving.

PRESENTATION

Well-chilled dry white wine and French bread are necessary accompaniments.

P.S. *The Spaniards spend hours making this, but with a blender, you get the same effect in minutes.*

Leeks Vinaigrette

TIME: 20 minutes, plus overnight   SERVES: 4

COMPOSITION

2 pounds leeks
½ cup chicken stock
½ cup Vinaigrette Sauce
  (p. 22)
1 2-ounce can anchovies
2-3 pimiento slices

PREPARATION

Wash the leeks and cut off all but 1-2 inches of the green. Drain. Place in a large shallow pan and cover with chicken stock. Simmer until tender, 15-20 minutes. Drain again and let them cool.

Cover with the vinaigrette sauce and marinate overnight.

Before serving, garnish with strips of anchovy filets and pimiento slices.

Cold Potatoes

If you have some on hand, eat them as a salad. Cover them first with sour cream and chives or with cold Hollandaise (p. 19).

A cold carrot, a cauliflower, or a few peas are delicious the same way.

P.S. *And they all go well together!*

Rice Salad

TIME: ½ hour plus chilling time   SERVES: 4-6

COMPOSITION

2 cups cooked rice
10-12 water chestnuts
½ cup chopped parsley
½ cup chopped green onions (scallions)
½ cup chopped (pitted) ripe olives
½ cup chopped (pitted) green olives
⅓ cup olive oil
2 tablespoons wine vinegar
salt
pepper
basil

PREPARATION

Cook the rice according to the directions on page 374.
Drain and cool it while you work at the cutting board.
Work over the chestnuts, the herbs, the vegetables and fruits, chopping coarsely.
Combine all ingredients thoroughly with the oil and vinegar. Season.
Chill before serving.

TOSS AND SERVE

Spinach Salad

TIME: 5 minutes   SERVES: Any number

COMPOSITION

fresh spinach   French dressing or oil and vinegar

PREPARATION

Wash the spinach thoroughly.
Dry it well.
Eat it undressed, or with French dressing (p. 401), or let each person apply his own combination of oil and vinegar.

Chilled Stuffed Tomatoes

TIME: 1 hour   SERVES: 6

COMPOSITION

6 large tomatoes
½ pint sour cream
½ teaspoon fresh dill
1 teaspoon horse-radish
½ teaspoon Dijon mustard

½ teaspoon curry powder
salt
pepper
paprika

PREPARATION

Peel and quarter the tomatoes, leaving the wedges joined at the base.
Combine all other ingredients to taste, except the paprika.
Fill the tomato cavities. Top with paprika.
Chill and serve.

French Tomato Salad

TIME: 4½-12½ hours   SERVES: 6-8

COMPOSITION

6 large tomatoes
3 large sweet onions
1 cup fresh parsley
1 teaspoon oregano

salt
pepper
¾ cup olive oil
¼ cup red wine vinegar

PREPARATION

Peel and slice tomatoes and onions paper thin.
Chop parsley.
Prepare the dressing using all other ingredients.
In a large bowl alternate layers of tomatoes and onions, topping each with parsley.
Cover with the dressing.
Marinate overnight if possible, but at least 4 hours.
Toss lightly just before serving.

Tomato Babiche

TIME: 80 minutes   SERVES: 6

COMPOSITION

6 large tomatoes
salt
pepper
powdered dill
6 artichoke hearts

1 pint mayonnaise
½ pint sour cream
1 teaspoon curry powder
1 teaspoon grated onion
1 teaspoon lemon juice

TOSS AND SERVE

PREPARATION

Peel, scoop out, and drain the tomatoes.

Season them inside and out with salt, pepper, and powdered dill.

Place a cooked artichoke heart in each. Chill thoroughly.

Prepare a sauce with the remaining ingredients. Pour it over the tomatoes just before serving.

Turnip Salad

TIME: 2 hours for salting down
5 minutes for dressing
25 minutes for chilling

SERVES: 4-6

COMPOSITION

1½ pounds young tender turnips
salt
3 tablespoons olive oil
1 pint sour cream
3 tablespoons white wine vinegar

1 tablespoon sugar
juice of ½ lemon
basil
monosodium glutamate
pepper

PREPARATION

Peel the turnips. Slice them paper thin. Salt them well and forget them for 2 hours.

Combine all ingredients to make a salad dressing.

Drain the turnip slices, coat them with dressing, chill and serve.

Marinated Zucchini

TIME: 15 minutes plus 12 hours or more   SERVES: 6-8

COMPOSITION

6 zucchini
2-3 parsley sprigs
1 cup olive oil
1-2 large garlic cloves

1 tablespoon chopped basil
½ teaspoon salt
½ teaspoon pepper
1 cup red wine vinegar

PREPARATION

Chop the zucchini into chunks about ½ inch thick.

Chop parsley.

Heat the oil. Sauté the zucchini until both sides are lightly browned. Drain well.

Place the zucchini in a deep dish, in layers. Sprinkle each layer with pressed garlic, basil, parsley, salt, and pepper.

Boil the vinegar for about 5 minutes. Pour it over the zucchini.

Marinate overnight, drain, and serve. (Or keep it for a week if you prefer. It not only keeps, it improves.)

PRESENTATION

Delicious as an hors d'oeuvre. Also very good as salad, especially with spaghetti.

MORE THAN BREAD

THERE ARE many burdens for mortals to bear: nonresident taxes and resident relatives, stalled trains and traffic snarls, even warm martinis. These appear inescapable. Add to them our daily bread, and what have you got? A man with a stomach growling with dyspepsia—a dangerous citizen, that's what.

It must have been B.C.B. (Before Commercial Bread) that Conrad Aiken wrote his eulogy: "Music I heard with you was more than music. Bread I broke with you was more than bread." Today, the more is less. Bread, the institution, is now a cube of soggy sterile pap encased in cellophane. There is little support from the staff of life except for the bakers of the land.

With decidedly little respect for them (and no taste for their products), I offer three solutions to the apparently unsolvable problem.

1. Go without. Pool all the money you spend each year on what is called bread. Save it. Then

2. Move to France where bread is bread with no foolishness about it. Or

3. Bake your own. Why not? To bake is not impossible. It requires little but time, a commodity that even working people can spare. Roll up your sleeves. Bake something more than bread—good bread—the kind Grandfather didn't get around to making. Add to this bread for breakfast with many variations, biscuits and rolls, even pretzels. When you realize your potential, you may want to open a bakery.

White Bread

TIME: 3½-4 hours   YIELD: 2 loaves

COMPOSITION

1 package yeast (fresh or powdered)
1 cup lukewarm water
1½ tablespoons salt
3½ tablespoons sugar
3 tablespoons vegetable shortening

4 cups milk
10-12 cups flour
butter
patience
fortitude

PREPARATION

Dissolve the yeast in the water. Add the salt and the sugar. Stir well.

Drop the shortening into the milk and bring it to scalding temperature. Don't let it boil. Cool to lukewarm.

Combine the two mixtures in a large bowl.

Sift the flour into the bowl gradually, stirring with a wooden spoon or with your presumably lily-clean hand. Keep the flour to a minimum quantity and avoid tough bread. The dough should just stick together.

Stir, and keep stirring, until you have a smooth dough.

Time up to now: 30 minutes.

When you can no longer stir easily, remove the dough to a lightly floured surface.

Now knead. Good bread requires good kneading. It is a simple process.

Fold the dough-ball toward you. Press down and away on it with the heel of your clean and floured hand (or hands).

Turn the ball a quarter circle. Press again.

Continue until the dough is smooth and shiny. Flour the work surface (and your hands) as necessary, but sparingly. Use as little extra flour as possible.

MORE THAN BREAD

Time: about 10-12 minutes.

Form a ball. Place it in a greased bowl and cover with a towel.

Let it rise in a warm place for about 45 minutes. (The oven is a good spot—*if* it lacks a pilot light. If it seems too cold, turn the heat on and off for a second or two before putting in the dough.)

The bulk of the dough should double. Poke it. If a hole remains, it is fat enough. Get back to work.

Punch it lustily and knead again, this time for 5 minutes.

Put it back in the bowl and cover as before.

Let it rise in a ball for about 30 minutes. Punch and knead it again 3-4 times.

Mould it into loaves. Divide it into halves and shape each into an oblong. Fold the ends to the middle with a slight overlap. Pinch the ends together. Press the long sides firmly to keep the dough in shape.

Deposit the loaves in well-buttered bread pans, sealed edges down. Paint them liberally with melted butter.

Time: another 15 minutes.

Let the loaves rise for a third time until doubled in bulk: about 25 minutes or so.

Now bake, at 375°. (If the bread has been rising in the oven, allow 5 minutes for preheating.)

Forty-five to 60 minutes should turn the trick. You know what good bread should look like. Tap the top of a loaf. A hollow thump indicates doneness.

Cool the loaves out of the pan before serving.

P.S. *Remember that the kneading process is a great ulcer preventative. Take out your pet peeve on dough and the bread is that much better!*

Brown Bread
(To Be Served with Almost Anything Except Baked Beans)

TIME: About 1¼ hours   YIELD: 1 small loaf—
better make two

COMPOSITION

- 1 cup flour
- 1 teaspoon salt
- 2 teaspoons soda
- 6 tablespoons powdered buttermilk
- ½ cup brown sugar
- 2 cups graham flour
- 2 cups water

PREPARATION

Preheat your oven to 400° before doing a thing.

Butter a small bread pan lavishly.

Sift the flour, salt, soda, and powdered buttermilk together. Repeat several times.

Add the sugar, graham flour and water. This now looks and smells like dog meal. Continue: it *is* (or will be) bread.

Pour into the pan. Slide it into the oven. Immediately reduce the heat to 350°.

Bake for at least 50 minutes.

PRESENTATION

Hot, warm, or cold.

Frenchified Bread

TIME: 2½ hours   YIELD: 1-2 loaves

COMPOSITION

2 cups water
1 cake yeast (or 1 package dry yeast)
1¼ tablespoons salt
2 tablespoons sugar
7-10 cups flour
butter

PREPARATION

Assemble the ingredients, the pots, the pans, the bowls, and the energy.

Heat the water just to lukewarm. Remove the pan from the fire. Add the yeast. Dissolve it.

Add the salt and the sugar. Stir well.

Sift in the flour as you continue to stir. When a smooth ball is formed, set it aside to rise for an hour.

Poke it. If it's ready, punch it. Knead for several minutes, then form "French" loaves, either round or long and narrow. Lay the loaves on a floured baking sheet, lave them with butter, and sprinkle them with flour. Let them rise for 5 minutes.

Shove them into a cold oven. Add a pan of boiling water. Turn the heat on at 400°.

Bake the bread for about 45 minutes.

PRESENTATION

Eat immediately.

Garlic Bread

TIME: 40 minutes in all   YIELD: 1-2 loaves

This is very likely the best garlic bread you will ever eat. Help yourself. Better double the quantity, however. Once the first guest samples it, others will follow in self-defense. They may clean you out too soon.

COMPOSITION

1 pound butter
1½ cups chopped parsley
4-6 garlic cloves
a large pinch of curry powder
1-2 unsliced loaves of French bread, depending on size

PREPARATION

Soften the butter.
Chop parsley until you ache. Blend the two together.
Squeeze in the garlic. Add the curry. Combine completely.
Slice the bread very thin. Avoid cutting through the bottom crust.
Butter each slice liberally on both sides.
Place the bread in a pan.
Bake it at 275° for about 30 minutes.

Popovers

TIME: 40-50 minutes   YIELD: 6-8

COMPOSITION

3 tablespoons butter
1 cup flour
½ teaspoon salt
2 eggs, room temperature
1 cup milk, room temperature

PREPARATION

First of all, stoke the oven. To you this means preheating it to 450°.

Drop some butter into 6-8 muffin tins (or popover pans or custard cups), using 1 tablespoon. Put them in the oven to get sizzling hot while you make the batter.

Melt 2 tablespoons of butter as you see fit.

Sift the flour and the salt.

Beat the eggs thoroughly.

Add the flour to the eggs, and then add the milk. Mix and beat until you have a rich liquid about the consistency of heavy cream. Stir in the melted butter, blending thoroughly.

Retrieve the hot muffin tins from the oven. Fill each about a half full.

Bake for 5 minutes.

Turn the heat down to 350°. Bake for another 30 minutes.

Resist the temptation to peek. Popovers should be browned, crisp, crunchy, and undeflated.

Cornbread

TIME: No more than 30 minutes   SERVES: 4-6

This is cornbread for special occasions. Nothing prosaic here.

COMPOSITION

⅓ cup melted butter
½ cup sifted flour
3 teaspoons baking powder
1½ cups yellow corn meal
1 teaspoon salt

2 teaspoons sugar
3 eggs
1 cup milk
¼ cup heavy cream

Muffins

PREPARATION

Melt the butter.

Sift the flour and the baking powder together. Combine them with the corn meal, the salt, and the sugar.

Beat the eggs into the milk. Blend these into the flour-meal mixture.

Stir in the heavy cream.

Add the melted butter.

Spread the mix in a shallow buttered pan.

Bake at 400° for about 20 minutes. The bread should be crisp and well tanned.

PRESENTATION

Cut into squares and serve from the pan.

P.S. *If you want to be fancy, wrap the pan in a napkin.*

Muffins

TIME: About 25 minutes   YIELD: Depends upon your muffin tins

COMPOSITION

4 eggs	*salt*
2 cups flour	*1 pint light cream*

PREPARATION

Separate the eggs.
Beat the whites until stiff.
Sift the flour and the salt three times.
Preheat the oven to 425°.
Butter muffin tins liberally.
Beat the egg yolks lightly. Stir them into the cream.

MORE THAN BREAD

Stir in the flour until smooth.
Fold in the egg whites.
Fill the tins about two-thirds full.
Bake for 12-15 minutes.

PRESENTATION

Serve immediately.

Pretzels

TIME: 30 minutes   YIELD: Never enough

Making pretzels is not all beer and skittles, but they are less trouble than you now think. The beer helps, of course. You will find the stale packaged variety loses much in comparison with these.

COMPOSITION

2 eggs
⅛ pound butter
2 cups flour
salt

pepper
milk
coarse salt

PREPARATION

Soften the butter.
Separate the eggs.
Beat the whites until stiff.
Beat the yolks until lemony in color.
Work (with hands or a spoon) the butter and the egg yolks into the flour.
Fold in the egg whites. Season with a generous pinch of salt and freshly-ground pepper.
Roll out the dough. Slice and shape it as you desire. Sticks are simple. If you must have bowknots, have them.

Brush the pretzels with milk. Sprinkle them with coarse salt. Bake them on a cookie sheet. About 10 minutes in a 350° oven, turning once, should do them well.

PRESENTATION

Mit beer, of course.

Grapenut Bread

TIME: 1 hour 25 minutes   YIELD: 2 small loaves

COMPOSITION

1 cup grapenuts
2 cups buttermilk
1 cup sugar
1 teaspoon soda

4 teaspoons baking powder
3½ cups flour
½ teaspoon salt
1 egg

PREPARATION

Butter 2 small bread pans.
Preheat the oven to 325°.
Mix together the cereal and the buttermilk. Let the mixture stand for about 10 minutes.
Sift together the sugar, the soda, the baking powder, the flour, and the salt.
Blend the dry ingredients into the milk mixture.
Stir in the egg.
Pour the batter into the pans. Let it stand for another 10 minutes.
Bake for 55-60 minutes.

P.S. *This is something new for breakfast eating. Made the day before, there is no early-rising problem for breakfast baking.*

Cinnamon Toast

TIME: 10 minutes flat   SERVES: 4

COMPOSITION

¼ pound butter   nutmeg
1 tablespoon cinnamon   12 slices bread
4 tablespoons sugar

PREPARATION

Blend the softened butter into the cinnamon, the sugar, and a healthy grinding of fresh nutmeg.
Toast the bread—good bread—on one side only.
Spread the paste on the reverse side. Cover it completely from crust to crust.
Place under the broiler for a few minutes until the sugar is melted and caramelized.

PRESENTATION

Hot, with plenty of coffee.

P.S. *For really easy living, divide this proposition into two parts, leaving only the final broiling for just-before serving.*

Cinnamon Bread

TIME: 15 minutes   SERVES: 4-6

As your guests will tell you, this *is* cinnamon bread. Make plenty. You'll still need more.

COMPOSITION

1 cup powdered sugar
1 tablespoon (or more) cinnamon

1 loaf sliced bread
½ pound butter

PREPARATION

Mix the cinnamon and the sugar together in a brown paper bag.

If bread crusts bother you, remove them. Cut each bread slice in half.

Melt the butter in a skillet, starting with a small amount and adding more as necessary.

Sauté the bread on each side until beautifully browned.

As each slice attains perfection, drop it into the bag.

Shake well, but gently, before serving.

Coconut French Toast

TIME: 15 minutes   SERVES: 4

COMPOSITION

3 eggs
1⅓ cups milk
½ cup flour
½ teaspoon salt

½ teaspoon baking powder
¼ pound (or more) butter
8 slices bread
½ package coconut

PREPARATION

Beat the eggs with ⅓ cup of milk.

Combine, sift, and add the flour, the salt, and the baking powder.

Stir in the rest of the milk until well blended.

Melt the butter as needed in a skillet.

MORE THAN BREAD

Dip the bread, one side at a time (and one slice at a time) into the milk mix and then into the coconut.

Sauté over low heat until golden on both sides.

PRESENTATION

Serve immediately with powdered sugar, preserves, or syrup (preferably maple).

Delectable French Toast

TIME: 15 minutes SERVES: 6

COMPOSITION

4 eggs
½ cup cream
salt
juice and grated peel of 1 orange

¼ teaspoon nutmeg
12 slices bread
butter
powdered sugar

PREPARATION

Beat the eggs. Gradually add the cream, the salt, the orange juice and grated peel, and the nutmeg.

Plunge the bread slices into the mixture briefly.

Sauté them in butter until delectable.

PRESENTATION

Serve with powdered sugar.

TAMPERING WITH BISCUITS

Before you start tampering, you need a good biscuit. The do-it-yourself brand is best. There is nothing as easy to make. If you absolutely cannot spare an extra few minutes, resort to a prefab tube or a packaged mix.

If time is no object (8-10 minutes extra, that is) then don your apron. Make these, the best biscuits you can sink your teeth into, and at the same time bolster your own self-esteem. (This in itself should be worth the little time required.) The first time you'll eat them as are. Once sated, proceed with one or more of the tampered variety.

Basic Baking Powder Biscuits

TIME: About 20 minutes   YIELD: 14-16

COMPOSITION

¼ pound butter
2 cups flour
¾ teaspoon salt
4 teaspoons baking powder

4 tablespoons vegetable shortening
⅔ to ¾ cup milk

PREPARATION

Preheat the oven at 475°.
Melt half of the butter.
Sift the flour, the salt, and the baking powder.
With two knives (or a pastry blender), cut the rest of the butter and the shortening into the flour. Work until you obtain pea-size bits.

MORE THAN BREAD

Stir in the milk by degrees. Stop adding before mixture becomes a paste.

Knead a bit if you feel the urge, or merely press the dough into a ½-inch thick sheet.

Cut into shapes which please you (circles seem to be most acceptable, but don't feel hampered).

Dip each into melted butter.

Pack side by side on a floured baking sheet.

Bake for 5 minutes at 475°, then 7-8 minutes at 450°.

PRESENTATION

Hot. With plenty of butter.

Butterscotch Rolls

TIME: 25 minutes   YIELD: 14-16

COMPOSITION

basic dough   *¾ cup brown sugar*
⅛ pound butter

PREPARATION

Make the dough.
Pat it into a sheet.
Spread the surface with the softened butter mixed with the brown sugar.
Roll into a cylinder.
Slice into ½-inch thick rounds.
Bake.

Cheese Biscuits

TIME: 25 minutes   YIELD: 14-16

COMPOSITION

basic dough
1 cup grated sharp cheese

cayenne, curry powder
dry mustard

PREPARATION

Prepare the dough.
Add the cheese and the seasonings.
Cut and bake.

Herb Biscuits

TIME: 25 minutes   YIELD: 14-16

COMPOSITION

basic dough
chopped parsley

additional herbs to taste

PREPARATION

Mix well-chopped parsley into the dough.
Add almost anything else in the herb line. Experiment cautiously until you ascertain your personal preference.
Bake.

MORE THAN BREAD

wwwwwwwwwwwwwwwwwwwwwwwwwwwwwwwwwwwwwwwwwwwwwwwwww

Jam Biscuits

TIME: 20 minutes   YIELD: 14-16

COMPOSITION

basic dough   *marmalade, jam, or jelly*

PREPARATION

Pay your money and take your choice. Again, it's up to you. Simply put a gob of whatever marmalade or jelly or jam you have or prefer on top of each biscuit before baking.

Onion Cakes

TIME: 25 minutes   YIELD: 14-16

COMPOSITION

1 onion   *basic dough*
coarse pepper   *coarse salt*
1 egg

PREPARATION

Chop the onion very fine.

Add it, together with a heavy dash of coarse pepper and the well beaten egg, to the dough.

Sprinkle each buiscuit top with salt (the coarser the better) before baking.

Sausage Rolls

TIME: 30 minutes   YIELD: 12

COMPOSITION

12 small sausages   basic dough
white wine

PREPARATION

Simmer the sausages in white wine for about 10 minutes.
    Drain off the wine. Let the sausages brown.
Roll the biscuit dough about ¼ inch thick. Cut it into strips.
Encase each sausage in dough.
Bake like basic biscuits.

Individual Shortcakes

TIME: About 20 minutes   YIELD: 6-8-10

COMPOSITION

½ pound butter   6 tablespoons sugar
2 cups flour   4 tablespoons vegetable short-
¾ teaspoon salt   ening
4 teaspoons baking powder   ⅔ to ¾ cup cream

PREPARATION

Prepare the dough.
Flatten it.
Cut it into rounds in two sizes.
Bake it in pairs, the larger round on the bottom, separated from
    its smaller mate by a healthy smear of butter.
When done, separate each duo with a spatula.

MORE THAN BREAD

Continue on your way with any fruit or berry in or out of season.

Sour-Dough Starter

TIME: 3-4 days   YIELD: Never ending

Please take note: this is the starter and not the bread. As you use it, add a similar batch of flour, sugar, salt, and water to the remainder. You will never then be without one of the best breads you have ever tasted.

COMPOSITION

2½ cups water
1 cake (or enveloped) yeast
2 cups flour

2 tablespoons sugar
1 tablespoon salt

PREPARATION

Arm yourself with a crock, pottery variety with cover.
Prepare for a ferment.
Heat the water to just lukewarm.
Dissolve the yeast in ½ cup of the water.
Sift the flour, the salt, and the sugar.
In the crock, mix the yeast and the flour. Add the remaining warm water. Blend well.
Cover the crock. Store it in a warm place (80°) for 3 days. Stir once each day for as long as you keep it on hand. Replace with a proportionate amount of flour, sugar, salt and water each time the *starter* is used.

Sour-Dough Bread

(Assuming that you have read the previous page)

TIME: 4 hours over all
30-35 minutes actual working time
YIELD: 1 honest loaf

COMPOSITION

½ cup milk
2 tablespoons butter
2 tablespoons sugar
1 cup sour-dough starter
3½ cups sifted flour

PREPARATION

Get over your prejudice against the time-consuming part of breadmaking.

Scald the milk with the butter and the sugar. Stir well. Let cool to lukewarm.

Place the sour-dough starter in a large bowl. Add the milk mixture. Stir in the flour.

Turn onto a floured work surface and knead briefly.

Place the dough in a bowl. Cover it with a towel. Let it rise until the bulk is doubled (about 1½ hours).

Punch it down, replace it in the bowl, and let it rise again for about 45 minutes.

Shape it into a round loaf, turning in the sides and ends. Seal the edges and place it, edges down, on a lightly buttered baking sheet.

Let it rest for another 45 minutes covered with the towel. Brush the top once or twice with cold water.

Bake in a preheated 400° oven for 45-50 minutes.

Pastel de Elote
(Mexican Corn Pie)

TIME: 1½ hours SERVES: 6-8

COMPOSITION

½ pound butter
1 4-ounce can chili peppers
1½ cups grated sharp cheese
1 cup flour
1 cup yellow corn meal
4 teaspoons baking powder

1 cup sugar
4 eggs
1 16-ounce can cream-style corn
¼ teaspoon salt

PREPARATION

Soften the butter.
Chop chili peppers.
Grate cheese.
Sift together the flour, the corn meal, and the baking powder.
Preheat the oven to 300°.
Butter and flour an 8-x-12-inch baking dish.
Cream together the butter and the sugar.
Add the eggs, one at a time. Beat well after each addition.
Mix in the chopped chili peppers and the undrained corn.
Blend in the flour mixture. Season.
Pour into the baking dish. Bake for 1 hour.

PRESENTATION

Prepare this in advance and reheat it. Serve it in place of potatoes, especially with char-broiled meat.

Operation Croissant

TIME: First stage: 1½ hours
Second stage: 2-3 hours or overnight
Third stage: 2½ hours
Fourth stage: 25 minutes to bake
Final stage: 2-3 bites each to eat

YIELD: Never enough, but approximately 18

When you're full of culinary confidence, do this. A man who makes a flaky *croissant* is a man indeed.

COMPOSITION

4 cups plus 1 tablespoon milk
1 cake (or envelope) yeast
4 cups all-purpose flour
¾ pound butter
½ teaspoon salt
1 tablespoon sugar
1 egg

PREPARATION

Heat ½ cup of the milk just to lukewarm. Pour into mixing bowl. Add the yeast and let it dissolve.

Add 1 cup of sifted flour. Stir to form a smooth ball of sponge. Let the sponge rise until double in bulk. (You have about 30 minutes, but don't go away. There is work to do.)

With your hands, knead the butter into a flat rectangle. This done, you may stop for a cigarette.

Sift the remaining flour, the salt, and the sugar into a large bowl. Slowly add 3½ cups of milk. Stir until smooth.

Combine with the sponge, beat well, and let the dough rest in a warm spot for 10-15 minutes. Meanwhile, if you think along my lines, have a drink. There is still work to do.

Sprinkle flour lightly on a work surface or board.

Get out your favorite rolling pin. Roll the dough into a ½-inch-thick rectangle.

MORE THAN BREAD

Lay the butter fairly in the center of the rectangle. Fold all but one end of the dough-sheet over the butter, making three layers.

Turn the slab so an open end faces you. Roll it out with a light but firm stroke taking care not to roll over the ends far edge (stopping about ½ inch from the end). Fold it into three layers again. (If this seems repetitive, it is. It is also more than worth all the effort.)

Turn and roll the dough once more. Set it aside for 2-3 hours. Better yet, refrigerate it overnight. Forget it. You've earned a rest.

Your energy restored, repeat the folding-turning-rolling operation two more times.

Chill the dough for an hour.

Now comes the countdown.

Roll the dough into a ⅛-inch-rectangle. Cut it up into triangles about 6-8 inches on each side. Roll each triangle toward the tip, making a cylinder. Bend each cylinder into a curve.

Place the crescents on a floured baking sheet and let them rise for 30-45 minutes. (Now is the time to start the fires: preheat the oven to 400°).

Paint the surface of each with beaten egg mixed with a tablespoon of milk.

Bake for 5 minutes at 400°, then for 15-20 minutes at 350°.

PRESENTATION

Serve with utmost pride.

Quick Coffee Cake

TIME: 35-40 minutes SERVES: 4-6

COMPOSITION

TOPPING	CAKE
2 tablespoons butter	1½ cups flour
¼ cup brown sugar	3 tablespoons baking powder
1 tablespoon flour	¾ teaspoon salt
1 teaspoon cinnamon	6 tablespoons butter
	¾ cup sugar
	1 egg
	1½ cups milk

PREPARATION

Melt the topping butter. Mix it together with the other ingredients. Set aside.

Set the oven at 400°.

Sift the flour. Measure it. Resift it with the salt and the baking powder.

Butter a 9-inch-square baking pan.

Blend 6 tablespoons of butter into the sugar.

Beat the egg into the milk.

Combine the two mixtures and stir into the flour. This should be a thick dough.

Pat the dough into the pan. Brush it with a little melted butter.

Spread the crumbly topping over the top.

Bake for 25 minutes.

Filled Coffee Cake

TIME: 40-50 minutes   SERVES: 4-6

COMPOSITION

| FILLING | COFFEE CAKE DOUGH *(p. 000)* |

½ cup brown sugar
2 teaspoons cinnamon
2 tablespoons flour
2 tablespoons butter
¾ cup chopped nuts

PREPARATION

Stir the ingredients until crumbly.
Prepare the dough. Divide it into two parts.
Spread half of it in a buttered 9-inch-square baking pan.
Add about two-thirds of the filling.
Pat (or roll out) the remaining dough. Lay it over the filling.
Top with the rest of the filling (now renamed topping).
Bake for 35-40 minutes at 375°.

Utopian Pancakes

TIME: 20 minutes   SERVES: 4-6

COMPOSITION

4 eggs   ¼ teaspoon salt
¾ cup flour   ½ pint sour cream
1 tablespoon sugar   ½ pint cottage cheese

PREPARATION

Separate the eggs. Beat the yolks until lemony. Whip the whites
    until stiff and shiny.

Utopian Pancakes

Sift the flour. Measure it. Resift with the sugar and the salt.
Blend (by hand or blender) the sour cream and the cheese until creamy.
Stir in the flour. Add the yolks. Beat until smooth.
Fold in the whites.
Cook quickly on a hot greased griddle.

PRESENTATION

Serve with a sweetening of your choice: syrup (maple or otherwise), honey, marmalade, sour cream, maple sugar, fresh fruit, or a dessert sauce.

GOURMET GOLD: CHEESE

AGE cannot wither nor custom stale the delights of cheese. Civilized taste buds belonging to men of the world esteem them highly. To satisfy said buds there are over a hundred and fifty varieties of cheese. What other single food can appear in so many guises on the dinner table? Indeed, what other food can boast a patron saint?

> "Saynt Whyte muste have a
> chese once in a yere and
> that of the greatest sorte:
> it shall be given unto the
> poore in hyr name saye they."
> —WILLIAM TYNDALE
> fifteenth century

In exploring cheese there are two infallible instruments —the palate and the nose. These two trusty servants can tell

GOURMET GOLD: CHEESE

you all you need to know about—where to start and when to stop. Choosing a cheese is a solemn matter. At the outset polish your taste and sensitize your nose on the underripe varieties. Work up very gradually to the ultimate refinements of the fully mature and stronger cheeses. The delectation of such cheese is based on experiment and experience.

Good cheese is best experienced when eaten at room temperature, *au naturel.* Serve it on a board with French bread —seldom crackers. Accompany it with a crisp apple, a pear, or some perfect grapes. Supply copious quantities of wine— white or red—with which to savor the cheese. This is the perfect ending to a meal—perfect for rich and poor. As a matter of fact, it is a superb meal in itself.

As a general rule, cheese to be eaten in this manner should be *bien fait*—well aged, sometimes runny, often noisome. Cheese for cooking should be very tasty and rather dry. The rewards of cooking with cheese are very great in respect to the little amount of work involved. To this you will attest when you use the following recipes ranging from cocktail-time edibles through main dishes and on through desserts.

Cheese Puffballs

TIME: 15-20 minutes   SERVES: 4, with drinks

COMPOSITION

lots of fat or oil in a deep pot
2 eggs
2 tablespoons flour
1 cup milk

1 cup grated sharp cheese
salt
cayenne

PREPARATION

Let the fat or oil be heating to 375° (If you lack a thermometer, test with a bread cube. The oil is ready for use when it crisps the bread in about 30 seconds.)

Separate eggs. Beat the whites until very stiff.

Mix together the flour, the egg yolks, the milk, and the grated cheese. Blend them into a smooth paste. Season with salt and cayenne.

Fold in the egg whites.

Form balls, or drop spoonsful into the fat.

Fry quickly, drain quickly, and serve quickly.

Cheese Dabs

TIME: About 25 minutes   SERVES: 4

COMPOSITION

1 cup grated sharp cheese
¼ pound butter
1 small garlic clove
½ teaspoon grated onion
2 cups flour

½ cup sherry
½ teaspoon salt
½ teaspoon paprika
½ teaspoon Worcestershire sauce

GOURMET GOLD: CHEESE

PREPARATION

Preheat the oven to 450°.

Grate cheese. Combine with the softened butter.

Add the pressed garlic and the grated onion. Mix.

Work everything together in a large mixing bowl, using your hands.

Make balls of dough about 1 inch in diameter. Place them on an ungreased baking sheet. Squash them with a fork.

Bake for about 10 minutes.

Cheese Rounds

TIME: Less than an hour   SERVES: 4-6

COMPOSITION

½ pound sharp cheese
1 cup flour
¼ pound soft butter

½ teaspoon salt
paprika

PREPARATION

Grate the cheese.

Combine all ingredients.

Form marbles. Place them on a baking sheet. Flatten them with a fork.

Chill for at least 30 minutes.

Bake at 450° for 8-10 minutes.

Welsh Rabbit for Four (M-in-I)

TIME: About 20 minutes

SERVES: 4—only because it is unwise to prepare it in larger quantities. Don't be surprised if this is sufficient for 2 only

COMPOSITION

1 pound sharp cheese
1 egg
1 teaspoon dry mustard
2 teaspoons Worcestershire sauce
butter
1 wedge Bleu cheese
1 12-ounce can beer or ale

PREPARATION

Grate the sharp cheese into a large measuring cup. Pack it loosely. Measure it.

Start water to heat in the base of a double boiler or chafing dish.

Beat together the egg, the dry mustard, and the Worcestershire.

Melt butter in the top of the double boiler, using ¼ pound of butter to 1 cup of cheese.

Add the cheeses. Stir until they melt and become well blended with the butter.

Add the beer, slowly. Blend it in thoroughly.

Add the egg mixture, again slowly.

Don't let the rabbit get too hot.

Don't stop stirring constantly.

Don't let the boiler-water boil.

PRESENTATION

Don't fail to eat immediately. Have a tossed salad or Leeks Vinaigrette (p. 414) waiting and ready.

GOURMET GOLD: CHEESE

Cheese Fondue
(M-in-I)

There must be as many recipes for cheese fondue as there are lovers of cheese. Here are some variations. I refuse categorically to vouch for the origin of any of them. Each is good. Each is dependent upon the available cheese and your liquor supply. Once cooked, eat at once by dipping hunks of French bread in the pan. Fondue gets increasingly good as the bottom of the pot (or the chafing dish) appears. Cool fruit is the perfect sequitur to this dish.

I

TIME: About 20 minutes   SERVES: 4

COMPOSITION

½ *pound Gruyère*	6 *eggs*
1 *garlic clove*	*salt*
½ *cup dry white wine*	*pepper*
⅛ *pound butter*	*French bread in quantity*

PREPARATION

Grate the cheese.

Press the garlic into the wine. Cook over a high heat until the wine is reduced by half. Set it aside to cool.

Melt the butter. Beat it together with the cheese and the eggs. Season with salt and pepper. Pour into a sturdy pot and stir in the reduced wine.

Cook over a very low flame until a creamy, scrambled-egg-looking mass is obtained.

Cheese Fondue II

TIME: 20 minutes   SERVES: 4

COMPOSITION

1 garlic clove
½ bottle white wine
1 pound Swiss cheese
1¼ teaspoons flour

nutmeg
salt
pepper
1 jigger brandy
bread

PREPARATION

Squeeze the garlic into the wine. Bring it to a boil.
Stir in the cubed or grated cheese. Bring to a boil again, stirring constantly.
Make a thin paste of flour and water. Stir it into the cheese.
Season to taste with nutmeg, salt, and pepper.
Add the brandy just before serving.

Cheese Fondue III

TIME: 15-20 minutes   SERVES: 4

COMPOSITION

1 garlic clove
1½ cups Chablis wine
1 teaspoon Dijon mustard
½ teaspoon salt
¼ teaspoon pepper

1 pound Gruyère
1 teaspoon cornstarch
½ teaspoon soda
⅛ cup kirsch

PREPARATION

Rub a chafing dish with the garlic.
Add the wine, the mustard, the salt and the pepper. Bring them to a boil.

GOURMET GOLD: CHEESE

Stir in the grated cheese. Stir steadily until the fondue is smooth and bubbling. Keep the flame low.

Mix together the cornstarch and the soda with the kirsch. Add it slowly. *Voilà!*

Cheese Soufflé

TIME: 35 minutes, beginning to end   SERVES: 4

COMPOSITION

½ pound sharp cheese   ⅛ pound butter
2 cups sifted flour   5 eggs
2 cups milk

PREPARATION

Grate the cheese.
Sift the flour. Measure it.
Heat the milk in a double boiler.
Preheat the oven to 350°.
Stir the flour into the simmering milk. Use care. Add the butter. Let it melt.
Continue cooking and stirring until the paste leaves the sides of the pan. Remove the pan from the fire and let it cool.
Separate the eggs. Beat in the egg yolks, one at a time.
Stir in the cheese.
Beat the egg whites until stiff. Fold them into the batter.
Pour the mixture into a well-buttered soufflé dish.
Bake for about 20 minutes.

PRESENTATION

Be prepared to eat immediately.

P.S. *This is a new system for making a soufflé. It's easy and it works!*

Cottage Cheese Soufflé

TIME: 1 hour   SERVES: 4-6

COMPOSITION

2 pounds cottage cheese
½ cup grated Parmesan cheese
6 eggs
nutmeg
1 tablespoon cream
2 heaping tablespoons flour

PREPARATION

Whip the cottage cheese until it is smooth.

Grate the Parmesan cheese.

Separate the eggs, dropping the yolks into individual cups. Whip the whites in a community bowl.

Beat the egg yolks into the cottage cheese one at a time.

Add the nutmeg (a stiff pinch), the cream, the Parmesan cheese, and the flour.

Fold in the whites.

Turn the mixture into a soufflé dish. Bake 30-40 minutes at 350°.

P.S. *A blender does a splendid job of smoothing cottage cheese.*

Croustade Jurasienne
(M-in-I)

TIME: 10 minutes to get up steam
and to make the dough
2 hours to relax
15 minutes to organize
30 minutes to bake

SERVES: 4-6

COMPOSITION

1½ cups sifted flour	1¼ cups diced ham
¼ pound butter	1½ cups grated Gruyère
1 egg yolk	2 cups cream
salt	4 eggs
water	salt
2-3 parsley sprigs	pepper

PREPARATION

Combine the flour, the softened butter, the egg yolk, a pinch of salt, and enough water to hold them together.

Mince the parsley. Add it.

Form a ball. Let it chill for 2 hours.

Roll out a thick crust and line a deep 10-inch pie tin.

Dice the ham.

Grate the cheese. Mix them together and spread in the pastry shell.

Beat together the cream, the eggs and the seasonings. Pour over the ham-cheese base.

Bake at 375° until golden. Insert a knife. If it comes out clean, the *croustade* is ripe and ready to eat.

PRESENTATION

Toss a salad and you have your meal.

Quiche Lorraine
(M-in-I)

TIME: 50 minutes   SERVES: 4-6

COMPOSITION

pastry for a 9-inch pie
6 bacon slices
12 slices Swiss cheese
2 tablespoons butter
4 eggs

1 tablespoons flour
½ teaspoon salt
cayenne
nutmeg
2 cups cream

PREPARATION

Line the pie tin with pastry. (Please see pages 516–518 before running out to purchase a prefab crust mix.)

Broil and drain the bacon. Overlap slices of bacon and cheese in the pie tin.

Melt the butter.

Preheat the oven to 400°.

Beat the eggs. Blend in the flour, the salt, and a dash each of cayenne and nutmeg. Stir in the cream and the butter.

Pour the custard into the pie shell.

Bake at 400° for 8-10 minutes. Reduce the heat to 350°. Continue baking for about 30 minutes or until the custard is firm and the top well tanned.

P.S. *Very filling. This just needs something cool and crisp to level off a meal.*

GOURMET GOLD: CHEESE

Macaroni and Ricotta Cheese

TIME: 30-40 minutes   SERVES: 4-6

This, in my opinion, is much better than the standard recipe you were probably expecting. Try it and come to your own conclusions.

COMPOSITION

½ cup grated Parmesan cheese
1 pound macaroni
⅛ pound (or more) butter
1 pound ricotta

½ cup milk
1-2 tablespoons sugar
1 teaspoon cinnamon

PREPARATION

Grate the cheese.
Cook the macaroni until tender in rapidly boiling salted water. Drain it. Toss it back into the pot.
Add the butter.
Mix the ricotta with the milk until it is smooth. Season with the sugar and the cinnamon. Stir into the macaroni.
Cover and cook for about 3 minutes.
Sprinkle each serving with Parmesan.

P.S. *Ricotta, similar to cottage cheese, is available in many supermarkets and all Italian food stores.*

Toasted Cheese Sandwiches

TIME: 15-20 minutes   SERVES: 3

For those who dislike the soggy and sodden toasted cheese sandwiches available at any corner drugstore.

COMPOSITION

1 cup grated sharp cheese   *salt*
1 egg   *pepper*
cream   *2 bacon slices*
Worcestershire sauce   *6 bread slices*
cayenne

PREPARATION

Grate the cheese.

Add the beaten egg and enough cream to make a spreadable mixture. Season it to taste.

Dice the bacon.

Trim the bread and toast it on one side only. Spread the cheese paste on the untoasted side. Sprinkle with the diced bacon.

Place under the broiler until the cheese is bubbly and the bacon is crisp.

PRESENTATION

Each person receives 2 open-face sandwiches, of course.

Dessert Cheese I

TIME: 20-30 minutes, plus time to chill   SERVES: 4-6

COMPOSITION

¾ pound Camembert   *¼ pound butter*
¼ pound Roquefort   *½ pint heavy cream*

GOURMET GOLD: CHEESE

PREPARATION

Combine all ingredients in the top of a double boiler. Cook and stir until hot and well blended.
Cool.
Beat until creamy.
Chill before using.

PRESENTATION

Serve with fresh fruit and (in this case only) crisp crackers.

Dessert Cheese II

TIME: 5-6 minutes other than time to chill well   SERVES: 4-6

COMPOSITION

1 pound dry cottage cheese or *ricotta*
½ cup heavy cream
3 tablespoons sugar

3-4 tablespoons rum, brandy, or *bourbon*
semisweet chocolate
nutmeg

PREPARATION

Beat the cheese until it is curdless and creamy.
Blend in the cream, the sugar, and the booze.
Taste. Add more of each if you like.
Put into a dessert bowl. Top with grated chocolate and nutmeg.
Chill before serving.

P.S. *This takes a matter of seconds if you have a blender.*

DESSERTS THAT DESERVE ATTENTION

DESSERTS of one kind or another enter into almost every man's gastronomical scheme of life. Their purpose is to crown with contentment the beatific mood that follows a good and satisfying meal.

Some people are made happy, and rightly so, with fruit and cheese. Others feel that to-end-with-a-sweet is indispensable. There are even those who want all three. With no attempt to lay down a gastronomical law, I simply recommend that the dessert keep balance with the rest of the meal. Something refreshing and light should follow a heavy, hearty first and second (and possibly third) course. If you have limited the menu to a comparatively light choice of foods, there should be no bars held on a rich and fullsome dessert. Most desserts fall into categories—ice cream, pies, cakes, or fruit-based— but there are a few that don't fit into any particular slot, and

DESSERTS THAT DESERVE ATTENTION

those you find at the end under Sweet Endings. Don't make up your mind until you have leafed through all the pages that follow.

I would never advise anyone getting into a swivet over dessert. It just isn't necessary. For those pressed for time, there is always the baker or the grocery shelf. Neither, however, can provide anything comparable to a comely creation concocted at home. There is no greater complement to guests than such an effort.

All food, and especially desserts, should be made to be seen as well as eaten. This does not imply long hours with a pastry tube turning out patchwork valentines, as you will observe in the following pages, where you will find an entire gamut of desserts, including some ideas, I think, neither you or anyone else ever thought of before.

FRUITS, THE ESSENCE OF ELEGANCE

The best fruit is ripe fruit. In season. If this sounds elementary, it is. I mention it as a reminder. It may seem impressive to serve beautiful hothouse or out-of-season fruit, but the taste seldom if ever lives up to the appearance. If it is looks you're after, invest in wax fruit; serve something else for dessert. Nothing can make up for the shortcomings of fruit picked too green and shipped too far, or for middle-aged fruit which has lingered long on the market shelf. Fruit must be treated with the respect it deserves.

There is nothing more elegant than fresh fruit, particularly served with one of the special fruit sauces (beginning page 493). In its natural state and with an appropriate cheese, it is a perfect ending for a meal. Nothing provides a better antidote for too much food.

There may be little need to advise anyone on what to do with fruit besides eating them in their natural fresh state, but I hereby do so. If any eyebrows are arched at these efforts to improve on the efforts of nature, they will be raised in delight.

DESSERTS THAT DESERVE ATTENTION

Baked Apples

TIME: 50 minutes   SERVES: 6

COMPOSITION

6 firm apples
1 cup mincemeat or 1 cup chopped raisins and chopped nuts
½ cup brown sugar
1½ cups white wine
1 tablespoon white sugar
1 jigger rum

PREPARATION

Peel and core the apples. Fill the hollow centers with mincemeat.

Fit the apples into a buttered flame-proof dish so they remain upright. Sprinkle with the brown sugar. Add 1 cup of the wine.

Bake, covered, at 350° for 40 minutes.

Remove the apples to a serving dish. Toss any leftover mincemeat into the baking dish. Add the rest of the wine. Cook over a high flame for about 5 minutes to reduce the sauce.

Pour the sauce around and over the apples.

Sprinkle them with sugar.

Warm the rum. Pour it over the apples.

Light a fire and serve.

Stuffed Apples

TIME: 25-30 minutes   SERVES: 6

COMPOSITION

6 firm apples
juice and grated rind of 1 lemon
1 cup sugar
¼ cup sherry
½ cup strawberry preserves
½ cup chopped dates
½ cup chopped nuts

PREPARATION

Pare and core the apples. Sprinkle them with lemon juice.

Mix together the sugar, the sherry, ½ cup of water, the strawberry jam and the grated lemon rind. Heat the mixture until it is liquid.

Poach the apples in the sherry mixture for 10-12 minutes, turning once. Remove them to a serving platter when tender but not mushy.

Chop and mix the nuts and dates. Stuff the apples.

Cook down the poaching liquid to about half its original quantity. Pour it over the apples.

PRESENTATION

Serve with a minimum of modesty. Eat hot or cold.

P.S. *This is when looks and flavor compete for top honors.*

Applejack Crisp

TIME: 50 minutes   SERVES: 4-6

COMPOSITION

3 pounds tart apples (around 1 dozen)
½ pound butter
3 jiggers apple jack or brandy
1¼ cups sugar
juice of ½ lemon
1 cup flour
½ cup brown sugar

PREPARATION

Peel, core, and chop the apples. Turn them into a well-buttered heat-proof serving dish.

Melt ¼ pound of the butter. Into it stir 2 jiggers of the applejack, the sugar, and the lemon juice. Mix with the apples.

Combine ¼ pound of softened butter with the flour and the

DESSERTS THAT DESERVE ATTENTION

brown sugar until crumbly. Spread over the apples. Press it down lightly.

Bake, uncovered, at 350° for about ½ hour.

PRESENTATION

Just to be sure, add another jigger of applejack or brandy before serving.

P.S. *This needs no embellishment, but cold heavy cream, vanilla ice cream, or Donn's Dessert Sauce (p. 23) are good, just for variety.*

Apple Thing

TIME: 50 minutes to make and bake
About 25 minutes to cool

SERVES: 8-10

COMPOSITION

- 12 tart apples
- ½ cup brown sugar
- 1 cup sugar
- 1 tablespoon whole cloves
- 1 teaspoon nutmeg
- 1 cup rum
- 1 cup graham-cracker crumbs
- ¼ pound butter
- 6 egg whites
- 1 pint heavy cream
- 1 cup chopped nuts
- ½ cup brandy

PREPARATION

Peel and core the apples. (If you are a blender-owner, skip the peeling process.)

Cover them with water. Add the brown sugar, ½ cup of the white sugar, the spices, and the rum. Cook until they are very soft. Obtain a smooth purée by forcing them through a sieve, a food mill, a potato-ricer, or your blender.

Meanwhile, melt the butter.

Crush the crackers. Mix the crumbs with the butter and ½ cup of sugar.

Butter a deep casserole liberally. Press the crumbs on the bottom and sides, saving some for later use.

Beat the egg whites until frothy.

Whip the cream. Fold half of the whipped cream into the egg whites.

Place half of the apple purée into the casserole.

Place half of the egg white-and-cream mixture on top of the purée.

Place half of the nuts on top of the egg whites.

Sprinkle with half of the brandy.

Repeat the layers. Top with the reserved cracker crumbs.

Bake at 325° for about 25 minutes.

Cool.

PRESENTATION

Get out that unused whipped cream. Sweeten it with sugar and a dash of brandy. Use it to crown the thing.

P.S. *Plan this with a meal that calls for a Béarnaise or Hollandaise. This is a practical and delicious solution to the egg-white problem.*

Alchemy for Canned Applesauce

TIME: 7-10 minutes   SERVES: 2-4

COMPOSITION

- 1-pound can of applesauce
- ½ cup brown sugar
- ¼ cup chopped candied (or fresh) orange peel
- ½ cup chopped nuts
- ¾ cup bread crumbs
- 2 tablespoons butter
- 1 jigger brandy, rum, or applejack
- sour cream

DESSERTS THAT DESERVE ATTENTION

PREPARATION

Mix the component parts, excluding the sour cream.
Heat until thoroughly warmed.
Ladle into individual bowls.

PRESENTATION

Top with a dollop of sour cream.

Apricot Soufflé

TIME: 1½ hours   SERVES: 4-6

COMPOSITION

1 pound dried apricots
½ cup nutmeats
1 tablespoon grated lemon rind
5 egg whites
¼ teaspoon cream of tartar
½ cup sugar
⅛ teaspoon salt

PREPARATION

Stew the apricots until soft. Force them through a sieve or a food mill, or purée in a blender.
Chop nuts.
Grate lemon rind.
Whip the eggs until stiff but moist. Beat in the cream of tartar, the sugar, and the salt.
Add the nuts and the lemon peel to the plup.
Fold the egg whites into the pulp.
Pour the mixture into a soufflé dish. Place the dish in a water bath.
Bake in a 275° oven for 1 hour.

PRESENTATION

Serve while hot and fluffy.

Avocado Sherbet

Avocado Sherbet

TIME: Minutes to prepare 1-2 hours to freeze   SERVES: 6-8

COMPOSITION

2 cups buttermilk
¼ cup lemon juice
¼ cup orange juice
¼ cup pineapple juice

¾ cup sugar
½ cup light corn syrup
1 cup mashed avocado

PREPARATION

Mix together the buttermilk, the juices, the sugar, and the corn syrup. When well blended, taste. Add more sugar if necessary.

Pour the amalgamation into a refrigerator tray.

Freeze until it is mushy.

Meanwhile, chill a large mixing bowl.

Peel and mash the avocado.

Empty the partially frozen mush into the bowl. Beat it smooth. Add the avocado. Beat again. Return the mush (now called avocado mush) to the tray.

Freeze until firm.

Banana Flambé

TIME: 15 minutes   SERVES: 6

COMPOSITION

6 ripe bananas
¼ pound butter
½ cup brown sugar

1 cup rum
about ⅔ cup granulated sugar
brandy

DESSERTS THAT DESERVE ATTENTION

PREPARATION

Peel, but do not slice, the bananas.

Melt the butter in a wide, shallow pan (or be dramatic and use a chafing dish).

Add the bananas. Sprinkle them with the brown sugar.

Pour in the rum. Let the bananas simmer for 8 to 10 minutes, basting occasionally. When cooked (with some "bite" left to them, sprinkle with white sugar.

PRESENTATION

Remove the bananas to the serving dish, cover with warmed brandy.

Serve with a flame and a flair.

Bananas à la West Indies

TIME: 20 minutes   SERVES: 6

COMPOSITION

6 ripe bananas
salt
1 cup white wine (or, more correctly, rum)
1 tablespoon butter

2 tablespoons flour
nutmeg
cinnamon
cloves
cayenne

PREPARATION

Peel and slice the bananas. Lay them in a shallow pan. Sprinkle them with salt. Add the wine or rum. Simmer for about 15 minutes.

Mix together the butter and the flour, with a dash each of nutmeg, cinnamon, cloves, and cayenne.

Stir this into the sauce. Cook for 2-3 more minutes.

Serve very hot.

Candied Bananas

P.S. *You can also serve this with broiled chops or steak and you have a banquet!*

Candied Bananas

TIME: 10-15 minutes   SERVES: 4

COMPOSITION

⅔ cup cider vinegar
⅔ cup brown sugar
1 tablespoon cornstarch
½ teaspoon fresh or candied (not powdered) ginger

⅛ pound butter
2 tablespoons sugar
4 bananas

PREPARATION

Combine the vinegar, the brown sugar, the cornstarch, and the ginger in a saucepan. Let it come to a boil and continue boiling for about 3 minutes.

Melt the butter and the sugar in a skillet.

Peel the bananas. Slice them lengthwise.

Sauté in the butter (over a very low flame) until they become a rich light brown.

Cover them with the vinegar mixture. Cook for another 3 minutes.

Fill a bowl with ice water.

Remove the banana sections one by one. Dip them into the ice water for a minute.

PRESENTATION

Place the now crunchy-coated sections on individual serving dishes.

Distribute the sauce equally.

DESSERTS THAT DESERVE ATTENTION

Cantaloupe Escoffier

TIME: 15 minutes to 1 hour   SERVES: 6

COMPOSITION

3 cantaloupes (small to medium)
the plup of 1 pineapple (or 1½ cups of the crushed variety)
1 pint strawberries, fresh or frozen
sugar
kirsch
sour cream

PREPARATION

Halve the cantaloupes. Remove the seeds.
Attack the pineapple. Scrape or mince the pulp very fine.
Combine the strawberries, the pineapple, and very little sugar.
Fill the cantaloupes. Add as much kirsch as possible—at least
    1 tablespoon per serving.
Permit the flavors to ripen before serving.

PRESENTATION

With a gobbet of sour cream on each.

Casaba Rafraîchi

TIME: 1 hour to chill the melon   SERVES: 6-8
      5 minutes to prepare

COMPOSITION

1 casaba melon
powdered ginger
limes
fresh mint

PREPARATION

Chill the melon.
Cut it into portions.
Sprinkle each with ginger, lime juice, and chopped mint.

Cranberry Ambrosia

TIME: 15 minutes to make SERVES: 6-8
1—? hours to Chill

COMPOSITION

4 cups cranberries
2 large oranges
2 cups sugar

½ teaspoon nutmeg
1 jigger kirsch
1 jigger Cointreau

PRESENTATION

Wash the cranberries.
Peel and deseed the oranges.
Put both through the coarse blade of a food grinder.
Add the sugar and the nutmeg.
Lubricate with the liquors.
Mix and chill in a silver or glass bowl.

Baked Brandied Cranberries

TIME: 1 hour and 5 minutes SERVES: 6-8

COMPOSITION

2 cups cranberries
2 cups sugar

1 cup brandy

PRESENTATION

Clean the berries.
Place them in a well-buttered baking dish. Add the sugar and
  ½ cup of the brandy.
Bake, covered, for 1 hour at 350° F. The berries should remain
  fat and plump.

PRESENTATION

Just before serving, pour on the rest of the brandy.

DESSERTS THAT DESERVE ATTENTION

Date Delight

TIME: 80 minutes   SERVES: 6-8

COMPOSITION

2 cups chopped dates
¾ cup chopped nuts
3 cups soft bread crumbs
⅛ pound butter
⅔ cup sugar
2 eggs
⅔ cup milk

¼ cup flour
1 teaspoon powdered ginger
½ teaspoon salt
2 teaspoons baking powder
⅛ teaspoon baking soda
½ teaspoon cinnamon

PREPARATION

Pit and chop dates.
Crack and chop nuts.
Make bread crumbs.
Butter a casserole.
Cream together the butter, the sugar, and the eggs. Add, alternately, the bread crumbs, the dates, the nuts, and the milk.
Sift the dry ingredients. Add to the date mix.
Pour the batter into the casserole.
Bake for 1 hour at 325°.

PRESENTATION

Serve hot with a hard sauce.

Figs

Fresh figs are fabulous to eat, but they don't require recipes. Consider the following as suggestions from Paradise.

FIGS ADAM:

Marinate fresh peeled figs in rum for an hour or so. Sauce them with red currant jelly thinned with kirsch or brandy.

AND EVE:

Marinate figs as above. Serve them with whipped cream and grated sweet chocolate.

FIGS EDEN:

Don't marinate peeled figs. Accompany them with a thin syrup of honey and sherry.

JUST FIGS:

Peel figs. Eat them with nothing more than sugar and good rich cream.

If fresh figs are not available, try the canned variety this way: Drain them.
Add a healthy slug of brandy or rum to the syrup. Boil rapidly to reduce the quantity.
Add the figs.
Serve with sour cream.

Fig Pudding

TIME: 3½ hours   SERVES: 6-8

COMPOSITION

½ pound butter
1 cup chopped nuts
1 pound dried figs
1½ tablespoons flour
1 cup brown sugar

3 eggs
2 cups soft bread crumbs
½ teaspoon cinnamon
1 tablespoon molasses
½ teaspoon soda

DESSERTS THAT DESERVE ATTENTION

PREPARATION

Let the butter relax and soften.

Chop the nuts.

Cut up the figs. Combine figs and nuts. Sprinkle the flour over them.

Butter a casserole unsparingly.

Set the oven at 300°. Turn it on.

With the back of a spoon, combine the butter and the sugar.

Separate the eggs. Add the egg yolks, one at a time, to the sugar. Beat well after each addition.

Add the bread crumbs, the cinnamon, the molasses, and the soda (dissolved in a tablespoon of hot water).

Add the fig-nut mixture.

Whip the egg whites until very stiff. Fold them into the batter.

Place the batter in the casserole.

Place the casserole in a pan of hot water.

Place both in the oven. Go away for 3 hours. (Not too far away; you may have to replenish the water in the pan.)

PRESENTATION

Serve hot or cold with Donn's Dessert Sauce (p. 23).

Lemon Pudding

TIME: 45-60 minutes   SERVES: 4-6

COMPOSITION

¾ cup sugar
2 tablespoons sifted flour
½ teaspoon cinnamon
½ teaspoon salt
3 eggs

juice and grated rind of 1 lemon
1 jigger sherry
1 cup milk

PREPARATION

Get out your largest mixing bowl. Blend together the sugar, the flour, the cinnamon, and the salt.

Get out two other bowls.

Separate the eggs. Beat the yolks. Add the lemon juice and rind and the sherry.

Beat the egg whites until very stiff.

Add the yolk mixture to the sugar mixture alternately with the milk. Stir until the sugar is well dissolved.

Fold in the egg whites.

Pour into a well-buttered baking dish.

Bake in a 350° oven for about 35 minutes.

P.S. *No one will ever buy lemon pudding in a package once he (or she) has tasted this.*

Peaches in Champagne

TIME: Long enough to chill both peaches and wine   SERVES: 8

COMPOSITION

peaches   *brandy*
1 bottle champagne

PREPARATION

Purchase the peaches—nine fine beauties. Eat one. Reserve eight.

Chill the champagne.

Drop the peaches in boiling water. Slip off their skins. Halve them and remove the stones.

Place the sections in a flat, shallow dish. Sprinkle with 2-3 jiggers of brandy.

Chill for an hour.

DESSERTS THAT DESERVE ATTENTION

PRESENTATION

Slosh the peaches with the champagne. Be generous; use it all.

Packed Peaches au Xérès

TIME: 30 minutes or less   SERVES: 6

COMPOSITION

½ cup finely ground almonds
1 tablespoon candied orange peel

6 peaches
⅓ cup powdered sugar
1 cup dry sherry

PREPARATION

Chop and grind almonds. If you have a blender, it will do the job, in seconds.

Chop the orange peel very fine.

Remove skins and stone from the peaches, cutting them in halves.

Mix together the almond meal, the orange peel, and the sugar.

Fill the peach halves. Place them in a shallow baking dish.

Add the sherry.

Bake at 300° for no more than 10 minutes. Pour off the wine into a pan and boil it down to half its quantity. Pour over the peaches and serve.

Pears in Red Wine

TIME: Approximately 35 minutes (plus chilling time)   SERVES: 6

COMPOSITION

6 firm pears
1½ cups sweet red wine

½ cup brown sugar
1 jigger brandy

Pears in Red Wine and Applesauce

PREPARATION

Peel the pears. Don't bother to core or cut them. Put them upright in a buttered baking dish. Add the wine, sugar, and brandy.

Bake, uncovered, at 300° until most of the liquid has disappeared.

PREPARATION

Hot or cold.

Pears in Red Wine and Applesauce

TIME: 1½ hours   SERVES: 6

COMPOSITION

5 cooking apples	6 pears
3 tablespoons butter	1 cup red wine
1¼ cups sugar	chunk of lemon peel
1 teaspoon cinnamon	1 jigger rum or brandy
¼ cup chopped walnuts	

PREPARATION

Peel and mince the apples.

Melt the butter. Add ¼ cup of the sugar and ½ teaspoon of the cinnamon. Add the apples. Simmer. When soft, stir in the walnuts.

Meanwhile peel the pears. Halve and core them. Poach them until soft in the wine, the remaining sugar and cinnamon, and the lemon peel.

Remove the pears and cook the sauce briskly to reduce it by half.

DESSERTS THAT DESERVE ATTENTION

PRESENTATION

Spread the apples in a serving dish.
Arrange the pears on top of the applesauce.
Pour the wine sauce over all. Serve hot or chilled.
Warm the rum. Pour it over the pears and ignite.

Pears Poached in Sauterne

TIME: ½ hour   SERVES: 6

COMPOSITION

6 pears	1-2 strips orange peel
⅓ cup seedless raisins	1 cup sauterne
⅓ cup brown sugar	1 6-ounce package semisweet chocolate bits
1 teaspoon grated lemon rind	
2 jiggers (or more) brandy	1 tablespoon butter
¾ cup sugar	

PREPARATION

Peel, halve, and core the pears.
Mix the raisins, the brown sugar, the lemon grating, and 1 jigger of brandy.
Bring to a boil ¾ cup of water, the sugar, and the orange peel. Poach the pears in it until they are soft yet firm.
Remove them, fill with filling, and place in a baking dish. Pour in the sauterne. Add the remaining pear-poaching juice.
Cover and bake at 350° for about 10 minutes.
Make a chocolate sauce by melting the chocolate bits with the butter and a jigger of brandy in a double boiler.

PRESENTATION

Place each pear in a small bowl.
Cover each with sauce.

Stuffed Pears

TIME: 30-40 minutes   SERVES: 6

COMPOSITION

½ cup toasted almond meal
½ cup chopped maraschino cherries
6 pears
¼ teaspoon almond extract
⅓ cup powdered sugar
butter
½ cup dry sherry

PREPARATION

Toast some almonds. Cleave, hack, chip, and grind them to granules or spin them in the blender.

Chop cherries.

Pare, core, and halve the pears.

Mix together the almonds, the cherries, the almond extract, and the sugar.

Stuff the pear halves. Place them in a shallow baking dish. Top each with a generous amount of butter. Distribute the sherry evenly over all.

Bake, covered, at 300° for 15-20 minutes (until the pears are tender but not mushy).

PRESENTATION

Serve hot or cold.

DESSERTS THAT DESERVE ATTENTION

Pineapple Kauai

TIME: 25 minutes to prepare   SERVES: 4-6
Chilling time indefinite

COMPOSITION

1 ripe pineapple of adequate size	*the meat of 1 coconut (or 1 package flaked coconut)*
3-4 ripe bananas	*juice of a lemon or lime*
3-4 oranges	*sugar*
	brandy, kirsch, or rum

PREPARATION

Go to the fields: swipe a fine pineapple, pluck a lime, a few bananas, and several oranges. Shinny up the nearest tree for a fresh coconut. If you cannot enter into the spirit of the thing, hie yourself to a market.

Attack the pineapple. Leave the leaves intact but cut an oval "lid" from one side. Remove the pulp in the easiest way, without poking through the shell.

Mash the bananas.

Remove the pulp from the oranges.

Chop the coconut meat.

Combine these with the pineapple pulp.

Season with lemon or lime juice, sugar, and booze. Do not stir without tasting.

Place the fruit mixture in the pineapple shell. Replace the lid and chill for several hours.

PRESENTATION

Use the pineapple as part of a fruit centerpiece. Let the guests help themselves freely.

Prunes in Wine

TIME: Overnight, plus 30 minutes
SERVES: 6-8

COMPOSITION

1 pound jumbo prunes
1 bottle sweet red wine
½ cup sugar
grated peel of 1 lemon
½ stick cinnamon
1 bay leaf
sour cream

PREPARATION

Invest in a pound of the largest prunes you can find. Soak them overnight in wine in a stainless-steel saucepan.

Add the sugar, the lemon peel, the cinnamon, and the bay leaf.

Simmer gently until the prunes are tender.

Remove them to a serving bowl.

Cook the syrup until it is reduced by half. Fish out the used cinnamon stick and the bay leaf.

PRESENTATION

Pour the sauce over the prunes.

Serve with plenty of sour cream.

Prunes Whipped

TIME: 1 hour to produce
1 hour to chill
SERVES: 4-6

COMPOSITION

¾ pound dried prunes
rind of 1 lemon
¾ cup sugar
⅔ cup brandy
½ teaspoon salt
2 tablespoons lemon juice
6 egg whites
1 cup whipped cream
1 jigger rum

DESSERTS THAT DESERVE ATTENTION

PREPARATION

Cook the prunes (and the lemond rind) in water until very tender.
Drain them. Drink the juice. Get rid of the pits and squash the prunes into a pulp.
Add the sugar and the brandy to the pulp. Bring it to a boil.
Stir in the salt and the lemon juice.
Remove from heat and beat until the pulp is light and frothy.
Whip the egg whites until stiff.
Fold in the hot pulp.
Chill thoroughly.
Whip the cream. Flavor it with rum.

PRESENTATION

Top the whipped prunes with the whipped cream.

Wined Strawberry Shortcake

TIME: Overnight plus 30 minutes   SERVES: 4

COMPOSITION

1 pint box strawberries	⅓ cup plus 4 tablespoons rum
sugar	4 shortcakes
⅓ cup brandy	⅛ pound butter
⅓ cup sherry	1 cup whipped cream

PREPARATION

Clean the berries. Sweeten them to taste with sugar. Marinate overnight in equal parts of brandy, sherry, and rum.
Make and bake shortcakes. The best recipe for them is to be found on p. 441.
Drain the berries.
Whip the cream. Fold some of the berry juice into it.

Melt the butter with 4 tablespoons of rum. Pour it over the cakes. Add the berries.
Crown with the whipped cream.

P.S. *This is a dish fit for a very fancy dinner party. Double or triple the recipe if necessary.*

FOUR SAUCES FOR FRUIT

I

Blend together ½ pint of sour cream and ½ cup of honey. Serve over fresh fruit.

II

TIME: Less than an hour (including chilling)   SERVES: 4-6

COMPOSITION

2 tablespoons sugar	*2 tablespoons liqueur (any kind you have or like)*
2 egg yolks	
1 cup hot milk	*2 cups whipped cream*

PRESENTATION

Beat the sugar into the egg yolks.
Heat the milk. Stir into the egg mixture. Cook until it is about the consistency of mayonnaise.
Cool.
Add the liqueur to taste.
Chill.
Blend in the whipped cream just before serving.

DESSERTS THAT DESERVE ATTENTION

III

TIME: About an hour (including chilling)   SERVES: 4-6

COMPOSITION

1 *8-ounce package cream cheese*
1 *tablespoon grated orange peel*
¼ *cup (or more) orange juice* or *curacao*
cream
sugar

PREPARATION

Combine the ingredients, using cream to thin and sugar to sweeten.
Beat until mixture is light.
Chill before serving.

IV

TIME: 10 minutes   SERVES: 4-6

Use this as a dessert dunk, with such things as pineapple spears, orange sections, and apple quarters.

COMPOSITION

½ *pint sour cream*
1 *teaspoon lemon juice*
1 *teaspoon grated lemon peel*
½ *cup sifted powdered sugar*
nutmeg

PREPARATION

Combine and mix the sour cream, the lemon juice and peel, and the powdered sugar.
Place in individual dunking bowls.
Sprinkle with nutmeg.

CAKE COMMENTS

For many good reasons, not the least of which is that they are too readily available, people rely on prepackaged mixes for cakes. With them, everything is built in—except the pride of accomplishment and the satisfactions of turning out a really good cake. Packaged mixes are not a swindle. In cases of emergency they come in handy. If you've been led to believe that they take less time and are less expensive than the real thing, think again. You save time, perhaps five to ten minutes, and for what? Someone has to do the premixing; you pay for it. If you want and can afford a cook, why not have a personal one?

There are cooks who do as the books say and those who do as they please. Experiment if you must (and if you enjoy it) with other things. With cakes, stick to the rules. They can be found in every cook book. At the risk of being a bore, I submit them again for convenience.

The lack of an ingredient can be a traumatic shock if the discovery is made in the midst of mixing a cake. Read the recipe. Check your cupboard. Assemble the necessary ingredients and the utensils in plain sight. Pitch into those requiring chopping or other attention. Let the eggs, the milk, the butter come to room temperature. Prepare the pans for use.

Follow directions exactly. Measure accurately. Use the ingredients called for in the amounts specified. Before proceeding with the actual operation, start the oven. Give it time to come up to the correct temperature.

Bake at the temperatures specified. Bake for the length of time specified (with some doubts) as well. Do your own testing with a cake tester or a finger. Insert the tester (or a

DESSERTS THAT DESERVE ATTENTION

toothpick or a broom straw). If it comes out clean, let the cake out of the oven. Or poke it with a finger. If the hole remains, bake the cake longer. If the hole disappears immediately, the cake is done. Remove it from the oven and cool it (in the pan or on a rack) according to the recipe directions. Experiment now, with frosting and filling to the content of your heart and your palate. You'll end up with a whole dessert or, if you prefer, a dessert accompaniment.

At this point it's up to you. Take off in a cloud of flour dust and bake a cake.

Sponge Cake

TIME: About 1¾ hours   SERVES: 6-8

COMPOSITION

1 teaspoons lemon juice
grated rind of 1 lemon
1 cup flour
1 teaspoon baking powder

¼ teaspoon salt
2 eggs
1 cup sugar
⅜ cup hot water

PREPARATION

Get out an 8-x-12-inch cake pan. Butter it. Sprinkle it with flour.
Start the oven, set at 350°.
Squeeze the lemon and grate its rind.
Sift the flour. Measure it. Sift it again, this time with the baking powder and the salt.
Separate the eggs. Beat the whites into stiff but moist peaks.
Beat the yolks until lemon colored, adding the sugar gradually.
Add the hot water, the lemon juice, and rind, then stir in the sifted flour. Mix well.

Fold in the egg whites.

Pour the batter into the pan. Bake the cake for 25-30 minutes.

PRESENTATION

Cool and frost it as you like, or sprinkle with powdered sugar. If you prefer, serve with a sauce or with fruit, or soaked in brandy or rum.

Genoise

TIME: 1½-1¾ hours   SERVES: 6-8

COMPOSITION

grated rind of 1 lemon
1 cup sugar
6 eggs

1 cup flour
⅛ pound butter

PREPARATION

Grate the lemon peel.

Stoke the oven (350°).

Heat water in the bottom of double-boiler.

Butter and flour two 9-inch round cake pans.

Combine the sugar, the eggs, and the lemon peel in the top of the double boiler and place over gently boiling water.

Beat for 15 minutes or so until the eggs are light and fluffy. Remove the top part of the double boiler and continue beating until the mixture is thick and ribbonlike.

Sift the flour. Resift it into the egg mixture. Fold it in with a rubber scraper or large spoon. Fold and refold until it is well blended.

Melt the butter without letting it boil. Fold it into the batter.

Pour the batter into the pans. Bake for 40-45 minutes.

DESSERTS THAT DESERVE ATTENTION

Remove the cakes from the pans immediately. Cool them on a rack.

PRESENTATION

Cover and fill with any frosting (pp. 508–511).

Orange Dessert Chiffon Cake

TIME: About 2½ hours   SERVES: 6-8-10-12

COMPOSITION

2 tablespoons grated orange rind	3 teaspoons baking powder
¾ cup fresh orange juice	1 teaspoon salt
5 egg yolks	½ cup vegetable oil
1 cup egg whites (7 or 8 in all)	1 teaspoon cream of tartar
2¼ cups cake flour	2 cups heavy cream
1½ cups sugar	1 cup powdered sugar
	½ cup unsweetened cocoa

PREPARATION

Heat the oven to 325°.

Grate the orange rind. Squeeze the oranges.

Separate eggs.

Sift flour. Add the sugar, the baking powder, and the salt. Sift it again into a large bowl.

Stir the oil, the egg yolks, the orange juice and rind into the flour. Beat until smooth.

Whip the egg whites and the cream of tartar together until stiff. (At the risk of repeating myself, I repeat—very stiff.)

Fold the whites into the batter, gently and without stirring.

Pour into an ungreased tube pan. Bake for 65-70 minutes. Cool upside down.

Pecan Cake

PRESENTATION

Whip the heavy cream together with the powdered sugar, the cocoa, and a pinch of salt. When it is stiff enough to spread, frost the cake.

P.S. *This is perfect dessert if the first part of the meal has been on the light side. After a heavy dinner the cake, without topping, makes a fine finish and goes wonderfully with strong black coffee.*

Pecan Cake

TIME: About 2¼ hours   SERVES: 10-12 or less

COMPOSITION

2 teaspoons nutmeg	1 teaspoon baking powder
½ cup bourbon	3 eggs
1 pound pecans	1 cup plus 2 tablespoons sugar
½ pound seedless raisins	¼ pound butter
1½ cups flour	Rum-Butter Cream (p. 510)

PREPARATION

Grind the nutmeg into the bourbon. Set it to one side for a while.

Shell and chop pecans. Chop raisins.

Line the bottom of a tube pan with wax paper.

Sift the flour together with the baking powder.

Separate the eggs, beating each part as usual: the whites very stiff and the yolks very little.

Set the oven at 300°.

Cream together the sugar and the softened butter. Add the egg yolks. Beat well and thoroughly.

DESSERTS THAT DESERVE ATTENTION

Stir in the spiced whisky. Blend in the nuts and the raisins. Fold in the egg whites.
Pour the batter into the pan. Bake for 1¼ hours.
Invert the pan. Cool the cake in it for about ½ hour.
Make the frosting, using bourbon in place of rum.
Eject the cake from the pan. Frost it.

Black Walnut Cake

TIME: 1½ hours   SERVES: 6-8-10

COMPOSITION

1 cup black walnut meats
3 eggs
¼ pound butter
1 cup sugar

1¾ cups flour
1½ teaspoons baking powder
½ cup milk
heavy cream

PREPARATION

Chop the nuts coarsely.
Separate the eggs. Beat the whites until very stiff.
Set the oven at 350°. Turn it on.
Butter and flour a tube ban.
Cream together the softened butter and the sugar. Add the egg yolks. Beat thoroughly.
Sift the flour and the baking powder together two times. Sift it again, into the batter. Add it alternately with the milk.
Stir in the nuts.
Fold in the egg whites.
Pour the batter into the pan.
Bake the cake for about 1 hour. Turn out on a cake rack to cool.

Cheese Cake

PRESENTATION

Serve this rich cake with more richness: heap sweetened whipped cream on each slice.

Cheese Cake

TIME: The crust: 15 minutes
The filling: 15 minutes
The baking: 30 minutes
The cooling: 30 minutes
The chilling: 3-4 hours
The eating: 10 minutes

SERVES: 6-8-10

COMPOSITION

THE CRUST	THE FILLING	THE TOP
1 cup graham-cracker or zwieback crumbs	*2 8-ounce packages cream cheese*	*1 pint sour cream*
2 tablespoons sugar	*½ teaspoon salt*	*2-3 tablespoons powdered sugar*
½ teaspoon cinnamon	*juice of ½ lemon*	*2 tablespoons sherry*
⅛ pound butter	*¼ cup rum (or sherry or a combination of both)*	
	4 egg whites	
	1 cup sugar	

PREPARATION

Let the butter soften. Crush the crackers. Mix the crust ingredients together. Press the mixture into the bottom an 8-inch spring-form pan.

Preheat the oven to 350°.

Combine the cream cheese, the salt, the lemon juice, and the liquor. Stir until smooth.

Beat the egg whites very stiff. Beat the sugar into the whites. Fold into the cheese mixture.

DESSERTS THAT DESERVE ATTENTION

Pour into the crust. Bake until the cheese is firm (about 25 minutes). Remove from oven and increase heat to 450°.
Blend together the sour cream, the powdered sugar, and the sherry. Spread it on top of the cake.
Bake for 5 minutes.
Remove, cool, and chill before serving.

Date Nut Cake

TIME: 1½ to 2 hours   SERVES: 10-12

COMPOSITION

butter
1 cup flour
2 teaspoons baking powder
¼ teaspoon salt
1 pound pitted dates

1½-2 cups walnuts
4 eggs
½ cup sugar
1½ ounces rum

PREPARATION

Preheat the oven to 350°.
Butter and flour a tube pan.
Sift, then measure the flour.
Add the baking powder and the salt. Sift again.
Pit and chop dates.
Chop nuts. Toss them into a bowl together. Sift the flour mixture over them. Stir with a fork to separate the sticky mass.
Separate the eggs. Beat the whites until very stiff yet moist.
Add the sugar to the yolks. Beat them until lemony. Stir in the rum.
Blend the yolk mixture into the flour-nut-date mixture. Fold in the egg whites.

Pour the batter into the pan. Bake it for 1 hour.
Invert the pan over a cake rack and cool.

PRESENTATION

Whipped cream, hard sauce, rum sauce, or no sauce are good accompaniments.
Serve the cake the day you bake or save it for next Christmas. It keeps safely in an air tight container, and mellows with age.

Hazlenut Torte

TIME: Under 2 hours   SERVES: 6-8-10

COMPOSITION

3 cups hazelnuts
½ cup flour
½ teaspoon salt
1 teaspoon baking powder
6 eggs

1½ cups sugar
⅓ cup vegetable oil
1 jigger rum
½ pint heavy cream

PREPARATION

Chop the nuts into pieces, very fine pieces.
Butter and flour three 8-inch square or round cake pans.
Preheat the oven to 350°.
Sift, measure, and resift the flour with the salt and the baking powder.
Separate the eggs. Beat the yolks briefly while adding the sugar. Gradually beat in the oil. Blend in the flour. Stir in the rum and the nuts (withholding a tablespoon of the former and about ¼ cup of the latter).
Beat the egg whites until stiff. Fold them into the batter. Pour it into the pans.

DESSERTS THAT DESERVE ATTENTION

Bake for 30 minutes.
Cool.

PRESENTATION

Shortly before serving time, whip the cream. Season it with a tablespoon of rum.

Split each cake in half horizontally. Spread the whipped cream between the 4 layers. Sprinkle the top with the remainder of the hazelnuts.

Babas au Rhum—vite faits

TIME: 1½ hours   SERVES: 6-8

COMPOSITION

1 teaspoon lemon juice
grated rind of ½ lemon
2 cups flour
2 teaspoons baking powder
¾ teaspoon salt
¼ pound butter
2¼ cups sugar

1 teaspoon vanilla
¾ cup milk
2 eggs
small handful of currants
½ cup (plus) rum
whipped cream

PREPARATION

Butter individual *baba* molds or muffin tins.
Squeeze the lemon. Grate its rind.
Sift flour, baking powder, and salt together.
Combine the softened butter and the lemon peel. Add 1¼ cups of sugar. Stir in the flour.
Combine the vanilla and the milk. Add this to the sugar-flour mix.
Beat in the eggs.

Upside-Down Cake (Preferably Pineapple)

Pour the batter into the molds. Sprinkle a few currants on top of each.

Bake at 350° for about 55 minutes.

Meanwhile prepare a rum syrup: cook together 1 cup of sugar, 1½ cups of water, the lemon juice, and the rum.

When done, let the cakes cool in their tins for about 10 minutes.

Remove them to a platter or to individual serving dishes. Poke them with a sharp tined fork in 2 or 3 places and spoon the hot syrup over them several times.

PRESENTATION

Serve with whipped cream and additional rum. Or skip the cream, warm some rum, pour it over the *babas,* light and serve forth.

P.S. *One and a half hours may not seem very* vite, *but compared to the yeast version of this dessert, it* is.

Upside-Down Cake (Preferably Pineapple)

TIME: 60-75 minutes   SERVES: 6-8, plus
(25-30 minutes to prepare
30-35 minutes to cook
5-10 minutes to cool)

COMPOSITION

1 cup nuts (walnuts, pecans or almonds)
fresh or canned fruit (judge the quantity by the size of your skillet)
¼ pound butter
1-pound box brown sugar

1 cup flour
1 teaspoon baking powder
½ teaspoon salt
3 eggs
1 cup sugar
1 teaspoon rum

DESSERTS THAT DESERVE ATTENTION

PREPARATION

First, crack and chop the nuts.

Second, prepare the fruit. (If it is canned, drain it. If it is fresh, peel, pit, and prepare it for cooking.)

Melt the butter in a heavy 10-12-inch skillet. Add the brown sugar. Toss in a cup of nutmeats. Stir. When the sugar has melted, set the pan aside to cool.

Preheat the oven to 375°.

Sift together the flour, the baking powder, and the salt.

Separate the eggs. Beat the yolks until light. Stir in the sugar and the rum. Beat some more.

Whip the whites until they stand in peaks.

Blend the flour into the yolks. Fold in the whites, gently.

Lay the fruit over the sugar in the skillet. Add the batter.

Bake the cake for 30-35 minutes.

Let it cool in the pan for 5 minutes.

Invert a platter on top of it, flip, and eject the cake.

PRESENTATION

Serve as is, or with whipped cream.

Brandied Chocolate Bars

TIME: 45 minutes plus . . .   SERVES: 6-8

COMPOSITION

1 cup walnuts
½ cup flour
¼ teaspoon salt
2 1-ounce squares unsweetened chocolate

⅛ pound butter
2 eggs
1 cup sugar
1 teaspoon vanilla
2 jiggers brandy

Brandied Chocolate Bars

PREPARATION

Chop walnut meats.

Sift flour and salt.

Line the bottom and sides of an 8-inch square pan with wax paper.

Preheat the oven to 350°.

Melt the chocolate and the butter together. Cool slightly.

Beat the eggs. Add the sugar and the vanilla. Blend well. Stir into the chocolate-butter mixture.

Add the flour. Stir in the walnuts.

Pour into the pan.

Bake for about 30 minutes.

Remove the cake from the pan, pull off the wax paper, and let it cool on a rack.

Return it to the pan, poke holes with a fork, pour the brandy over all, and let it soak.

PRESENTATION

Cut into bars. Sample before serving. If the liquor has evaporated, add more.

CROWNS FOR CAKES

Making frosting is an art that fascinates very few men, but these fillings and frostings and toppings are quick and easy. They are also good. Use them to vary any good basic cake. Each will more than cover (or fill) a cake eight inches in diameter. Each will take no more than 10 minutes to prepare.

Cream Cheese Frosting

COMPOSITION

1 3-ounce package softened cream cheese
1½ cups powdered sugar
1 teaspoon vanilla (or *rum*, etc.)

PREPARATION

Mix thoroughly.
Spread.

Chocolate Cheese Frosting

COMPOSITION

2 1-ounce squares unsweetened chocolate
2 tablespoons cream
1 3-ounce package cream cheese
2 cups powdered sugar
salt

PREPARATION

Melt the chocolate with the cream over a very low flame. Cool.
Work in the softened cheese.
Gradually add the sugar and the salt.
Mix well and spread.

Date Topping

COMPOSITION

1 cup chopped nuts
1 cup chopped dates
½ pint heavy cream
1 cup powdered sugar
¼ pound butter
1 egg

PREPARATION

Chop nuts and dates.
Whip the cream.
Cream the sugar and the butter. Add the egg. Beat well.
Stir in the dates and nuts. Fold in the cream.

DESSERTS THAT DESERVE ATTENTION

Fabulous Frosting

COMPOSITION

1 6-ounce-package semi-sweet chocolate bits
½ cup sour cream
⅛ teaspoon salt
rum, brandy, or sherry

PREPARATION

Melt the chocolate over hot water.
Mix in the sour cream and the salt. Stir and blend until smooth and creamy.
Add a dash of booze.

Lemon-Butter Frosting

COMPOSITION

juice and grated rind of 1 lemon
¼ pound butter
2 cups powdered sugar

PREPARATION

Squeeze the lemon. Grate its rind.
Soften the butter. Sift the sugar.
Combine the ingredients.

Rum-Butter Cream

COMPOSITION

¼ pound butter
⅛ teaspoon salt
1 pound powdered sugar
2 egg yolks
2 tablespoons rum

Sour Cream Frosting

PREPARATION

Cream the softened butter with the salt and the sifted sugar. Add the sugar gradually and stir to a smooth paste after each addition.

Stir in the egg yolks.

Season (to taste) with rum.

Sour Cream Frosting

COMPOSITION

6 tablespoons butter	*¼ teaspoon salt*
3 cups powdered sugar	*½ teaspoon vanilla*
6 tablespoons sour cream	or *booze*

PREPARATION

Cream the softened butter and the sugar thoroughly.

Stir in the sour cream.

Add the salt and the vanilla.

INIMITABLE
ICE CREAMS

Ice cream classically consists of cream, sugar, eggs and flavoring—frozen. New things have been added. One is air. In 1894 a method blowing it into the cream was patented. After seventy years and much research the final and economically correct proportion (about 99 per cent air) has been found.

Some air, as supplied by whipped egg whites, is all well and good and delicious. Most air, is less than good. It is atrocious. Of necessity, flavored and frozen air needs something to give it stability. Tortured seaweed does the job well. Ice cream containing it remains repulsively erect even when left to melt. Seaweed is economical, too. With it, an absolute minimum of cream is required.

If you want real ice cream, make your own. It's a man's job, anyway. The only needs, other than the classical ingredients, are ice, rock-salt, a freezer, elbow grease, and time.

Ice can be purchased or made. Even a middle-aged refrigerator will turn out sufficient quantity in a few hours. The salt is a mere nothing. No excuses accepted on that basis. A proper freezer costs less than three jugs of good bourbon. (If this idea is too far-fetched, one can accumulate sufficient trading stamps—pink, green, gold, red—in no time. Less time by far is needed for the freezing process itself.

Who has the time to do everything he thinks he should be doing (or would like to do) anyhow? A continuous supply of martinis will oil the elbow and noticeably shorten freezing time.

All arguments defeated, shall we proceed to make honest-to-Grandfather old-fashioned ice cream?

Vanilla Ice Cream

TIME: 25-30 minutes   SERVES: 4-6-8

COMPOSITION

2 *pints heavy cream*
6 *eggs*
2½ *cups sugar*

1 *pint light cream*
1 *tablespoon vanilla*

PREPARATION

Whip 1 pint of the heavy cream.
Separate the eggs.
Beat the yolks until very light. Add 2 cups of the sugar. Continue beating until the sugar is well amalgamated.
Beat the egg whites until stiff. Continue beating with the rest of the sugar until very, very stiff.
Stir the light cream and the remaining pint of heavy cream into the yolk mixture.
Fold in the whipped cream and then the egg whites. Stir in the vanilla gently.
Freeze.
Too much rock salt produces very grainy ice cream. One cup of salt should be sufficient for a half-gallon freezer.
Turn and crank until it becomes a struggle, remove the paddle for that first taste, fill the hole in the lid with butter, and pack ice solidly over the top of the inner can.
After ripening for at least an hour, the ice cream is ready to eat. Enjoy it.

DESSERTS THAT DESERVE ATTENTION

Coffee Ice Cream

Season basic vanilla ice cream to taste with instant coffee and brandy before freezing.

Ginger Ice Cream

Before freezing, add ⅓ cup chopped candied ginger and 2 tablespoons sherry to vanilla ice cream.

Maple Ice Cream

Use maple syrup in place of sugar for the vanilla ice cream recipe.

Mocha Ice Cream

Refer to the vanilla ice cream recipe again. Omit the vanilla. Melt 6 ounces of semisweet chocolate in 2 tablespoons of *very strong* black coffee. Add it to the vanilla mixture.

Fresh Peach Ice Cream

Add 2 cups crushed ripe peaches (or 1 frozen package, defrozen) to vanilla ice cream. Spark by adding 1 teaspoon of almond extract also.

Strawberry Ice Cream

Mash 1 quart of strawberries. Cover them with ½ cup sugar. Let stand 20 minutes, strain, and add to vanilla ice cream before freezing.

Chocolate Ice Cream

TIME: 30-50 minutes　　SERVES: 4-6-8

COMPOSITION

½ pound sweet chocolate
1 pint heavy cream
4 eggs
1 cup sugar

1 pint light cream
1 tablespoon vanilla
⅛ teaspoon salt

PREPARATION

Cook and stir the chocolate and the heavy cream in the top of a double boiler until it is thick and smooth.

Beat together the eggs and the sugar. Add the light cream, the vanilla, and the salt.

Combine the two mixtures thoroughly. Strain them.

Freeze.

TARTS AND PIES

There is one thing to say about pies. They are indubitably and undisputedly the American dessert. Resistance to pies is useless; escape impossible. To be socially (if not gastronomically) secure, one might as well learn how to make them. It is not really difficult. The difficulty is in making one fit to eat.

The basic thing is the crust, of which there are dozens of upper and lower variations. For some people the problem is solved by a store-bought mix. If this suits you, use it. If you prefer one like Mother used to make, make it. Use her recipe, or mine.

Donn's Pastry Mix

TIME: 15 minutes to prepare
24 hours to season

SERVES: 3-4 pie crusts

COMPOSITION

5 *cups flour*
1 *teaspoon salt*

2 *cups vegetable shortening*

PREPARATION

Sift together the flour and the salt.
Cut the shortening into the flour with a pastry blender or two knives.
The size of the lumps will determine the quality of the crust. Pea-size bits make a flaky pie crust. Large pieces make a useless crust. Meal-like bits will turn out a very crumbly crust. Use your own judgment.

Let the mix stand, covered and unrefrigerated, for at least 24 hours before using. Keep it, also unrefrigerated but in a cool place, for 2-3 weeks if necessary.

Pie Crust

TIME: 10 minutes   SERVES: 1 pie

COMPOSITION

2 *heaping cups Donn's Pastry Mix*   5 *tablespoons* cold *water*

PREPARATION

Measure out the mix.

Add the water gradually.

Work the paste into a ball. It should stick together but not be doughy. Let it rest for a few minutes in or out of the refrigerator.

Flour a pastry board, a rolling pin, and your hands, very lightly.

TWO-CRUST PIE

Divide the pastry ball into two parts. Roll. Work from the center toward the edges. Stop rolling when the circle is about ¼ inch thick.

Line the pie tin. Trim the edges, leaving an overhang. Add the filling.

Roll out the top crust. Lay it on the pie. Press the edges to seal it with the lower crust. Trim the excess dough. Decorate the border by pressing with the tines of a fork or your own big thumb. Gash the top and bake.

DESSERTS THAT DESERVE ATTENTION

PIE SHELL

Prepare half of the recipe. Roll the dough and lay it in the tin. Poke it with a fork. Brush it with butter. Weight it down with rice or dry beans. Bake it in a 425° oven for 10-12 minutes or until beautifully (but lightly) browned.

Simple Pastry

TIME: 45 minutes or less   SERVES: 2-crust pie

COMPOSITION

2½ cups flour
1 teaspoon salt
12 tablespoons butter (lard, margarine, vegetable shortening or a combination)
4 tablespoons cold (ice) water

PREPARATION

Let the butter get soft enough to work.

Sift, then measure the flour. Sift it again with the salt.

Blend the fat into the flour. Use two knives, a pastry blender, or your fingers. Obtain a mealy mixture, not a paste.

Add the water gradually, the less the better.

Form a ball which just sticks together. If it becomes a soggy sticky-ball, toss it out. Otherwise, chill it for 20-25 minutes before rolling and using as indicated above.

Crumb Pie Crusts

TIME: 30 minutes   YIELD: 1 9-inch pie

COMPOSITION

1½ cups crushed crumbs*
¼ pound butter
½ cup brown sugar

1-2 teaspoons cinnamon
2 tablespoons vanilla, rum, or brandy

PREPARATION

Crush crumbs. Use a plastic bag (to cut down on the mess) and wield a cleaver or flat side of a knife. Better yet, spin them in the blender.

Melt the butter.

Combine crumbs, sugar, cinnamon, and butter. Moisten them with vanilla, rum or brandy.

Spread the mixture in a 9-inch pie tin.

Bake it at 325° for about 10 minutes.

Let it cool before filling with filling.

P.S. *Choose the crumb material to match the filling.

Use graham crackers for Apple-Crumb Tarts, Cheese Cake, Lime Pie or Walnut Pie. Gingersnaps or chocolate cookies make a great base for Chocolate Cream Pie. Zwieback is good for Apple Crumb Tarts, Cheese Cake or Walnut Pie.

Meringue Pie Crust

TIME: Under 2 hours   SERVES: 2 8-inch pie shells

COMPOSITION

4 egg whites
¼ teaspoon cream of tartar

1 cup fine granulated sugar
sweet butter

DESSERTS THAT DESERVE ATTENTION

PREPARATION

Beat the egg whites until frothy. Add the cream of tartar gradually.

Add the sugar gradually, beating constantly.

Continue beating until the meringue is extremely smooth and extremely stiff.

Spread it in two 8-inch pie tins which have been slathered with sweet butter.

Bake in a very slow oven for 1¼ hours.

PRESENTATION

To be filled to taste.

Wined Apple Tart

TIME: 2 hours in all   SERVES: 6-8

COMPOSITION

1 9-inch prebaked pie shell	*½-⅔ cup red wine*
10-12 tart apples	*Rum-Butter Cream*
½-¾ cup sugar	*additional rum*

PREPARATION

Read pp. 516–518. Make and bake the pie shell.

Peel, core, and slice the apples.

Make applesauce, using the sugar and the wine. Cook the apples to your own degree of doneness.

Ladle the sauce into the shell.

Chill.

Top with Rum-Butter Cream (p. 510). Chill again.

PRESENTATION

Pour additional rum over the pie just before serving.

Apple Crumb Tart

TIME: Just over an hour SERVES: 6-8

COMPOSITION

- 1 9-inch graham-cracker or zwieback pie crust
- 10-12 tart apples
- 1 teaspoon grated lemon rind
- 1 cup white sugar
- ¼ cup brown sugar
- ½ teaspoon nutmeg
- 2 tablespoons butter
- ½ pint whipping cream
- 1 tablespoon powdered sugar
- 1 jigger rum

PREPARATION

Prepare the crumb crust of your choice (p. 519). Let it cool. Chill well.

Peel and core the apples. Slice them as thin as paper. Cook them with the lemon peel, the sugars, the nutmeg, and the butter. Use an absolute minimum of water, barely enough to cover. In about 20 minutes you should have a delicious applesauce.

Let it cool. Pour it into the crust. (If the crust has become too crumbly, stir everything together. Here are the makings for a good Brown Betty.)

PRESENTATION

Top with the whipped cream, strengthened with powdered sugar and rum.

DESSERTS THAT DESERVE ATTENTION

Chocolate Cream Pie

TIME: 1½-2 hours   SERVES: 6-8

COMPOSITION

1 9-inch pie shell (prebaked or prefabricated chocolate crumb)
4 eggs
1¼ cups sugar
½ teaspoon salt
4 tablespoons flour

2½ cups milk
2 1-ounce squares unsweetened chocolate
2 tablespoons butter
1 jigger rum
⅛ teaspoon cream of tartar

PREPARATION

Turn out the pie shell of your choice (pp. 516–519).

Separate the eggs.

Combine and sift 1 cup of sugar, the salt, and the flour. Sift several times.

Beat the egg yolks. Stir them into the sugar-flour mixture.

Scald the milk and the chocolate. Stir steadily until the combination is smooth.

Add the chocolate milk to the egg-flour-sugar mixture. Beat thoroughly. Return it to the stove. Cook and stir until thick. Don't cease stirring and don't give up too soon. During the process, add the butter and the rum.

Pour the mixture into the pie shell.

Beat the egg whites until very stiff. Gradually add ¼ cup of sugar, the cream of tartar, and a dash of salt plus a teaspoon of rum.

Continue beating until the froth stands in stiff peaks.

Spread the meringue over the pie.

Place it under the broiler until the top is tanned.

Chill before serving.

Lemon Tarts

TIME: 40 minutes SERVES: 2-6

COMPOSITION

pastry for 12 tarts
⅓ cup lemon juice
grated rind of ½ lemon
¼ pound butter

2 cups sugar
4 eggs
1 tablespoon flour

PREPARATION

Prepare sufficient pastry for a two-crust pie after reading pp. 516–518. Use it to line 12 muffin tins, custard cups or tart tins.

Obtain lemon juice.

Grate the lemon.

Cream together the butter and the sugar. Add the eggs, one at a time. Beat hard after each addition.

Stir in the juice and the grated rind.

Sift in 1 (only) tablespoon of flour.

Spoon the batter into the shells. Fill each one about seven-eighths full.

Bake them for 25 minutes at 350°. Both shell and filling should be tawny but not browned.

P.S. *These are gems. If two people cannot consume the entire batch at one sitting, we lose money.*

Don't overlook the possibility of making them beforehand, to pop into the oven when your guests are just sitting down to dinner.

DESSERTS THAT DESERVE ATTENTION

Almond Tarts

TIME: About an hour, plus an hour to chill
SERVES: 12, supposedly 6, probably

COMPOSITION

pastry for a 2-crust pie
1 cup finely chopped almonds
⅛ pound butter
¼ cup flour
⅓ cup sugar

½ pint cream
salt
2 egg yolks
almond extract

COMPOSITION

Prepare enough pastry for a two-crust pie (pp. 516–518). Line 12 2-inch tart tins with round of pastr 3½ to 4 inches in diameter. Weight and bake them like a single-crust pie.

Chop almonds.

Melt the butter. Blend in the flour.

Add the sugar, the salt, and the cream. Cook until the sauce is thick. Stick with it: stir constantly.

Whip the egg yolks. Add them to the sauce. Beat until it is smooth and creamy.

Add the almonds and the almond extract to taste. Taste. If more flavor is needed (or more sugar), add it now.

Cool the sauce.

Chill it thoroughly.

Fill the shells shortly before serving.

Pear Tarts

TIME: Less than an hour SERVES: 6

COMPOSITION

pastry for 12 tarts (enough for a 2-crust pie)
6 pears
1 tablespoon chopped candied ginger or lemon peel
1¼ cups brown sugar
¼ cup vinegar
¼ teaspoon cinnamon
⅛ teaspoon allspice
6 whole cloves
1 tablespoon flour
heavy cream

PREPARATION

First, prepare the pastry (pp. 516–518). Line muffin tins or tart shells. Do not bake them.

Peel, core, and halve the pears.

Chop ginger or lemon peel (or a combination of the two).

Bring the sugar, the vinegar, and the spices to a boil. Add the pears. Simmer for 5 minutes.

Place the pears in the tart shells, half a pear per shell.

Fish the cloves out of the syrup.

Mix the flour to a paste with a bit of water. Add the paste to the syrup. Cook and stir until it is thick. Pour some into each shell.

Bake the tarts at 425° for about 15 minutes.

PRESENTATION

Serve very hot with cold thick cream.

DESSERTS THAT DESERVE ATTENTION

Lime Pie

TIME: 20 minutes to turn out
1 hour to chill

SERVES: 6-8

COMPOSITION

1 9-inch baked pie shell
⅓ cup fresh lime juice
3 eggs
1 can (15 oz.) sweetened condensed milk

½ pint heavy cream
2 tablespons sherry
cinnamon

PREPARATION

Make ready the 9-inch pie shell (pp. 516–518).

Squeeze fresh limes. (Please do not attempt this with canned, processed, or otherwise degraded lime juice.)

Separate the eggs. Beat the yolks until lemon colored. Whip the whites very stiff.

Combine and mix the milk, the lime juice, and the egg yolks.

Fold in the egg whites.

Pour the mixture into the pie shell.

Bake it for 8-10 minutes in a 250° oven.

Cool, then refrigerate the pie before serving.

PRESENTATION

Whip the cream. Season it with sherry and a pinch of cinnamon. Heap it on the pie.

Rum Pie

TIME: 20 minutes to make the shell
       15 minutes to make filling
       30-60 minutes to chill

SERVES: 6-8

COMPOSITION

1 9-inch baked pie shell
2 eggs
½ pint heavy cream
2 teaspoons gelatin
¼ cup milk
⅓ cup sugar
salt
¼ cup rum
½ teaspoon vanilla

PREPARATION

Obtain the pie shell. Make it as per pages 516–518, buy it, or unfreeze it.

Separate the eggs. Whip the whites until stiff.

Whip the cream until it is very thick.

Soak the gelatin in the cold milk for about 5 minutes. Melt it in the top of a double boiler over hot water.

Beat the egg yolks together with the sugar and the salt. Add the gelatin.

Stir in the rum and the vanilla.

Fold in the egg whites.

Fold in the whipped cream.

Fill the shell.

Chill it well before serving.

DESSERTS THAT DESERVE ATTENTION

~~~~~~

Ice-Cream Pie

TIME: 1½-2 hours   SERVES: 4-8

COMPOSITION

1 crumb crust
ice cream

imagination

PREPARATION

Make the crust that fancy dictates (pp. 516–519).

Make (or buy) ice cream. Spread it in the crust. Use almost anything in the cupboard (with reservations, of course) to mix into or spread over the ice cream: strawberries, rum, brandy, chocolate chips, nuts, powdered coffee.

Freeze until ready to serve.

P.S. *For a safe version of Baked Alaska, cover the ice cream with meringue. Cover it completely, from crust to crust.*

Brown it in a very hot oven, very briefly and very quickly.

Pecan (or Walnut) Pie

TIME: 1½ hours   SERVES: 6-8

COMPOSITION

pastry for a 1-crust pie
1½ cups coarsely chopped pecans or walnuts
¼ pound butter

½ cup sugar
1 cup dark corn syrup
½ teaspoon salt

PREPARATION

Make and bake the pie crust, after reading pages 516–518.
Chop nuts.

Combine and mix together everything but the nuts.

Spread the nuts evenly in the bottom of the pie shell. Cover them with the butter-sugar mixture.

PRESENTATION

Bake at 350° for 50-60 minutes.

Serve hot or cold. Stretch it to the limit. A tiny sliver is sufficient.

Cream Puff Pie

TIME: Just under 1½ hours   SERVES: 8-10

PREPARATION

CREAM PUFF PASTRY	THE FILLING
½ *cup boiling water*	2 *cups milk*
⅛ *pound butter*	¾ *cup sugar*
⅛ *teaspoon salt*	⅓ *cup flour*
½ *cup flour*	⅛ *teaspoon salt*
2 *eggs*	2 *eggs*
	1 *tablespoon (or more) rum*
	1 *pint heavy cream*

PREPARATION

Heat water in a double-boiler bottom.

Mix ½ cup of boiling water with the butter and the salt in the top part of the boiler. Cook over simmering water until the butter melts.

Stir in the flour. Beat until the mixture forms a ball which leaves the sides of the pan. (This reads like work. It takes little more time than you have just spent reading about it.)

DESSERTS THAT DESERVE ATTENTION

Add the eggs, singly, beating well after each addition. Continue to beat and cook until the paste is very smooth and velvety.

Butter a 9-inch pie tin. Spread the paste on the bottom only. Bake it for 50-60 minutes in a 400° oven with no peeking or prying. Remove it from the oven and let it cool.

To make the filling, scald the milk in a saucepan.

In the double boiler, mix the sugar, the flour, and the salt. Beat in two eggs.

Add the scalded milk slowly. Cook and stir until the mixture thickens (about 10 minutes).

Remove it from the fire. Let it cool.

Add the rum. Cool it further.

Whip 1 cup of heavy cream. Fold it into the custard. Enjoy a well-earned libation while the custard chills.

PRESENTATION

When the time is ripe, pile the filling on top of the crust.

Whip another cup of heavy cream and slather it thickly over the top of the filling.

SWEET ENDINGS

Almond Cheese

TIME: 1½ hours   SERVES: 4-6

COMPOSITION

½ cup finely ground almonds   ¾ cup water
grated rind of 1 lemon   7 egg yolks
2 cups sugar

PREPARATION

Grind almonds, by hand or in blender.
Grate lemon peel.
Butter a mold.
Boil the sugar with the water. Stir it constantly. When the sugar is dissolved, add the almonds and the lemon peel.
Beat together the egg yolks. When the sugar mixture has thickened, add them, slowly. Cook, stirring constantly, over a very low fire until the mixture comes away from the pan.
Pour it into the mold.
Let it chill thoroughly.

PRESENTATION

Unmold and decorate or not as you see fit.

DESSERTS THAT DESERVE ATTENTION

Walnut Pudding

TIME: 1 hour   SERVES: 6-8

COMPOSITION

1½ cups chopped walnuts
1 teaspoon cinnamon
1⅓ cups brown sugar
⅛ pound butter
2 eggs

1 cup flour
2 teaspoons baking powder
½ teaspoon salt
brandy

PREPARATION

Chop walnuts, the finer the better. (A blender will grind them too fine).

Butter a shallow baking dish.

Mix the nuts with the cinnamon.

Combine the brown sugar, the softened butter, and the slightly beaten eggs. Add the walnuts.

Sift the dry ingredients. Add to the walnut mixture. Stir well. Add the vanilla. Stir some more.

Pour the batter into the casserole and bake at 350° for 40 minutes or until it is set.

Poke a multitude of holes into the pudding with a fork. Pour in as much brandy as will be absorbed.

The pudding will improve if you can let it age for a few hours before serving.

Crème Brûlée

TIME: Several hours. Sorry.   SERVES: 4-6

COMPOSITION

4 eggs
3-4 tablespoons brown sugar
salt
1 pint heavy cream

PREPARATION

Beat together the eggs, the brown sugar, and a pinch of salt.
Heat the cream to scalding in the top of a double boiler.
Combine the eggs with the hot cream slowly. Watch the pot.
  Don't let it boil. Don't let it overcook. Don't stop stirring.
  When the mixture coats the spoon, it is done.
Pour it into a shallow oven-proof dish. Cool it for 1-2 hours.
  Sprinkle the top with additional brown sugar. Give it a
  quick trip under the broiler to glaze the top.
Chill thoroughly and serve in slices.

P.S. *There's nothing to be sorry about. "Most of the several hours" the crème is sitting in the refrigerator.*

Tortoni

TIME: Only a few minutes, but well ahead of serving time. It must freeze.   SERVES: 4-6

COMPOSITION

½ cup currants
brandy
½ cup macaroon or graham-cracker crumbs
1 egg white
1 cup whipped cream
¼ cup powdered sugar
1 tablespoon sherry
additional whipped cream
additional brandy

DESSERTS THAT DESERVE ATTENTION

PREPARATION

Drop the currants into enough brandy to cover. Let them soak.
Crush macaroons.
Beat the egg white until stiff.
Whip the cream. Fold the sugar into it.
Fold the egg white into the whipped cream. Stir in the crumbs.
 Add the sherry. Fold in the currants, including any unabsorbed brandy.
Pour the mixture into individual molds.
Freeze for at least 1½ hours.

PRESENTATION

Serve with brandy-flavored whipped cream.

P.S. *The easiest molds are straight-side large paper baking cups—available everywhere. These keep beautifully in the freezer for a long time.*

Brandy Pecan Waffles

TIME: 15-20 to prepare   SERVES: 4-6

COMPOSITION

½ *cup pecans (or other nuts, excluding peanuts)*
1 cup flour
2 teaspoons baking powder
2 tablespoons butter

2 eggs
1 tablespoon sugar
1 jigger brandy
1 teaspoon vanilla
1 cup whipped cream

PREPARATION

Chop the nuts.
Sift the flour and the baking powder together.
Melt the butter.

Separate the eggs. Beat the yolks and whites separately and thoroughly.

Add the butter, the sugar, the brandy, and the vanilla to the yolks, blending after each addition. Stir in the flour. Add the nuts. Fold in the stiff whites.

Bake the batter as usual.

PRESENTATION

Serve with whipped cream.

Cream Puffs

TIME: 20 minutes to beat
45 minutes to bake

YIELD: 10 puffs

COMPOSITION

1 cup water
¼ pound butter
1 cup sifted flour

1 teaspoon salt
5 eggs

PREPARATION

Bring the water to a boil. Add the butter. Let it melt.

Add the flour and the salt all at once.

Stir like a fool until the paste leaves the sides of the pan and forms a ball around the spoon.

Remove the pan from the fire. Let it cool slightly.

Preheat the oven to 375°.

Add the eggs to the paste in single file, beating well after each addition.

Drop small mounds of paste onto a well-buttered baking sheet, about 2 inches apart. (You should have at least 10.) Shape them into balls or cylinders by hand or with a spoon.

DESSERTS THAT DESERVE ATTENTION

Bake them for about 45 minutes. The puffs should be puffed. They should also be dry, tanned, and rigid to the touch.
Split the puffs. Cool. Fill them, using ice cream, whipped cream, or custard (vanilla or chocolate), depending upon your mood. Sauce them, frost them, or sprinkle with confectioners' sugar before serving.

Coffee Jelly

TIME: 15 minutes to whip up
60 minutes to chill

SERVES: 4

COMPOSITION

2 cups strong coffee
sugar
1 tablespoon unflavored gelatin

¼ cup brandy
whipped cream
instant coffee

PREPARATION

Make coffee—very strong coffee.
Sweeten it to taste.
Soften the gelatin in the brandy. Stir it into the hot coffee.
Pour the brew into a mold.
Chill it thoroughly.

PRESENTATION

Serve with cream, whipped and seasoned with brandy and sugar.
Sprinkle the top with instant coffee.

Wine Jelly

TIME: 10-15 minutes, plus chilling time   SERVES: 4-6

COMPOSITION

1½ tablespoons unflavored gelatin
water

1½ cups sherry
brandy
1 tablespoon sugar

PREPARATION

Stir the gelatin into ⅓ cup of cold water.
Stir this into 1 cup of boiling water. Continue stirring until the gelatin is completely dissolved.
Add the sherry, a slug of brandy, and the sugar.
Mix well.
Pour into individual molds.
Chill.
Serve.

Chocolate Soufflé

TIME: About 1 hour   SERVES: 4-6

COMPOSITION

1 cup rich milk
3 tablespoons butter
2 squares baking chocolate
2 tablespoons flour

½ cup sugar
¼ teaspoon salt
1 teaspoons vanilla
4 eggs

PREPARATION

Scald the milk.
Melt the butter with the chocolate. Stir in the flour. Add the

milk, the sugar, the salt, and the vanilla. Stir until the sauce is very smooth and somewhat thick. Remove it from the fire. Let it cool.

Butter a soufflé dish.

Separate the eggs. Beat the yolks briefly. Beat the whites until stiff and frothy. Add the yolks to the batter, stir well, then fold in the whites.

Pour the combination into the soufflé dish. Place it in a shallow pan of hot water. Place both in a 400° oven. After 15 minutes, reduce the heat to 375°.

In another 15-20 minutes you should have a beautiful soufflé.

PRESENTATION

Serve it immediately, with or without whipped cream.

P.S. *Believe it or not, a chocolate soufflé is one of the easiest party desserts. Along with final preprandial (post-cocktail) ministrations, the egg whites are beaten stiff and folded into the previously prepared chocolate mixture. Thirty-five to forty minutes later you have a perfect soufflé and astonished guests.*

Cointreau Soufflé

TIME: 1¼ hours   SERVES: 4

COMPOSITION

4 eggs   1¼ cups **Cointreau**
¾ cup powdered sugar

PREPARATION

Separate eggs. Beat the whites very stiff. Beat the yolks until thick.

Add the sugar to the yolks.

Add the liqueur to the yolks.

Add the whites to the yolks, gently.

Butter a soufflé dish. Turn the batter into it and place it in a shallow pan of hot water.

Bake it for an hour at 325°.

P.S. *The P.S. on the previous page applies to this soufflé except that you have more time—perhaps an extra course—at your disposal.*

Lemon Soufflé

TIME: 15 minutes and 1 hour   SERVES: 4-6

COMPOSITION

⅓ cup flour
⅛ teaspoon salt
5 eggs
1 cup milk

juice and grated peel of 1 lemon
3 tablespoons butter
1 cup sugar
⅓ cup flour

PREPARATION

Sift the flour and the salt together.

Separate the eggs. Beat the yolks into the milk. Whip the whites until frothy and stiff.

Squeeze and grate the lemon.

Butter a soufflé dish.

Mash the butter into the sugar.

Work the flour into the sugar mixture with a fork.

Add the egg yolk-milk mixture.

Add the lemon juice and peel.

Mix again.

DESSERTS THAT DESERVE ATTENTION

Fold in the egg whites.
Bake for an hour at 300°.

PRESENTATION

As with all soufflés, eat immediately.

Soufflé Flambé

TIME: 15-20 minutes   SERVES: 2

COMPOSITION

4 eggs
butter
3 tablespoons sugar
½ cup rum

PREPARATION

Separate the eggs.
Butter a soufflé dish.
Add 2 tablespoons of sugar to the egg yolks. Beat them until thin and ribbony.
Whip the whites until very stiff. Fold the whites into the yolks. Pour into the buttered dish.
Bake at 350° for 10 minutes.
Let the rum be warming.

PRESENTATION

Pour the rest of the sugar over the top of the soufflé. Flood it with rum. Ignite. Run to the table. Serve forth immediately.

Index

A

Aïoli, 20
  Pseudo-, 20
Ale, Eggs in, 58
Almond
  Cheese, 531
  Chicken, 211
  Chicken Soup, 45
  Sauce
    for Fish, 11
    for Meat, 10
  Tarts, 524
Appetizers
  Cheese
    Dabs, 455
    Puffballs, 455
    Rounds, 456
  Eggplant Caviar *pour l'homme sans Sous*, 348
  I'a Maka, 87
  Mushrooms
    Cooked, 355
    Les Champignons de Mon Ami, 354
    Raw, 355
  Pâté
    Chicken Liver, 214
    Liver, 154
    Maison, 155
    Shrimp, 93
  Shrimp
    Balls of, 90
    Butter, 91
    Cajun, 94
    in Beer, 92
    Pâté, 93
Apple(s)
  Applejack Crisp, 473

Apple(s)—*Continued*
  Baked, 472
  Crumb Tart, 521
  Stuffed, 472
  Tarts, Wined, 520
  Thing, 474
Applesauce
  Alchemy for Canned, 475
  with Pears in Red Wine, 487
Apricot Soufflé, 476
Arroz con Pollo, 299
Artichoke(s), 317
  and Romaine Salad, 409
  Boiled, 318
  Cold, 320
  Roast, 318
  Stuffed, 319
Asparagus, 320
  Casserole, 274
  Parmigiana, 321
  Pie, 322
Aspic, Salmon, 85
Avocado
  Baked, 323
  Eggs, 60
  Sherbert, 477

B

Babas au Rhum—*vite faits*, 504
Baking Powder Biscuits, 437
Banana(s)
  à la West Indies, 478
  Candied, 479
  Flambé, 477
Barbecue(d)
  Fish, Hawaii, 83
  Sauce, 11

i

INDEX

Bean(s)
  Baked, Authoritative, 275
  Cassoulet, One Version of, 238
  Green, see Green Beans
  Lima, see Lima Beans
  Salad, Kidney, 405
  Soup
    Black, 40
    Lentil, 36
Bean Sprout(s)
  Salad, 411
  with Green Beans and Water Chestnuts, 325
Béarnaise Sauce, 18
Béchamel Sauce, 8
Beef
  à la mode du Barry, 233
  Boeuf Bourguignon, 232
  Chateaubriand en Casserole, 234
  Chow Mein, 311
  Curry, 304
  Filet of
    aux Champignons, 105
    Flambé, 106
    in a Crust, 107
  Flank Steak I, 110, II, 110, III, 111
  Fondue Bourguignonne, 295
  Ground Beef
    Delight, 235
    Pie, 115
  Hamburgers Big Sur, 113
  Hash
    Baked, 180
    Chestnut, 176
    Corn Beef, 179
    in Sour Cream, 177
  Meat Loaf
    Italian, 166
    Pain de Boeuf
      (cold), 165
      (hot), 162
        Variation I, 164
        Variation II, 165
    Plain, More or Less, 160
  Pastetseo, 246
  Pot-au-Feu, 29
  Pot Roast
    in Beer, 116
    in Beer Casserole, 248
    Left-Over in Wine Sauce I 175, II 175

Beef—Continued
  Shortribs
    in Burgundy, 120
    Marinated, 119
  Smothered, 117
  Steak(s)
    Chopped, 111
    Flank, 110, 111
    Garlic, Swiss Style, 112
    Sirloin, Brandied, 105
    Stuffed, 108
    with Cheese, 109
  Stew(s)
    Boeuf Bourguignon, 232
    Son-of-a-Bitch, 191
  Stroganov, 114
    Casserole, 249
    Tamara's, 118
  Sukiyaki, 178
  Vinaigrette, 180
Beer
  Crab Soup with, 41
  Eggs-in-your-Beer Soup, 67
  Shrimp in, 92
Beet(s), 327
  Borscht, 34
  California, 328
  Salad, 410
  Sauterne, 328
  with Orange, 329
Biscuits, 437
  Baking Powder, 437
  Butterscotch, 438
  Cheese, 439
  Herb, 439
  Jam, 440
  Onion Cake, 440
  Sausage Rolls, 441
  Shortcakes, Individual, 441
Bisque, Lobster-Pea, 40
Boeuf
  à la Mode du Barry, 233
  Bourguignon, 232
Bouillon, Court, 73
Brains
  à la Parisienne, 130
  Empty, 131
Brazil Nuts and Yams, 393
Bread(s)
  Biscuits, 437
  Brown, 427
  Cinnamon, 434

INDEX

Breads—*Continued*
  Coffee Cake
    Filled, 448
    Quick, 447
  Cornbread, 430
  Croissants, 445
  Frenchified, 428
  Garlic, 429
  Grapenut, 433
  Muffins, 431
  Pastel de Elote, 444
  Popovers, 429
  Pretzels, 432
  Sourdough, 443
    Starter, 442
  Toast
    Cinnamon, 434
    Coconut French, 435
    Delectable French, 436
  White, 425
Broccoli, 330
  à la Grecque, 330
Brown Sauce, 6
  on the Double, 6
Brown Stock, 4
Brussels Sprouts, 331
  Savory, 332
Butter(s)
  Lemon-Herb, 14
  Nut, for Vegetables, 18
  Shrimp, 91
Butterscotch Rolls, 438

C

Cabbage, 333
  Choucroute *à l'Alsacienne*, 309
  Coleslaw, Savory, 411
  Red, with Sour Cream, 334
  Sweetsour, Hot, 334
  with Caraway, 333
Caesar Salad, 407
Cake(s), 495
  Babas au Rhum—vite faits, 504
  Black Walnut, 500
  Cheesecake, 501
  Chocolate Bars, Brandied, 506
  Coffee Cake
    Filled, 448
    Quick, 447
  Date Nut, 502

Cake(s)—*Continued*
  Frostings
    Chocolate Cheese, 509
    Cream Cheese, 508
    Fabulous, 510
    Lemon-Butter, 510
    Rum-Butter Cream, 510
    Sour Cream, 511
  Genoise, 497
  Hazelnut Torte, 503
  Orange Dessert Chiffon, 498
  Pecan, 499
  Sponge, 496
  Topping, Date, 509
  Upside-Down, 505
Cantaloupe Escoffier, 480
Carrot(s), 335
  Brandied, 337
  Cold, 415
  Pierce Style, 336
  Salad, 412
Casaba *Rafraîchi*, 480
Casseroles
  Cheese
    and Egg, 271
    and No Wine, 273
    and Wine, 272
    Fondue, 271
    Onion Soufflé, 361
  Chicken
    and Corn, 254
    and Ham, 253
    Breasts, the Best in the World, 251
    en Cocotte, 256
    for Four, 255
    Newburgh, 255
    with Oysters, 252
  Egg(s)
    and Cheese, 270
    in Ale, 58
    in Cream, 59
    Swiss, 64
  Fish and Shellfish
    Clam and Eggplant, 276
    Crab, 261
    Crab *Chevalier*, 262
    Fish, Baked in Coconut Cream, 261
      Pudding, 260
    Flounder, Stuffed, 258
    Halibut, 259

INDEX

Casseroles—*Continued*
  Fish and Shellfish—*Continued*
    Oyster, 263
      with Chicken, 252
    Scallops, Baked, 264
    Seafood, Quick, 265
    Shrimp
      Casserole, 267
        Another, 268
        Still Another, 269
      Mornay, 266
  Fowl, Left-Over, 183
  Lasagna, 244
  Meat
    Beef
      Boeuf à la mode du Barry, 233
      Boeuf Bourguignon, 232
      Chateaubriand *en casserole*, 234
      Ground Beef Delight, 235
      Pot Roast in Beer, 248
      Smothered, 177
      Stroganov, 249
      Tamara's 118
    Ham
      and Chicken, 253
      and Egg Soufflé, 241
      Baked, *en Casserole*, 237
      Quick Casserole for Two, 240
      Sandwiches in a Casserole, 242
      Soufflé, 241
    Jambolaya, 243
    Lamb
      and Eggplant, 237
      Chops in Wine, 236
      Ragout, 190
      Shanks, Cora's, 137
    Liver, Baked, Casserole Style, 245
    Pork Chop(s), 247
      Wined, 145
      with Almonds, 143
    Veal
      Birds en casserole, 250
      Parmigiana, 123
  Paella, 297
  Pastetseo, 246
  Spaghetti, Baked, 292
  Vegetable
    Asparagus, 274
    Avocado Eggs, 60
    Beans, Baked, 275
    Cassoulet, 238

Casseroles—*Continued*
  Vegetables—*Continued*
    Choucroute à l'Alsacienne, 309
    Corn and Chicken, 254
    Eggplant, 276
      and Clam, 276
      and Lamb, 237
    Onion, 27
    Onion-Cheese Soufflé, 361
    Pea, 278
    Peppers
      Stuffed *à la Grecque*, 279
      Stuffed, Pierce Style, 280
    Potatoes, 281
    Rice *Pilaff*, 281
    Vegetable Mishmash, 282
    Zucchini Mousse, 283
Cassoulet, One Version of, 238
Cauliflower, 337
  à l'individu, 338
  Salad, Cold, 415
Caviar Mousse, 87
Celery, 339
  Amandine, 339
  Provençale, 340
Champagne Potato-Shrimp Salad, 408
Chateaubriand *en Casserole*, 234
Cheese
  Almond, 531
  and Egg Casserole, 270
  and No Wine Casserole, 273
  and Wine Casserole, 272
  Biscuits, 439
  Cake, 501
  Casserole, Fondue, 271
  Cottage Cheese Soufflé, 461
  Croque Madame, 302
  Croque Monsieur, 301
  Croustade Jurasienne, 462
  Dabs, 455
  Dessert I 465, II 466
  Fondue I 458, II 459, III 459
  Onion Soufflé, 361
  Puffballs, 455
  Quiche Lorraine, 463
  Ricotta and Macaroni, 464
  Rounds, 456
  Sandwiches, Toasted, 465
  Soufflé, 460
    and Onion, 361
  Welsh Rabbit for Four, 457
  with Steak, 109

INDEX

Chestnut(s)
　Beef Hash, 176
　Ham and Turkey with, 227
　Stuffing
　　à la Bourgeoise, 224
　　Brandied, 225
Chick Peas with Herbs, 349
Chicken
　Almond, 211
　Almond Soup, 45
　and Corn Casserole, 254
　and Ham Casserole, 253
　Arroz con Pollo, 299
　Brazil, 208
　Breasts
　　the Best in the World, 251
　　with Mushrooms, 201
　Cacciatora, 202
　Casserole
　　and Corn, 254
　　and Ham, 253
　　for Four, 257
　　for Left-Over Fowl, 183
　　Newburgh, 255
　Charcoaled, 201
　Chow Mein, 311
　Cold, with Tuna, 207
　Coq au Vin, 205
　Curry, 304
　En Cocotte, 256
　For Every Pot, The, 210
　Hash, Parmesan, 182
　in Marsala, 206
　Livers
　　and Mushrooms, 212
　　Pâté, 214
　　Risotto, 213
　Nasi Goreng, 308
　Oven Fried, 206
　Poule au Pot Henri IV, 210
　Tarragon, 203
　with Lemon Sauce, 204
　with Oysters, 252
Chocolate
　Bars, Brandied, 506
　Cheese Frosting, 509
　Cream Pie, 522
　Ice Cream, 515
　Soufflé, 537
Choucroute à l'Alsacienne, 309
Chow Mein, 311
Cioppino, 300

Clam(s)
　and Eggplant Casserole, 276
　Eggplant *aux Palourdes*, 349
Coconut Soup, 46
Coffee Cake
　Filled, 448
　Quick, 447
Coffee Jelly, 536
Cointreau Soufflé, 538
Cole Slaw, Savory, 411
Coq au Vin, 205
Corn, 341
　and Chicken Casserole, 254
　and Eggplant Pudding, 344
　Chowder, Canned, 43
　in Sour Cream, 343
　in the husk, 342
　on the cob, 341
　Pastel de Elote, 444
　Soup, Cream of, 42
　with Mushrooms, 345
Court Bouillon, 73
Crab(s)
　Casserole, 261
　Chevalier, 262
　Curry, 304
　Quick Luncheon, 90
　Soup with Beer, 41
Cranberry(ies)
　Ambrosia, 481
　Baked Brandied, 481
Cream Puffs, 534
Cream Puff Pie, 529
Crème Brûlée, 533
Croissants, 445
Croque Madame, 302
Croque Monsieur, 301
Croustade Jurasienne, 462
Cucumber Soup, 48
Curry(ied), 303
　Beef, 304
　Chicken, 304
　Crab, 304
　Eggs, 304
　Eggs, Quick, 61
　Fish Steaks, 80
　Lamb, 304
　Lobster, 304
　Sambals, 305
　Scallops, 304
　Shrimp, 304
　Soup Iced, 47

v

INDEX

D

Date Delight, 482
Demi-Glace, 7
Desserts, *see also* Cakes, Fruits, Pies, Pastry, Puddings, Soufflés, Tarts
  Almond Cheese, 131
  Cheese I 465, II 466
  Cream Puffs, 534
  Crème Brûlée, 533
  Coffee Jelly, 536
  Ice Creams, 512
  Pancakes, Utopian, 449
  Sauces
    Donn's, 23
    for Fruit, 493
    Hard, 23
  Tortoni, 533
  Waffles, Brandy-Pecan, 534
  Wine Jelly, 537
Duck(ling)
  Brandied, 216
  Roast with Oranges, 215

E

Egg(s)
  and Cheese Casserole, 270
  and Ham, Baked, 63
  and Ham Soufflé, 241
  Avocado, 60
  Curry, 315
    Quick Curried, 61
  Diable, 57
  Funghi, 58
  in Ale, 58
  in Beer, 67
  in Cream, 59
  In-Your-Beer Soup, 67
  Mornay, 64
  Obstaculos, 66
  Orsini, 65
  Ox-Eyes, 61
  Prarie Oyster, 66
  Riviera, 62
  Swiss, 64
  with Mushrooms, 62
Eggplant, 346
  and Clam Casserole, 276
  and Corn Pudding, 344
  and Lamb Casserole, 237
  and Shrimp, 347

Eggplant—*Continued*
  aux Palourdes, 349
  Casserole, 276
  Caviar pour l'homme sans Sous, 348
  Ratatouille, 307
  Tomato Surprise, 385

F

Figs, 482
  Adam, 483
  Eden, 483
  Eve, 483
  Just, 483
  Pudding, 483
  with Sour Cream, 483
Fish
  Almond Sauce for, 11
  Baked in Coconut Cream, 261
  Barbecued, Hawaii, 83
  Bluefish in Wine Sauce, 82
  Caviar Mousse, 87
  Cioppino, 300
  Court Bouillon, 73
  Fillets, *Marguéry,* 76
  Flounder
    in Wine Sauce, 82
    Stuffed, 258
  Haddock
    I'a Maka, 87
    Pudding, 260
  Halibut
    Baked in Coconut Cream, 261
    Barbecued, Hawaii, 83
    Casserole, 259
    in Wine Sauce, 82
    Pudding, 260
    Steaks
      Curried, 80
      Kazia's, 78
  I'a Maka, 87
  in Wine Sauce, 82
  Pompano, in Wine Sauce, 82
  Pudding, 260
  Raw, 87
  Salmon
    Aspic, 85
    Barbecued, Hawaii, 83
    in Wine Sauce, 82
    Pudding, 260
    Soufflé, 84

INDEX

Fish—*Continued*
  Salmon—*Continued*
    Steaks
      Curried, 80
      Kazia's, 78
    Shrimp Sauce for, 13
  Sole
    Baked in Coconut Cream, 261
    Casserole, 259
    I'a Maka, 87
    Raw, 87
    Stuffed, 258
    Véronique, 77
  Stew, 194
  Stuffed, 74
  Swordfish Steaks
    Broiled, 79
    Broiled with Olive Sauce, 81
    Curried, 80
    Kazia's, 78
  Trout, Poached, 75
  Tuna
    Barbecued, Hawaii, 83
    Steaks
      Broiled, 79
      Broiled with Olive Sauce, 81
      Curried, 80
      Kazia's, 78
      Terrific, 86
    Vitello Tonnato, 126
    with Cold Chicken, 207
  Whitefish
    Baked in Coconut Cream, 261
    Casserole, 259
    Fillets Marguéry, 76
    in Wine Sauce, 82
    Pudding, 260
    Stuffed, 258
  Yellowtail Steaks
    Curried, 80
    Kazia's, 78
Flank Steak I 110, II 110, III 111
Fondue Bourguignonne, 295
  Casserole, 271
Fowl, Left-over Casserole, 183
French
  Salad Dressing, 401
  Toast, Coconut, 401
  Toast, Delectable, 436
  Tomato Salad, 417
Frosting(s)
  Chocolate Cheese, 509
  Cream Cheese, 508

Frosting(s)—*Continued*
  Fabulous, 510
  Lemon Butter, 510
  Rum-Butter-Cream, 510
  Sour Cream, 511
Fruit Desserts
  Apple(s)
    Baked, 472
    Stuffed, 472
  Applejack Crisp, 473
  Applesauce, Alchemy for Canned, 475
  Apple Thing, 474
  Apricot Soufflé, 476
  Avocado Sherbet, 477
  Banana(s)
    à la West Indies, 478
    Candied, 479
    Flambé, 477
  Cantaloupe Escoffier, 480
  Casaba *Rafraîchi,* 480
  Cranberry
    Ambrosia, 481
    Baked Brandied, 481
  Date Delight, 482
  Figs
    Adam, 483
    Eden, 483
    Eve, 483
    Just, 483
    Pudding, 483
  Lemon Pudding, 484
  Peaches
    in Champagne, 485
    Packed *au Xérès,* 486
  Pears
    in Red Wine, 486
    in Red Wine and Applesauce, 487
    Poached in Sauterne, 488
    Stuffed, 489
  Pineapple *Kauai,* 490
  Prunes
    in Wine, 491
    Whipped, 491
  Wined Strawberry Shortcake, 492
Fruit Sauces, 493, 494

G

Garbanzos with Herbs, 349
Garlic
  Bread, 429
  Soup, 32

INDEX

Gazpacho, 413
Genoise, 497
Glace de Viande, 5
Gravy, Turkey, 221
Green Bean(s)
  au naturel, 324
  salad, 409
  with Water Chestnuts and Bean Sprouts, 325
Green Pepper(s), 365
  Sauté, 365
  Stuffed
    à la Grecque, 279
    Espagnole, 366
    Pierce Style, 280
    Tomato Salad, 404
    with Corn, 367

H

Ham
  and Beans, Steffy, 150
  and Chicken Casserole, 253
  and Eggs, Baked, 63
  and Eggs *en Soufflé*, 241
  and Turkey with Chestnuts, 227
  Baked *en Casserole*, 239
  Calvados, 148
  Casserole for Two, Quick, 240
  Croque Monsieur, 301
  Fresh, with Capers, 147
  Loaf, 167
  Meat Loaf, Jellied, 169
  Nivernaise, 149
  Sandwiches in a Casserole, 242
  Soufflé, 241
  with Bananas, 149
Hamburgers
  Big Sur, 113
  Chopped Steak, 111
Hard Sauce, 23
Hash
  Baked Beef, 180
  Chestnut Beef, 176
  Chicken, Parmesan, 182
  Corned Beef, 179
  Lamb, 185
Herb Biscuits, 439
Hollandaise, 19
  Simplified, 19
Hominy in Sour Cream, 350

I

Ice Cream(s), 512
  Chocolate, 515
  Coffee, 514
  Ginger, 514
  Maple, 514
  Mocha, 514
  Peach, Fresh, 514
  Strawberry, 515
  Vanilla, 513
Ice Cream Pie, 528

J

Jam Biscuits, 440
Jelly(ies)
  Coffee, 535
  Wine, 537

K

Kazia's Fish Steaks, 78
Kauai, Pineapple, 490
Kidney Bean Salad, 405

L

Lamb
  Anchovy Stuffed, 138
  and Eggplant Casserole, 237
  Chops
    Diable, 137
    in Wine Casserole, 236
  Curry, 304
  Hash, 185
  Leg of, Stuffed, 135
  Ragout, 190
  Shanks, Cora's, 139
  Shashlik, 140
  Shoulder Roast, 137
Lasagna, 244
Leeks
  in Red Wine, 351
  Mornay, 351
  Vinaigrette, 414
Lemon
  Butter Frosting, 510
  Herb Butter, 14

INDEX

Lemon—*Continued*
 Pudding, 484
 Sauce for Chicken, 204
 Soufflé, 539
 Tarts, 523
Lentil Soup, 36
Lima Beans, 326
 In Sour Cream, 326
Lime Pie, 526
Liver
 Baked, Casserole Style, 245
 Chanfaïna of, 133
 Herbed, 132
 in Sour Cream, 134
 Pâté, 154
Lobster
 Curry, 304
 Marsala, 89
 Pea Bisque, 40

M

Mayonnaise, 21
Meal-In-Itself
 Arroz Con Pollo, 299
 Boeuf Bourguignon, 232
 Casserole Fondue, 271
 Casserole for Left-Over Fowl, 183
 Cassoulet, 238
 Champagne Potato Shrimp Salad, 408
 Cheese and No Wine Casserole, 273
 Cheese and Wine Casserole, 272
 Cheese Fondue, 458
 Choucroute à l'Alsacienne, 309
 Chow Mein, 311
 Cioppino, 300
 Croque Madame, 302
 Croque Monsieur, 301
 Croustade Jurasienne, 462
 Curry, 303
 Egg and Cheese Casserole, 270
 Fondue Bourguignonne, 295
 Ground Beef Delight, 235
 Ham and Eggs en Soufflé, 241
 Ham Sandwiches in a Casserole, 242
 Lasagna, 244
 Nasi Goreng, 308
 Onion Cheese Soufflé, 361

Meal-In-Itself—*Continued*
 Onion Sludge, 360
 Paella, 297
 Quiche Lorraine, 463
 Ratatouille, 307
 Salade Niçoise, 406
 Sausage Pie, 280
 Spaghetti, 290
  Baked, 292
 Tomato Eggplant Surprise, 385
Meat
 Casseroles, *see* Casseroles
 Loaf
  Ham, 167
  Italian, 166
  Jellied, 169
  Pain de Boeuf, 163
   Variation I 164, II 165
  Plain (More or Less), 160
  Sauce, 161
 Marinating, A Witch's Brew for, 13
 Pâté
  Liver, 154
  Maison, 155
 Pie, Sausage, 289
 Rolls, Sausage, 441
 Sauces, *see* Sauces
Meats, *see* Beef, Ham, Lamb, Pork, Stews, Veal, Game, Poultry
Meringue Pie Crust, 519
Minestrone, 35
Mon Dieu Sauce, 17
Mornay Sauce, 8
Mousse
 Caviar, 87
 Zucchini, 283
Muffins, 431
Mushroom(s), 352
 and Chicken Livers, 212
 Baked and Stuffed, 354
 Cocktail
  Cooked, 355
  Raw, 355
 Eggs *Funghi*, 58
 in Brandy, 352
 Just, 356
 Les Champignons de Mon Ami, 354
 Sauce for Ham, 12
 Stuffing for Pork Chops, 143
 with Corn, 345
 with Eggs, 62
Mustard Sauce for Meat, 9

ix

INDEX

N

Nasi Goreng, 308
Noodles, Homemade, 293
Nut Butter for Vegetables, 18

O

Octopus in Wine, 99
Olive
    Sauce for Broiled Fish, 81
    Soup, Cream of, 44
Onion(s), 357
    Baked, 357
    Baked Brandied, 358
    Cakes, 440
    Casserole, 277
    Cheese Soufflé, 361
    Sludge, 360
    Soufflé, 359
    Soup, 30
    Soup, Quick for Two, 31
Osso Buco, 127
Ox-Eyes, 61
Oyster(s)
    Abstruse, 41
    Casserole, 263
    Poulette, 97
    Roffignac, 98
    Stew for Two, 194
    with Chicken, 252

P

Paella, 297
Pain de Boeuf, 162
    Cold, 165
    Variation I 164, II 165, III 165
Pancakes, Utopian, 449
Parsnip(s), 389
    Baked Purée of, 391
Paste(s)
    Lasagna, 244
    Macaroni and Ricotta, 464
    Noodles, 293
    Sauces for
        Meat, 291
        Tomato, 293
    Spaghetti, 290
        Baked, 292

Pastel de Elote, 444
Pastetseo, 246
Pastry, see also Pies and Tarts
    Crumb Crust, 519
    Crust, 517
    Meringue Crust, 519
    Mix, Donn's, 516
    Simple, 518
Pâtés
    Chicken Liver, 214
    Liver, 154
    Maison, 155
    Shrimp, 93
Peach(es)
    Ice Cream, Fresh, 514
    in Champagne, 485
    Packed au Xérès, 486
Pear(s)
    in red wine, 486
    in red wine and applesauce, 487
    Poached in Sauterne, 488
    Stuffed, 489
    Tarts, 525
Pea(s)
    à la Bonne Femme, 363
    Casserole, 278
    Creamed, 364
    Lobster Bisque, 40
    Perfect Plain, 362
    Salad, 415
Pecan Pie, 528
Peppers, Green, see Green Peppers
Pie(s), see also Tarts
    Asparagus, 322
    Chocolate Cream, 522
    Cream Puff, 529
    Crusts, see Pastry
    Ground Beef, 115
    Ice Cream, 528
    Lime, 526
    Pastel de Elote, 444
    Pecan, 528
    Rum, 527
    Sausage, 528
    Walnut, 528
Pilaff, Rice, 281
Pineapple
    Kauai, 490
    Upside-Down Cake, 505
Pine-Nut Sauce, 12
Popovers, 429

INDEX

Pork
  Chop(s)
    Casserole, 247
    Marinated, 144
    Stuffed, 142
    Wined, 145
    with Almonds, 143
  Chow Mein, 311
  Sausage
    Pie, 289
    Rolls, 441
  Spareribs
    Glazed, 145
    in Wine, 146
    Stuffing for, 142
Pot-au-Feu, 29
Potato(es), 368
  Baked, Perfect, 368
  Baked with Mushrooms, 370
  Casserole, 281
  Cold, 415
  Mashed, Perfect, 369
  Parmesan, 371
  Salad, 408
  Sauce for, 17
  Soufflé, 373
  Stuffed, 372
  with Shrimp, 371
Poule au Pot, Henri IV, 210
Poultry, *see* Chicken, Duck, Turkey, Rock Cornish Game Hen
Prairie Oyster, 66
Prunes
  in wine, 491
  whipped, 491
Pseudo-Aïoli, 20
Pudding(s)
  Fig, 483
  Fish, 260
  Lemon, 484
  Walnut, 532
Pumpkin Soup, 37

Q

Quiche Lorraine, 463

R

Rabbit Stew, 193

Ratatouille, 307
Rice, 374
  Arroz con Pollo, 299
  Baked, 374
  Boiled, 374
  Chicken Liver Risotto, 213
  Orange, 375
  Pilaff, 281
  Salad, 415
  Sauce for, 17
  Wild, *see* Wild Rice
Ricotta and Macaroni, 464
Rock Cornish Game Hens
  San Francisco, 218
  Vermouth, 217
Romaine and Artichoke Salad, 409

S

Salad(s), 399
  Artichoke and Romaine, 409
  Bean Sprout, 411
  Beet, 410
  Caesar, 407
  Carrot, 412
    Cold, 415
  Cauliflower, 415
  Champagne Potato-Shrimp, 408
  Cole Slaw, Savory, 411
  French Tomato, 417
  Gazpacho, 413
  Green Bean, 409
  Kidney Bean, 405
  Leeks *Vinaigrette,* 414
  Pea, Cold, 415
  Potato, Cold, 415
  Rice, 415
  Salade Niçoise, 416
  Spinach, 416
  Tomato, 417
    Babiche, 417
    Chilled Stuffed, 416
    French, 417
    Pepper, 404
  Turnip, 418
  Veal, Cold, 174
  Zucchini, Marinated, 419
Salad Dressings
  Anchovy-Caper, 402
  French, 401
  Roquefort, 401

xi

INDEX

Salad Dressings—*Continued*
  Sour Cream, 403
Sauce(s), Dessert
  Donn's, 23
  Four, for Fruit, 493
  Hard, 23
Sauces, *see also* Fish, Poultry, Meat, Vegetables, etc.
  Curry, 303
  For Fish
    A Sauce for, 15
    Almond, 11
    Mornay, 8
    Olive, 81
    Shrimp, 14
    Sweet-Sour, 13
  For Meat
    Almond, 10
    Anchovy, 15
    Barbecue, 11
    Brown, 6
      On the Double, 6
    Cold Meat, 10
    Demi-Glace, 7
    Espagnole, 6
    Glace de Viande, 5
    Hot Meat, 9
    Marinade, 13
    Meat Glaze, Quick, 5
    Meat Loaf, 161
    Mornay, 8
    Mushroom for Ham, 12
    Mustard, 9
    Pine-Nut, 12
    Shrimp, 14
    Tuna for Cold Veal, 181
    Vinaigrette, 22
    Witch's Brew for Marinating, 13
  For Poultry
    Lemon for Chicken, 204
    Mushroom for Turkey Soufflé, 184
  For Spaghetti, Noodles, etc.
    Meat, 291
    Tomato, 293
  For Vegetables
    Aïoli, 20
      Pseudo-*Aïoli*, 20
    Anchovy, 15
    Béarnaise, 18
    Béchamel, 8
    for Baked Potatoes, 17

Sauces—*Continued*
  For Vegetables—*Continued*
    for Rice, 17
    Hollandaise, 19
      Simplified, 19
    Lemon-Herb Butter, 14
    Mayonnaise, 21
    Mon Dieu, 17
    Mornay, 8
    Nut Butter, 18
    Sour Cream, Hot, 16
    Vinaigrette, 22
Sauerkraut
  Choucroute à l'Alsacienne, 309
Sausage
  Pie, 289
  Rolls, 441
Scallops
  Baked, 264
  Curry of, 304
  St. Jacques, 95
Seafood, *see also* Fish and Shellfish
  Curry, 304
  Casserole, 265
  Cioppino, 300
  Nasi Goreng, 308
  Paella, 297
Shashlik, 140
Shellfish, *see* Clam, Crab, Lobster, Oyster, Scallops, Shrimp
Sherbet, Avocado, 477
Shortcakes, Individual, 441
Shrimp
  and Eggplant, 347
  Balls of, 90
  Butter, 91
  Cajun, 94
  Casserole, 267
    Another, 268
    Still Another, 269
  Chow Mein, 311
  Curry, 304
  in Beer, 92
  Mornay, 266
  Pâté, 93
  Potato Salad, Champagne, 408
  Stuffed Potatoes, 371
  with Wild Rice, 378
Snow Peas, 377
  Chinese, 379
  with Wild Rice, 378

INDEX

Soufflés
  Apricot, 476
  Cheese, 460
  Chocolate, 537
  Cointreau, 538
  Cottage Cheese, 461
  Flambé, 540
  Ham, 241
  Ham and Eggs *en*, 241
  Lemon, 538
  Onion, 359
  Onion-Cheese, 361
  Potato, 373
  Salmon, 84
  Spinach, 382
  Turkey, with Mushroom sauce, 184
  Wild Rice, 376
Soup
  Almond Chicken, 45
  Black Bean, 40
  Borscht, 34
  Buttermilk, Cold, 51
  Cheddar, 38
  Chicken, 33
  Coconut, 46
  Corn
    Chowder, 43
    Cream of, 42
  Crab, with Beer, 41
  Cucumber, 48
  Curry, Iced, 47
  Egg-In-Your Beer, 67
  Garlic, 32
  Gazpacho, 413
  Lentil, 36
  Lobster Pea Bisque, 40
  Minestrone, 35
  Olive, Cream of, 44
  Onion, 30
    Quick for Two, 31
  Oysters *Abstruse*, 41
  Pot-au-Feu, 29
  Pumpkin, 37
  Singhalese, Simple, 44
  Tomato
    Cold, 50
    Exotic, 39
  Vichyssoise, 49
  Watercress, 46
Sourdough
  Bread, 443
  Starter, 442

Spaghetti, 290
  Baked, 292
  Meat Sauce for, 291
  Tomato Sauce for, 293
Spareribs
  Glazed, 145
  in Wine, 146
Spinach, 379
  Salad, 416
  Sesame, 382
  Simply, 380
  Soufflé, 382
  Valenciennes, 380
  with Savory Mushrooms, 381
Squash, *see* Zucchini
Steak(s)
  Chopped, 111
  Flank, 110, 111
  Garlic, Swiss Style, 112
  Sirloin, Brandied, 105
  Stuffed, 108
  with Cheese, 109
Stew(s)
  Boeuf Bourguignon, 232
  Fish, 194
  Oyster for Two, 194
  Rabbit, 193
  Son-of-a-Bitch, 191
  Veal, 192
    Ragout, 296
    Wine Stewed, 192
  Venison, 153
Stock, Brown, 4
Strawberry
  Ice Cream, 514
  Shortcake, Wined, 492
Sukiyaki, 178
Sweetbreads, Braised, 129
Sweet Potatoes, 392
  and Brazil Nuts, 393
  Sherried, 393

T

Tart(s), *see also* Pies
  Almond, 524
  Apple Crumb, 521
  Apple, Wined, 520
  Crusts, *see* Pastry
  Lemon, 523
  Pear, 525

INDEX

Tomato(es), 383
  Babiche, 417
  Chilled Stuffed, 416
  Eggplant Surprise, 385
  Fromagées, 386
  Pepper Salad, 404
  Salad French, 417
  Sauce for Spaghetti, 293
  Scalloped, 389
  Shrimp Stuffed, 388
  Soup, Cold, 50
    Exotic, 39
  Stuffed, 384
  with Sour Cream, 388
Tortoni, 533
Truffles, 222
Turkey, 219
  and Ham with Chestnuts, 227
  Florentine, 226
  Gravy, 226
  Roast, 219
  Soufflé with Mushroom Sauce, 184
  Stuffings, 223
    Chestnut *à la Bourgeoise,* 221
    Wine chestnut, 225
Turnips, 389
  Baked, 390
  Purée, 390
  Salad, 418

V

Veal
  Birds *en Casserole,* 250
  Cold, with Tuna Sauce, 181
  Les Oiseaux sans Têtes, 122
  Marsala, 124
  Osso Buco, 127
  Parmigiana, 123
  Ragout of, 296
  Roast, 121
  St. Marcoux, 124
  Salad, Cold, 174
  Salpicon of, 125
  Vitello Tonnato, 126
  Wine Stewed, 192

Vegetable(s), *see also* names of Vegetables
  Mishmash, 282
  Ratatouille, 307
Venison
  Roast Haunch of, 152
  Stew, 153
Vichyssoise, 49
Vinaigrette Sauce, 22
Vitello Tonnato, 126

W

Waffles, Brandy Pecan, 534
Walnut
  Cake, Black, 500
  Pie, 528
  Pudding, 532
Water Chestnuts with Green Beans and Bean Sprouts, 325
Watercress Soup, 46
Wild Rice
  Soufflé, 376
  with Mushrooms, 376
  with Shrimp, 94
  with Snow Peas, 378
Wine Jelly, 537
Witch's Brew for Marinating Meat, 13

Y

Yam(s)
  and Brazil Nuts, 393
  Sherried, 393

Z

Zucchini, 394
  in Sour Cream, 396
  Marinated, 419
  Mousse, 283
  Semplici, 395
  Stuffed, 395

A Note on the Type

THE TEXT of this book was set on the Linotype in a new face called PRIMER, designed by *Rudolph Ruzicka,* earlier responsible for the design of Fairfield and Fairfield Medium, Linotype faces whose virtues have for some time now been accorded wide recognition. The complete range of sizes of Primer was first made available in 1954, although the pilot size of 12 point was ready as early as 1951. The design of the face makes general reference to Linotype Century (long a serviceable type, totally lacking in manner or frills of any kind) but brilliantly corrects the characterless quality of that face.

Composed, printed, and bound by
The Haddon Craftsmen, Inc., Scranton, Pa.
Typography and binding design by
VINCENT TORRE

NOTES

NOTES

NOTES

NOTES

NOTES